A

LIST

OF THE

PROPER NAMES

OCCURRING IN THE

OLD TESTAMENT

WITH THEIR INTERPRETATIONS.

PRINCIPALLY COMPILED FROM

SIMONIS AND GESENIUS.

Wipf & Stock
PUBLISHERS
Eugene, Oregon

Wipf and Stock Publishers
199 W 8th Ave, Suite 3
Eugene, OR 97401

A List of Proper Names Occurring in the Old Testament with Their Interpretations
Principally Compiled from Simonis and Gesenius
ISBN: 1-59752-464-6
Publication date 2/16/2006
Previously published by J. Wertheimer and Co., 1844

PREFACE.

THE following Dictionary of the Proper Names, found in the Hebrew Bible, exhibits:—1st, the Names arranged in alphabetical order;—2nd, the pronunciation of the Hebrew name in English letters;—3rd, the form in which the name appears in the English authorised version;—and 4th, the meaning of the Hebrew names;—the especial object of this list has been to give the interpretations.

To some it might seem, at first sight, to be a thing of but little importance what the signification may be of the names used in the Scripture; but it is believed that but a little consideration will suffice to convince any Christian mind, that even such a thing as this, in the word of God, ought not to be overlooked. Indeed, the use made of proper names in the word of God, and arguments founded on their meaning, must prove sufficiently that even these things are "written for our instruction." For instance, in Heb. vii. 1, &c., we read "this Melchizedek, king of Salem, priest of the most high God," "first being by interpretation *king of righteousness*, and after that also king of *Salem*, which is king of *peace*." So too with regard to the change of the names of Abram and Sarai to Abraham and Sarah; and the additional name of Israel given to Jacob, "for as a prince hast thou power with God and with men, and hast prevailed."

The names given to our blessed Lord also mark the importance of attending to the meaning of the Hebrew proper names, for in them we find both the glory of His person and also His work pointed out in the express interpretations which the Scripture itself affords; thus we read in Mat. i. 21, &c., "She shall bring forth a son, and thou shalt call his name JESUS, for *he shall save* his people from their sins." Here we find the Hebrew name יֵשׁוּעַ so explained as to exhibit that its meaning was to be to us a source of instruction as to the work of Him who should bear it—"*he shall* SAVE." "Now all this was done that it might be fulfilled which was spoken of the Lord by the prophet, saying, Behold a virgin shall be with child, and shall bring forth a son, and they shall call his name *Emmanuel* עִמָּנוּאֵל, which being interpreted is GOD *with us*." This symbolic name is so explained by the Holy Ghost, as distinctly to shew, even in the account of our Lord's birth as man, that He was really and truly God; the symbolic name being shewn to involve most valuable and important doctrine, this first mention of *God* in the New Testament being used in speaking of our Lord.

It would be easy to increase the number of instances from Scripture of proper names, the meaning of which involves some truth of interest or importance, but the above may suffice to prove that they ought not to be overlooked.

It is true, that many of the proper names in the Old Testament, are of obscure derivation;—it should also be remembered that many of the persons whose names are mentioned are those of whom we are told scarcely anything further; and the fact that some part of the subject is obscure, is no reason for us to overlook that part which is clear and manifest; were we so to act, we might neglect the whole of the Scripture on account of the difficulties which we may find in particular portions.

In doubtful and difficult cases, Gesenius and J. Simonis have been consulted in drawing up the interpretations in the following list; the initials of these two writers indicate explanations given on their authority.

There yet exists a good deal of uncertainty as to the principles of composition and contraction of Hebrew proper names; attention being called to the subject, may lead to its being so fully investigated that we may arrive at settled principles of general application.

Some of the proper names in the Old Testament, are not Hebrew, but Babylonian, Egyptian, &c.; the explanations which are given of such, rests entirely on the authority of the writers who are cited at the close of each article.

INDEX TO THE PROPER NAMES.

***In the following Index to the Proper Names the references are made to the page and column in which the Hebrew word is to be found: the letters *a*, *b*, are used to denote the two columns into which the page is divided. When an English name occurs more than once in the following Index, even though in the same page and column, it will be found under different Hebrew headings. The variations of rendering found in the English translation are here given.

AAR — AHI

Name	Ref		Name	Ref		Name	Ref
Aaron	5 *b*		Abner	3 *b*		Adonijah, see Tob-adonijah	50 *a*
Abagtha	1 *a*		Abraham	4 *a*		Adonikam	5 *a*
Abana	3 *b*		Abram	4 *a*		Adoniram	5 *a*
Abarim	91 *a*		Absalom	4 *a*		Adonizedek	5 *a*
Abarim, see Ije-abarim	94 *b*		Accad	10 *a*		Adoraim	4 *b*
Abda	90 *b*		Accho	96 *a*		Adoram	5 *b*
Abdeel	90 *b*		Achan	96 *a*		Adrammelech	5 *b*
Abdi	91 *a*		Achar	96 *b*		Adriel	92 *a*
Abdiel	91 *a*		Achbor	96 *a*		Adullam	92 *a*
Abdon	91 *a*		Achish	10 *a*		Adullamite	92 *a*
Abed-nego	91 *a*		Achmetha	9 *a*		Adummim	5 *a*
Abel	3 *a*		"Achor, the valley of"	98 *a*		Agag	4 *a*
Abel	36 *a*		Achsah	96 *a*		Agagite	4 *a*
Abel-maim	3 *b*		Achshaph	10 *b*		Agee	4 *a*
Abel-meholah	3 *b*		Achzib	10 *a*		Agur	4 *a*
Abel-mizraim	3 *b*		Acrabbim, see Maaleh-acrabbim	79 *a*		Ahab	7 *a*
Abez	4 *a*		Adadah	92 *a*		Aharah	9 *a*
Abi	1 *a*		Adah	91 *b*		Aharhel	9 *a*
Abia	2 *a*		Adaiah	91 *b*		Ahasai	7 *b*
Abiah	2 *a*		Adaiah	91 *b*		Ahasbai	9 *a*
Abialbon	3 *a*		Adalia	4 *b*		Ahasuerus	9 *a*
Abiasaph	2 *a*		Adam	4 *b*		Ahava	5 *b*
Abiathar	3 *a*		Adam	2 *b*		Ahaz	7 *b*
Abib, see Tel-abib	127 *b*		Adamah	4 *b*		Ahaziah	7 *b*
Abida	2 *a*		Adami	5 *a*		Ahaziah	7 *b*
Abidah	2 *a*		Adar	5 *a*		Ahban	7 *a*
Abidan	2 *a*		Adar, see Ataroth-adar	94 *a*		Aher	9 *a*
Abiel	1 *b*		Adbeel	4 *b*		Ahi	7 *b*
Abiezer	3 *a*		Addan	5 *a*		Ahiah	7 *b*
Abiezrite	2 *a*		Addar	5 *a*		Ahiam	7 *b*
Abigail	2 *a*		Addar, see Ataroth-addar	94 *a*		Ahian	8 *a*
Abihail	2 *b*		Addar, see Hazar-addar	47 *a*		Ahiezer	8 *b*
Abihu	2 *a*		Addon	4 *a*		Ahihud	8 *b*
Abihud	2 *a*		Ader	92 *a*		Ahihud	8 *a*
Abijah	2 *a*		Adiel	91 *b*		Ahijah	7 *b*
Abijah	2 *a*		Adin	91 *b*		Ahijah	7 *b*
Abijam	2 *b*		Adina	91 *b*		Ahikam	8 *b*
Abimael	2 *b*		"Adino the Ezrite"	91 *b*		Ahilud	8 *a*
Abimelech	2 *b*		Adithaim	92 *a*		Ahimaaz	8 *a*
Abinadab	2 *b*		Adlai	92 *a*		Ahiman	8 *a*
Abinoam	2 *b*		Admah	4 *b*		Ahimelech	8 *a*
Abiram	3 *a*		Admathah	5 *a*		Ahimoth	8 *a*
Abishag	3 *a*		Adna	92 *a*		Ahinadab	8 *a*
Abishai	3 *a*		Adnah	92 *a*		Ahinoam	8 *a*
Abishalom	3 *a*		Adoni-bezek	5 *a*		Ahio	8 *a*
Abishua	3 *a*		Adonijah	5 *a*		Ahira	8 *b*
Abishur	3 *a*		Adonijah	5 *a*		Ahiram	8 *b*
Abital	2 *b*		Adonijah	5 *a*		Ahiramites	8 *b*
Abitub	2 *b*						
Abner (*marg.* Abiner)	2 *b*					Ahisamach	8 *b*

Ahishahar	8 b	Ammi, see Lo-ammi.	70 b	Aram	16 b
Ahishar	8 b	Ammiel	97 a	Aram, see Beth-aram	21 b
Ahithophel	8 b	Ammihud	97 b	Aram, see Padan-aram	102 a
Ahitub	8 a	Amminadab	97 b	Aram-naharaim	16 b
Ahlab	8 b	Ammishaddai	97 b	Aramitess	16 b
Ahlai	8 b	Ammizabad	97 b	Aran	17 a
Ahoah	7 a	Ammon	97 a	Ararat	17 a
Ahohite	7 a	Ammonite	97 a	Araunah	16 a
Aholah	5 a	Amnon	13 b	Arba	15 b
Aholiab	5 a	Amnon	13 b	Arba, see Kirjath-arba	112 a
Aholibah	5 a	Amok	97 a	"Arba, city of"	112 a
Aholibamah	5 a	Amon	13 b	Arbathite	100 a
Ahumai	7 a	Amorite	14 a	Arbel, see Beth-arbel	21 a
Ahuzam	7 b	Amos	97 a	Arbite	15 a
Ahuzzath	7 b	Amoz	13 b	Archevites	16 b
Ai	94 b	Amram	45 a	Archi	16 b
Aiah	9 a	Amram	98 b	Archite	16 b
Aiath	96 a	Amramites	98 b	Ard	15 b
Aija	94 b	Amraphel	14 a	Ardites	15 b
Aijalon	9 b	Amzi	13 b	Ardon	15 b
Ain	95 a	Anab	98 b	Areli	15 b
Ajah	9 a	Anah	98 b	Arelites	15 b
Ajalon	9 b	Anaharath	14 a	Argob	15 b
Akan	100 a	Anaiah	99 a	Aridai	16 a
Akkub	100 a	Anak	99 a	Aridatha	16 a
"Akrabbim, ascent of"	79 a	Anak	98 b	Arieh	16 a
"Akrabbim, going up to"	79 a	Anakims	99 a	Ariel	16 a
		Anamim	99 a	Arim, see Kirjath-arim	112 a
Alameth	96 b	Anammelech	99 a	Arioch	16 a
Alammelech	12 b	Anan	99 a	Arisai	16 a
Alemeth	96 b	Anani	99 a	Arkite	100 b
Alemeth	96 b	Ananiah	99 a	Armenia	17 a
Aliah	96 b	Anath	99 a	Armoni	16 b
Aliah	96 b	Anathoth	99 a	Arnan	17 a
Alian	96 b	"Anathoth, of"	99 b	Arnon	17 a
Allon	10 b	Anem	99 a	Arod	16 a
Allon-bachuth	10 b	Aner	99 a	Arodi	16 a
Almodad	12 b	Anethothite	99 b	Arodites	16 a
Almon	96 b	Anetothite	99 b	Aroer	100 a
Almon-diblathaim	96 b	Aniam	14 a	Aroer	100 a
"Aloth, in"	25 b	Anim	99 a	Aroerite	100 b
Alush	10 b	Antothijah	99 b	Arpad	17 a
Alvah	96 b	Antothite	99 b	Arphaxad	17 a
Alvan	96 b	Anub	98 b	Artaxerxes	17 a
Amad	98 a	Apharsachites	15 a	Aruboth	15 b
Amal	97 b	Apharsathchites	15 a	Arumah	16 a
Amalek	97 b	Apharsites	15 a	Arvad	16 a
Amalekite	98 a	Aphek	15 a	Arvadite	16 a
Amam	13 b	Aphekah	15 a	Arza	17 a
Amana	13 b	Aphiah	14 b	Asa	14 a
Amariah	14 b	Aphik	14 b	Asahel	100 b
Amariah	14 a	Aphrah	22 a	Asahiah	100 b
Amasa	98 b	Aphses	37 b	Asaiah	100 b
Amasai	98 b	Appaim	14 b	Asaph	14 b
Amashai	98 b	Ar	100 a	Asareel	17 a
Amasiah	98 a	Ara	15 b	Asarelah	18 a
Amaziah	13 b	Arab	15 b	"ascent of Akrabbim, the"	79 a
Amaziah	13 b	Arabah, see Beth-arabah	21 b		
Ami	13 b	Arabia	100 a	Asenath	14 a
Amittai	14 a	Arabian	100 a	Ashan	101 a
Ammah	13 b	Arabian	100 a	Ashbea	17 b
Ammah, see Metheg-ammah	83 a	Arad	100 a	Ashbel	17 a
		Arah	16 a	Ashbelites	17 a

Ashchenaz	18 a	Azem	99 b	Baladan, see Merodach-baladan	80 a
Ashdod	17 b	Azgad	93 a		
"Ashdod, of"	17 b	Aziel	93 a	Balah	24 b
"Ashdod, of"	17 b	Aziza	93 b	Balak	24 a
Ashdodites	17 b	Azmaveth	93 b	Bamoth	24 b
Asher	18 a	Azmaveth, see Beth-azmaveth	22 b	Bamoth Baal	24 b
Asherites	18 a			Bani	24 b
Ashima	18 a	Azmon	99 b	Barachel	28 a
Ashkelon	18 a	Aznoth-tabor	7 a	Barah, see Beth-barah	21 a
Ashkenaz	18 a	Azriel	94 a	Barak	28 a
Ashnah	18 a	Azrikam	94 a	Barak, see Bene-barak	25 a
Ashpenaz	18 a	Azubah	93 a	Barhumite	27 b
Ashtaroth	101 a	Azur	93 a	Bariah	28 a
Ashtaroth Karnaim	101 a	Azzah	93 a	Barkos	28 a
Ashterothite	101 a	Azzan	93 b	Barnea, see Kadesh-barnea	110 a
Ashtoreth	101 a	Azzur	93 a		
Ashur	18 a			Baruch	27 b
Ashvath	101 a	Baal	25 b	Barzillai	27 b
Asiel	100 b	Baal, see Gur-baal	30 b	Bashan	28 b
Askelon	18 a	Baal, see Kirjath-baal	112 a	Bashemath	28 b
Asnah	14 b			Basmath	28 b
Asnapper	14 b	Baal, see Merib-baal	81 b	Bath-rabbim	28 b
Aspatha	14 b	Baal, see Merib-baal	81 b	Bath-sheba	29 a
Asriel	17 a	"Baal, high places of"	24 b	Bath-shua	29 a
Asrielites	17 a			Bavai	20 a
Asshur	17 b	Baal-berith	25 b	Bazlith	27 a
Asshurim	17 b	Baal Gad	25 b	Bazluth	27 a
Asshurites	17 b	Baal Hamon	25 b	Bealiah	26 a
Assir	14 a	Baal-hanan	26 a	Bealoth	25 b
Assur	17 b	Baal-hazor	26 a	Bebai	19 b
Assyria	17 b	Baal-hermon	26 a	Becher	23 b
Assyrian	17 b	Baal-meon	26 a	Bechorath	23 a
Atarah	94 a	Baal-meon, see Beth-baal-meon	21 a	Bedad	20 a
Ataroth	94 a			Bedan	20 a
Ataroth-adar	94 a	Baal-peor	26 a	Bedeiah	20 a
Ataroth-addar	94 a	Baal-perazim	26 a	Beeliada	26 a
"Ataroth, the house of Joab"	94 a	Baal-shalisha	26 b	Beer	18 b
		Baal-tamar	26 b	Beer, see Baalath-beer	26 b
Ater	9 a	Baal-zebub	25 b	Beer-elim	19 a
Athach	101 a	Baal-zephon	26 a	Beer-lahai-roi	19 a
Athaiah	101 a	Baalah	25 b	Beer-sheba	19 a
Athaliah	101 a	Baalath	26 b	Beera	18 b
Athaliah	101 b	Baalath-beer	26 b	Beerah	19 a
Athlai	101 a	Baalim	25 b	Beeri	19 a
Atroth, Shophan	94 b	Baalis	26 a	Beeroth	19 a
Attai	101 a	Baana	26 b	"Beeroth of the children of Jaakan"	19 a
Ava	92 a	Baanah	26 b		
Aven, see Beth-aven	20 b	Baara	26 b	Beerothite	19 b
Avim	92 b	Baaseiah	26 b	Beeshterah	26 b
Avims	92 b	Baasha	26 b	Bel	23 b
Avites	92 b	Babel	19 b	Bela	24 b
Avith	92 b	Babylon	19 b	Belaites	24 a
Avith	94 b	Babylonians	19 b	Belshazzar	24 a
Azal	15 a	Bachrites	23 b	Belteshazzar	24 a
Azaliah	15 a	Baharumite	20 b	Ben	24 b
Azaniah	7 a	Bahurim	20 b	Ben-ammi	25 a
Azareel	93 b	Bajith	20 b	Ben-hadad	24 b
Azariah	94 a	Bakbakkar	27 a	Ben-hail	24 b
Azariah	94 a	Bakbuk	27 a	Ben-hanan	24 b
Azaz	93 a	Bakbukiah	27 a	Ben-oni	24 b
Azaziah	93 a	Balaam	24 a	Ben-zoheth	24 b
Azbuk	93 a	Baladan	23 b	Benaiah	25 a
Azekah	93 b	Baladan, see Berodach-baladan	27 b	Benaiah	25 a
Azel	15 a			Bene-barak	25 a

Bene-jaakan	25 a	Beth-nimrah	22 b	Cabbon	67 a
Beninu	25 a	Beth-palet	23 a	Cabul	66 b
Benjamin	25 a	Beth-pazzez	23 a	Cain	110 b
"Benjamin, of"	25 a	Beth-peor	23 a	Cain, see Tubal-cain	126 b
Benjaminite	25 a	Beth-phelet	23 a	Cainan	111 a
Benjamite	25 a	Beth-rapha, see Rapha	115 b	Calah	68 a
Benjamite	25 a	Beth-rehob	23 a	Calcol	68 a
Beon	26 b	Beth-shan	23 a	Caleb	68 a
Beor	25 b	Beth-shean	23 a	"Caleb, of the house of"	68 a
Bera	28 a	Beth-shemesh	23 a	Caleb-ephratah	68 a
Berachah	28 a	Beth-shemite	22 a	Calneh	68 b
"Berachah, valley of"	41 a	Beth-shittah	22 a	Calno	68 b
Beraiah	27 b	Beth-tappuah	23 a	Camon	111 b
Berechiah	28 a	Beth-zur	23 a	Canaan	69 a
Berechiah	28 a	Bethelite	21 a	Canaanite	69 a
Bered	27 b	Bethuel	28 b	Canneh	68 b
Beri	27 b	Bethul	28 b	Caphthorim	69 b
Beriah	28 a	Betonim	20 b	Caphtor	69 b
Beriites	28 a	Bezai	27 a	Caphtorim	69 b
Berites	28 a	Bezaleel	27 a	Captorims	69 b
Berith	28 a	Bezek	20 b	Car, see Beth-car	22 a
Berith, see Baal-berith	25 b	Bezer	27 a	Carcas	69 [b
Berodach-baladan	27 b	Bichri	23 b	Carchemish	69 b
Berothah	27 b	Bidkar	20 a	Careah	111 b
Berothai	28 b	Bigtha	20 a	Carmel	69 b
Berothite	28 b	Bigthan	20 a	Carmelite	70 a
Besai	25 a	Bigthana	20 a	Carmelitess	70 a
"besieged places"	80 a	Bigvai	19 b	Carmi	69 b
Besodeiah	25 a	Bildad	24 a	Carmites	69 b
Besor	28 b	Bileam	24 a	Carshena	70 a
Betah	20 b	Bilgah	23 b	Casiphia	69 b
Beten	20 b	Bilgai	24 a	Casluhim	69 a
Beth-anath	22 b	Bilhah	24 a	Cephar-haammonai	69 b
Beth-anoth	22 b	Bilhan	24 a	Chalcol	68 a
Beth-arabah	21 b	Bilshan	24 a	"Chaldea, inhabitants of"	70 a
Beth-aram	21 b	Bimhal	24 a		
Beth-arbel	21 a	Binea	25 a	Chaldeans	70 a
Beth-aven	20 b	Binnui	24 b	Chaldees	70 a
Beth-azmaveth	22 b	Birei, see Beth-birei	21 a	Charashim	48 b
Beth-baal-meon	21 a	Birsha	28 b	Charchemish	69 b
Beth-barah	21 a	Birzavith	27 b	Chebar	67 a
Beth-birei	21 a	Bishlam	28 b	Chedorlaomer	67 a
Beth-car	22 a	Bithiah	28 b	Chelal	68 b
Beth-dagon	21 a	Bithron	29 a	Chelluh	68 a
Beth-diblathaim	21 a	Bizjothjah	20 b	Chelub	68 a
Beth-el	21 a	Biztha	20 b	Chelubai	68 a
Beth-el, see El-beth-el	10 b	Boaz	25 b	Chemosh	68 b
eth-emek	21 b	Bocheru	23 b	Chemosh	68 b
Beth-ezel	21 b	Bochim	23 b	Chenaanah	69 a
Beth-gader	21 a	Bohan	20 a	Chenani	68 a
Beth-gamul	21 a	Boscath	27 a	Chenaniah	68 b
Beth-haccerem	21 b	Bozez	20 b	Chenaniah	68 b
Beth-hanan	22 a	Bozkath	27 a	Chephirah	69 b
Beth-haran	21 b	Boznai, see Shethar-boznai	126 a	Cheran	70 a
Beth-hoglah	22 a			Cherethims	70 a
Beth-horon	22 a	Bozrah	27 a	Cherethites	70 a
Beth-jeshimoth	21 b	Bukki	27 a	Cherith	69 b
Beth-lebaoth	22 b	Bukkiah	27 a	Cherub	69 b
Beth-lehem	22 b	Bunah	20 a	Chesalon	69 a
Beth-lehemite	21 b	Bunni	24 b	Chesed	70 a
Beth-maachah	22 b	Buz	20 a	Chesil	69 a
Beth-marcaboth	22 b	Buzi	20 a	Chesulloth	69 a
Beth-meon	22 b	Buzite	20 a	Chezib	67 b

Chidon	67 b	Darius	35 b	Eglah	91 b
"chief"	113 a	Darkon	35 b	Eglaim	4 b
"children of Gad"	30 a	Dathan	35 b	Eglaim, see En-eglaim	95 b
"children of Reuben"	112 b	"daughter of Shua, the"	29 a	Eglon	91 b
Chileab	67 b	David	34 a	Egypt	80 a
Chilion	68 a	Debir	33 b	"Egypt, of"	80 a
Chilmad	68 b	Deborah	33 b	Egyptian	80 a
Chimham	68 b	Dedan	33 b	Egyptians	80 a
Chimham	68 b	Dedanim	34 a	Ehi	7 b
Chinnereth	69 a	"defence"	80 a	Ehud	5 b
Chinneroth	69 a	Dehavites	34 a	Ehud	7 a
Chisleu	69 a	Dekar	35 b	Eker	100 a
Chislon	69 a	Delaiah	34 b	Ekron	100 a
Chisloth-tabor	69 a	Delaiah	34 b	Ekronites	100 a
Chittim	70 a	Delilah	34 b	El-beth-el	10 b
Chiun	67 b	Deuel	35 a	El-elohe-Israel	10 b
Chorashan	67 a	Diblaim	33 b	El-paran	9 b
Chozeba	67 b	"Diblath, towards"	33 b	Eladah	12 b
Chub	67 a	Diblathaim, see Almon-diblathaim	96 b	Elah	10 b
Chun	67 a			Elah	10 b
Cinneroth	69 a	Diblathaim, see Beth-diblathaim	21 a	Elam	94 b
"cities, fortified"	80 a			Elam	92 b
"city of Arba"	112 a	Dibon	34 b	Elasah	13 a
"city of salt, the"	96 a	Dibri	33 b	Elath	9 b
Colhozeh	68 a	Diklah	35 b	Elath	9 b
Coniah	68 b	Dilean	34 b	Eldaah	10 b
Cononiah	67 a	Dimnah	35 a	Eldad	10 b
Cononiah	69 a	Dimon	34 b	Elead	12 b
Coz	110 b	Dinah	34 b	Elealeh	13 a
Cozbi	67 a	Dinaites	34 b	Eleasah	13 a
"craftsmen"	48 b	Dinhabah	35 a	Eleazar	13 a
Cush	67 a	Dishan	34 b	Eleph	13 a
Cushan	67 b	Dishon	34 b	Elhanan	11 a
Cushan-rishathaim	67 b	Dizahab	34 b	Eli	96 b
Cushi	67 a	Dodai	34 a	Eliab	11 a
Cuth	67 b	Dodanim	34 a	Eliada	11 a
Cuthah	67 b	Dodavah	34 a	Eliahba	11 b
Cyrus	70 a	Dodo	34 a	Eliakim	12 a
Cyrus	67 a	Doeg	33 a	Eliam	11 b
		Dophkah	35 b	Eliasaph	11 b
Dabareh	33 b	Dor	34 a	Eliashib	16 a
Dabbasheth	33 b	Dor, see Hammoth-dor	45 b	Eliathah	11 a
Daberath	33 b	Dothan	35 b	Eliathah	12 b
Dagon	33 b	Dothan	35 b	Elidad	11 a
Dagon, see Beth-dagon	21 a	"dragon-well"	95 b	Eliel	11 a
"dale, the king's"	98 a	Dumah	34 a	Elienai	11 b
Dalphon	34 b	Dura	34 b	Eliezer	11 b
Damascus	35 a			Elihoreph	11 b
Damascus	35 b	Ebal	94 b	Elihu	11 a
Damascus	34 a	Ebed	90 b	Elijah	11 a
Dammim, see Pas-dammim	104 a	Ebed-melech	91 a	Elijah	11 a
		Ebenezer	3 b	Elika	12 a
Dan	35 a	Eber	91 a	Elim	9 b
Dan, see Mahaneh-dan	75 a	Ebiasaph	3 a	Elim, see Beer-elim	19 a
"Dan also"	38 b	Ebronah	91 b	Elimelech	11 b
"Dan, of"	35 a	"Edar, tower of"	73 a	Elioenai	11 a
Daniel	35 a	Eden	92 a	Elioenai	11 a
Danites	35 a	"Eden, house of"	22 b	Eliphal	11 b
Danjaan	35 a	Eder	92 a	Eliphalet	11 b
Dannah	35 a	Edom	4 b	Eliphaz	11 b
Dara	35 b	Edom, see Obed-edom	90 b	Elipheleh	11 b
Darda	35 b	Edomite	4 b	Eliphelet	11 b
Darius	35 b	Edrei	5 b	Elisha	12 a

Elishah	12	a	Er	100	a	Gad	29 b
Elishama	12	a	Eran	100	b	Gad, see Baal-gad	25 b
Elishaphat	12	b	Eranites	100	b	Gad, see Migdal-gad	72 b
Elisheba	12	a	Erech	16	b	"Gad, children of"	29 b
Elishua	12	a	Eri	100	b	Gaddah, see Hazar-gaddah	47 a
Elizaphan	12	a	Erites	100	b		
Elizur	12	a	Esar-haddon	14	b	Gaddi	30 a
Elkanah	13	a	Esau	100	b	Gaddiel	30 a
Elkohshite	13	a	Esek	100	b	Gader, see Beth-gader	21 a
Ellasar	12	b	Eshbaal	17	b	Gadi	30 a
Elnaam	12	b	Eshban	17	b	Gadites	30 a
Elnathan	12	b	Eshcol	18	a	Gaham	31 a
Elon	10	b	Eshean	18	a	Gahar	31 a
Elon	9	b	Eshek	101	a	Galal	31 b
Elon-beth-hanan, see Beth-hanan	22	a	Eshkalonites	18	a	Galeed, i.q. Gilead.	
			Eshtaol	18	a	Galilee	31 b
Elonites	12	b	Eshtaulites	18	b	Gallim	31 b
Eloth	9	b	Eshtemoa	18	b	Gamaliel	32 a
Elpaal	13	a	Eshtemoh	18	b	Gammadims	31 b
Elpalet	13	a	Eshton	18	b	Gamul	32 a
Eltekeh	13	a	Esther	14	b	Gamul, see Beth-gamul	21 a
Eltekon	13	b	Etam	94	b	Gannim, see En-gannim	95 a
Eltolad	13	a	Etham	18	b	Gareb	32 b
Eluzai	12	b	Ethan	10	a	Garmite	32 b
Elzabad	10	b	Ethbaal	18	b	Gashmu	33 a
Elzaphan	13	a	Ether	101	b	Gatam	32 b
Emims	9	b	Ethiopia	67	a	Gath	33 a
En-eglaim	95	a	Ethiopian	67	a	Gath, see More-sheth-gath	74 b
En-gannim	95	a	Ethiopians	67	a		
En-gedi	95	a	Ethnan	18	b	Gath-rimmon	33 a
En-haddah	95	a	Ethni	18	b	Gazah	93 a
En-hakkore	95	a	Euphrates	105	b	Gazathites	94 a
En-hazor	95	a	Eve	42	a	Gazer	31 a
En-mishpat	95	a	Evi	6	a	Gazez	31 a
En-rimmon	95	b	Evil-merodach	6	a	Gazites	94 a
En-rogel	95	b	Ezbai	6	b	Gazzam	31 a
En-shemesh	95	b	Ezbon	15	a	Geba	29 b
En-tappuah	95	b	Ezekiel	58	b	Gebal	29 a
Enam	95	a	Ezel	3	b	Gebal	29 b
Enan	95	b	Ezel, see Beth-ezel	21	b	Geber	29 b
Enan, see Hazar Enan	47	b	Ezem	99	b	Geber, see Ezion-geber	99 b
Enan, see Hazar Enan	47	b	Ezer	15	a	Geber, see son of Geber	24 b
Endor	95	a	Ezer	93	b	Gebim	29 a
Enoch	45	b	Ezer, see Romamti-ezer	113	b	Gedaliah	30 a
Enos	14	a	Ezion-geber	99	b	Gedaliah	30 a
Enosh	14	a	"Eznite, Adino the"	91	b	Geder	30 a
Ephah	95	b	Ezra	93	b	Gederah	30 b
Ephai	95	b	Ezra	94	a	Gederathite	30 b
Ephai	92	b	Ezrahite	7	a	Gederite	30 b
Epher	99	b	Ezri	94	a	Gederoth	30 b
Ephes-dammim	15	a				Gederothaim	30 b
Ephlal	15	a	"field, fruitful"	69	b	Gedi, see En-gedi	95 a
Ephod	14	b	"field, plentiful"	69	b	Gedor	30 a
Ephraim	15	a	"flock, tower of the"	73	a	Gedor	30 b
Ephraimite	15	a	"foreskins, hill of"	29	b	Gehazi	31 a
Ephraimites	15	a	"fortified cities"	80	a	Gemalli	32 a
Ephrain	99	b	"fruitful field"	69	b	Gemariah	32 a
Ephratah	15	a	"fruitful place"	69	b	Gemariah	32 a
Ephratah, see Caleb-ephratah	68	a	Gaal	32	a	"Gentiles, Haroseth of the"	48 b
			Gaash	32	b		
Ephrath	15	a	Gaba	11	a	Genubath	32 a
Ephrathite	15	a	Gabbai	29	a	Gera	32 b
Ephron	99	b	Gabriel	29	b	Gerar	32 b

Gerizim	32 b	"going up to Ak-rabbim, the"	79 a	Hakkoz	110 b
Gershom	32 b			Hakupha	47 b
Gershon	32 b	Golan	30 b	Halah	44 a
"Gershon, sons of"	32 b	"goldsmiths, the"	109 a	"half of the Manah-ethites"	46 b
Gershonite	32 b	Goliath	31 b		
Gesham	31 a	Gomer	32 a	"half the Manahethites"	46 b
Geshem	33 a	Gomorrah	98 a	Halhul	44 a
Geshur	33 a	Goshen	33 a	Hali	44 b
Geshuri	33 a	Gozan	30 b	Hallohesh	37 a
Geshurites	33 a	Grecians	57 a	Hallohesh	71 a
Gether	33 a	Gudgodah	30 a	Halohesh	37 a
Geuel	29 a	Guni	30 b	Ham	37 a
Gezer	31 a	Gunites	30 b	Ham	45 a
Gezrites	32 b	Gur	30 b	Haman	37 b
Giah	31 a	Gur baal	30 b	Hamath	45 a
"giant"	115 b			Hamathite	45 b
"giant, the"	115 b	Haahashtari	9 a	Hammath	45 a
"giants"	115 b	Haammonai, see Cephar-haammonai	69 b	Hammedatha	37 a
"giants, the valley of"	98 a			Hammedatha	73 b
Gibbar	29 b	Habakkuk	41 a	Hammoleketh	37 b
Gibbethon	29 b	Habaziniah	41 a	Hammoleketh	78 a
Gibea	29 b	Habor	41 a	Hammon	45 a
Gibeah	29 b	Hachaliah	43 b	Hammoth-dor	45 b
Gibeah	29 b	Hachilah	43 b	Hamon, see Baal-hamon	25 b
Gibeathite	29 b	Hachmoni	44 a		
Gibeon	29 b	Hachmonite	44 a	Hamonah	37 b
Gibeonite	29 b	Hadad	36 a	Hamor	45 a
Giblites	29 a	Hadad	41 b	Hamuel	45 a
Giddalti	30 a	Hadad	4 b	Hamul	45 a
Giddel	30 a	Hadad, see Ben-hadad	24 b	Hamulites	45 a
Gideon	30 a	Hadadezer	36 a	Hamutal	45 a
Gideoni	30 a	Hadadrimmon	36 a	Hamutal	45 b
Gidom	30 a	Hadar	36 b	Hanameel	45 b
Gihon	31 a	Hadar	42 a	Hanan	45 b
Gilalai	31 b	Hadarezer	36 b	Hanan, see Baal-hanan	26 a
Gilboa	31 a	Hadashah	42 a	Hanan, see Ben-hanan	24 b
Gilead	31 b	Hadassah	36 b	Hanan, see Beth-hanan	22 a
Gileadite	31 b	Hadattah, see Hazor-hadattah	46 b	Hananeel	46 b
Gileadite	31 b			Hanani	46 b
Gilgal	31 b	Haddah, see En-haddah	95 a	Hananiah	46 b
"Gilgal, house of"	21 b	Hadid	41 b	Hanes	46 b
Giloh	31 b	Hadlai	41 b	Haniel	45 b
Gilonite	31 a	Hadoram	36 a	Hannah	45 b
Gilonite	31 b	Hadrach	42 a	Hannathon	46 a
Gimzo	32 b	Hagab	41 b	Hanniel	45 b
Ginath	31 a	Hagaba	41 b	Hanochites	45 b
Ginnetho	32 a	Hagabah	41 b	Hanun	45 b
Ginnethon	32 a	Hagar	36 a	Haphraim	46 b
Girgashite	32 b	Hagarenes	36 a	Hara	38 a
Girgasite	32 b	Hagarite	36 a	Haradah	47 a
Gispa	33 a	Hagarites	36 a	Haran	38 a
Gittaim	33 a	Haggai	41 b	Haran	48 a
Gittite	33 a	Haggeri	36 a	Haran, see Beth-haran	21 b
Gizonite	30 b	Haggi	41 b	Hararite	17 a
Gizrites	31 a	Haggiah	41 b	Hararite	38 a
"Goath, to"	32 a	Haggites	41 b	Haraseth, see Kir-haraseth	111 a
Gob	29 a	Haggith	41 b		
"God"	53 b	Hagidgad, see Hor-hagidgad	47 b	Harbona	47 b
"God, house of"	21 a			Harbonah	47 b
Gog	30 b	Hai	94 b	Hareph	48 b
"going up of Adummim, the," see Adummim	5 a	Hail, see Ben-hail	24 b	Hareseth, see Kir-hareseth	111 a
		Hakkatan	110 b		
		Hakkatan	37 b	Haresh, see Kir-haresh	111 a

Haresha, see Tel-haresha	127 b	Hazerim	47 a	Hezekiah	43 b
Hareth	48 b	Hazeroth	47 a	Hezekiah	58 b
Harhaiah	48 a	Hazezon-tamar	47 a	Hezekiah	58 b
Harhas	48 a	Haziel	43 a	Hezion	43 a
Harhur	48 a	Hazo	43 a	Hezir	43 a
Harim	48 a	Hazor	46 b	Hezrai	47 a
Hariph	48 a	Hazor, see Baal-hazor	26 a	Hezro	47 a
Harnepher	48 b	Hazor, see En-hazor	95 a	Hezron	47 a
"Harod, the well of"	95 a	Hazor, Hadattah	46 b	Hezronites	47 a
Harodite	48 a	Hazzurim, see Helkath-hazzurim	44 b	Hiddai	36 a
Haroeh	38 a	Heber	41 a	Hiddekel	41 b
Haroeh	112 b	Heberites	41 b	Hiel	43 b
Harorite	38 a	Hebrew	91 a	"high places of Baal, the"	24 b
"Harosheth of the Gentiles"	48 b	"Hebrew woman"	91 a	Hilen	43 b
		Hebrewess	91 a	Hilkiah	44 b
Harsa, see Tel-harsa	127 b	Hebron	41 b	Hilkiah	44 b
Harsha	48 b	Hebron	91 b	"hill of the foreskins"	29 b
Harum	38 a	Hebronites	41 b	"hill, the"	29 b
Harumaph	48 a	Hegai	36 a	Hillel	37 a
Haruphite	48 a	Hege	36 a	Hinnom	App.
Haruz	48 a	Helah	44 a	Hirah	43 b
Hasadiah	46 a	Helam	43 b	Hiram	43 b
Hashabiah	49 a	Helam	44 a	Hittite	49 b
Hashabiah	49 a	Helbah	44 a	Hittites	49 b
Hashabnah	49 a	Helbon	44 a	Hivite	42 a
Hashabniah	49 a	Heldai	44 a	Hizkiah	58 b
Hashbadana	49 a	Heleb	44 a	Hizkijah	58 b
Hashem	38 a	Heled	44 a	Hobab	41 a
Hashmonah	49 b	Helek	44 b	Hobah	42 a
Hashub	49 a	Helekites	44 b	Hobaiah	41 a
Hashubah	49 a	Helem	37 a	Hod	36 b
Hashum	49 b	Helem	44 b	Hodaiah	36 b
Hashupha	49 a	Heleph	44 b	Hodaviah	36 b
Hasrah	46 a	Helez	44 b	Hodesh	42 a
Hassenaah	89 b	Helkai	44 b	Hodevah	36 b
Hasshub	49 a	Helkath	44 b	Hodevah	36 b
Hasupha	49 a	Helkath-hazzurim	44 b	Hodijah	36 b
Hatach	38 a	Helon	44 b	Hodshi	42 a
Hathath	49 b	Hemam	37 a	Hoglah	41 b
Hatipha	43 b	Heman	37 a	Hoglah, see Beth-hoglah	22 a
Hatita	43 b	Hemath	45 a	Hoham	36 b
Hattaavah, see Kibroth-hattaavah	109 b	Hemdan	45 a	Holon	44 a
		Hen	45 b	Homam	36 b
Hatticon, see Hazar-hatticon	47 b	Hena	37 b	Hophni	46 a
		Henadad	45 b	Hophra, see Pharaoh-hophra	105 a
Hattil	43 b	Hepher	46 b		
Hattush	43 b	Hepherites	46 b	Hor	37 b
Hauran	42 b	Hephzi-bah	46 b	Hor-hagidgad	47 b
Havilah	42 a	Heres	48 b	Horam	38 a
Hazael	43 a	Heres, see Kir-heres	111 a	Horeb	App.
Hazaiah	43 a	Heres, see Timnath-heres	128 a	Horem	48 a
Hazar-addar	47 a			Hori	42 b
Hazar Enan	47 b	Heresh	48 b	Hormah	48 a
Hazar Enan	47 b	Hermon	48 b	Horon, see Beth-horon	22 a
Hazar-gaddah	47 a	Hermon, see Baal-hermon	26 a	Horonaim	48 b
Hazar-hatticon	47 a			Horonite	48 b
Hazar-shual	47 b	Hesed	46 a	Hosah	46 a
Hazar-susah	47 b	Heshbon	49 a	Hosea	37 a
Hazar-susim	47 b	Heshmon	49 b	Hoshaiah	37 a
Hazarmaveth	47 a	Heth	49 b	Hoshama	36 b
Hazazon-tamar	47 a	Hethlon	49 b	Hoshea	37 a
Hazelel-poni	37 b	Hezeki	43 b	Hotham	43 a
Hazelel-poni	107 b	Hezekiah	43 b	Hothir	37 a

"house of Caleb, of the"	68 a	Ir	95 b	Jaakan, see "Beeroth of the children of Jaakan"	19 a
"house of Eden, the"	22 b	Ir-nahash	96 a		
"house of Gilgal, the"	21 b	Ir-shemesh	96 a	Jaakan, see Bene-jaakan	25 a
		Ira	95 b		
		Irad	96 a		
"house of God"	21 a	Iram	96 a	Jaakobah	61 a
"house of Joab," see Ataroth	94 a	Iri	96 a	Jaala	61 a
		Irijah	62 b	Jaalah	61 a
"house, shearing"	22 b	Iron	62 b	Jaalam	61 a
Hukok	42 b	Irpeel	64 a	Jaanai	61 a
Hul	42 b	Iru	96 a	Jaare-oregim	61 a
Huldah	44 a	Isaac	62 a	Jaasau	61 b
Humtah	45 a	Isaac	64 b	Jaasiel	61 b
Hupham	42 b	Isaiah	66 a	Jaazaniah	50 b
Huphamites	42 b	Iscah	60 a	Jaazaniah	50 b
Huppah	46 a	Ish-bosheth	9 b	Jaazer	60 b
Huppim	46 a	Ishaiah	65 b	Jaaziah	60 b
Hur	42 b	Ishbah	64 b	Jaaziel	60 b
Hurai	42 b	Ishbak	65 a	Jabal	51 a
Huram	42 b	Ishbi-benob	64 b	Jabbok	51 b
Huram	43 b	Ishbi-benob	65 a	Jabesh	51 b
Huri	42 b	Ishi	66 a	Jabez	60 a
Hushah	42 b	Ishijah	65 b	Jabin	51 a
Hushai	43 a	Ishma	65 b	Jabneel	51 a
Husham	43 a	Ishmael	65 b	Jabneh	51 a
Hushathite	49 b	Ishmaelites	65 b	Jachan	60 b
Hushim	43 a	Ishmaiah	65 b	Jachin	59 b
Hushim	49 b	Ishmeelites	65 b	Jachinites	59 b
Huzoth, see Kirjath-huzoth	112 a	Ishmerai	65 b	Jacob	61 a
		Ishod	10 a	Jada	52 b
		Ishpan	66 a	Jadau	52 a
Ibhar	51 a	Ishtob	10 a	Jaddua	52 a
Ibleam	51 a	Ishuah	65 a	Jadon	52 a
Ibneiah	51 b	Ishui	65 a	Jael	61 a
Ibnijah	51 b	Ismachiah	60 a	Jagur	51 a
Ibri	App.	Ismaiah	65 b	Jah	52 b
Ibzan	4 a	Ispah	66 a	Jahath	59 a
I-chabod	9 b	Israel	64 b	Jahaz	56 a
Idalah	52 a	Israel, see El-elohe-Israel	10 b	Jahazah	56 a
Idbash	52 a			Jahaziah	58 b
Iddo	52 a	"Israel, of"	64 b	Jahaziel	58 b
Iddo	60 a	Israelite	64 b	Jahdai	52 b
Iddo	91 b	Israelitish	64 b	Jahdiel	58 a
Iddo	4 b	Issachar	64 b	Jahdo	58 a
Idumea	4 b	Isuah	65 a	Jahleel	58 b
Igdaliah	51 b	Isui	65 a	Jahleelites	59 a
Igeal	51 b	Ithamar	10 a	Jahmai	59 a
Iim	94 b	Ithiel	10 a	Jahzah	56 a
Ije-abarim	94 b	Ithmah	66 b	Jahzeel	59 a
Ijon	94 b	Ithnan	66 b	Jahzeelites	59 a
Ikkesh	100 a	Ithra	66 b	Jahzeiah	58 b
Ilai	94 b	Ithran	66 b	Jahziel	58 b
Imla	60 a	Ithream	66 b	Jahziel	59 a
Imlah	60 a	Ithrite	66 b	Jair	50 b
Immanuel	98 a	Ittah-kazin	101 b	Jair	60 b
Immer	14 a	Ittai	10 a	Jairite	50 b
Imna	60 a	Ittai	18 a	Jakan	61 a
Imna	60 a	Ivah	92 b	Jakeh	62 a
Imrah	60 a	Izeharites	62 a	Jakim	62 a
Imri	14 a	Izhar	62 a	Jalon	59 b
India	36 a	Izharites	62 a	Jamin	59 b
"inhabitants of Chaldea"	70 a	Izrahiah	58 a	Jaminites	59 b
		Izrahite	58 a	Jamlech	60 b
Iphideiah	61 b	Izri	62 a	Janoah	60 a

JAN (230) JOE

Janum	60 a	Jehoahaz	53 a	Jesaiah	66 a
Japheth	61 b	Jehoahaz	56 a	Jeshaiah	66 a
Japhia	61 b	Jehoash	53 a	Jeshaiah	66 a
Japhlet	61 b	Jehohanan	55 a	Jeshanah	66 a
Japhleti	61 b	Jehoiachin	55 a	Jesharelah	66 a
Japho	61 b	Jehoiachin	56 b	Jeshebeab	64 b
Jarah	61 a	Jehoiada	55 a	Jesher	66 a
Jareb	62 b	Jehoiada	56 b	Jeshimoth, see Beth-jeshimoth	21 b
Jared	63 a	Jehoiakim	55 a		
Jaresiah	61 a	Jehoiarib	55 a	Jeshishai	65 b
Jarha	63 b	Jehonadab	55 a	Jeshohaiah	65 a
Jarib	63 b	Jehoram	55 b	Jeshua	65 b
Jarkon, see Me-jarkon	75 b	Jehoshabeath	55 b	Jeshurun	66 a
Jarmuth	64 a	Jehoshaphat	55 b	Jesimiel	64 b
Jaroah	63 a	Jehoshaphat	57 b	Jesse	65 b
Jashen	65 b	Jehosheba	55 b	Jesse	10 a
Jashobeam	65 a	Jehoshua	55 b	Jesui	65 a
Jashub	65 a	Jehovah	53 b	Jesuites	65 a
Jashub	65 b	Jehovah-jireh	54 b	Jesurun	66 a
Jashub, see Shear-Jashub	118 a	Jehovah-nissi	54 b	Jether	66 b
		Jehovah-shalom	55 a	Jetheth	66 b
Jashubi-lehem	65 a	Jehozabad	55 a	Jethlah	66 a
Jashubites	65 a	Jehozadak	55 b	Jethro	66 b
Jasiel	61 b	Jehu	53 a	Jethro	66 b
Jathniel	66 b	Jehubbah	41 a	Jetur	59 a
Jattir	66 a	Jehuchal	55 a	Jeuel	60 b
Javan	56 b	Jehud	53 a	Jeush	60 b
Jazer	60 b	Jehudi	53 a	Jeush	60 b
Jaziz	58 a	Jehush	60 b	Jeuz	60 b
Jearim, see Kirjath-jearim	112 a	Jeiel	60 b	Jew	53 a
		Jeiel	60 b	Jewry	53 a
Jeaterai	51 a	Jekabzeel	62 a	Jews	53 a
Jeberechiah	51 b	Jekameam	62 b	"Jews' language"	53 a
Jebus	51 a	Jekamiah	62 a	Jezaniah	58 a
Jebusite	51 a	Jekuthiel	62 a	Jezaniah	58 a
Jecholiah	59 b	Jemimah	59 b	Jezebel	9 b
Jecoliah	59 b	Jemuel	59 b	Jezer	62 a
Jecoliah	59 b	Jephthah	61 b	Jezerites	62 a
Jeconiah	59 a	Jephunneh	61 b	Jeziah	57 b
Jeconiah	59 b	Jerah	63 a	Jeziel	57 b
Jeconiah	59 b	Jerahmeel	63 b	Jezliah	58 a
Jedaiah	52 b	Jerahmeelites	63 b	Jezoar	107 a
Jedaiah	52 b	Jeremai	64 a	Jezreel	58 a
Jedeiah	58 a	Jeremiah	64 a	Jezreelite	58 a
Jediael	52 b	Jeremiah	64 a	Jezreelitess	58 a
Jedidah	52 a	Jeremoth	64 a	Jibsam	51 b
Jedidiah	52 a	Jeriah	64 a	Jidlaph	52 b
Jeduthun	52 a	Jeribai	63 b	Jimnah	60 a
Jeduthun	52 b	Jericho	63 b	Jimnites	60 a
Jeezer	9 b	Jericho	64 a	Jiphtah	61 b
Jeezerites	9 b	Jeriel	63 b	Jiphthah-el	61 b
Jegar Sahadutha	52 a	Jerijah	63 b	Joab	56 a
Jehadijah	52 b	Jerimoth	64 a	Joab, see Ataroth, the house of	94 a
Jehaleel	56 a	Jerioth	64 a		
Jehezekel	58 b	Jeroboam	62 b	Joah	56 a
Jehiah	58 b	Jeroham	63 b	Joash	56 a
Jehiel	58 b	Jerubbaal	62 b	Joash	57 b
Jehiel	58 b	Jerubbesheth	62 b	Job	9 a
Jehiel	60 b	Jeruel	63 a	Job	56 a
Jehiel	60 b	Jerusalem	63 a	Jobab	56 a
Jehieli	58 b	Jerusalem	63 b	Jochebed	56 b
Jehoadah	55 a	Jerusha	63 a	Joed	57 a
Jehoaddan	55 b	Jerushah	63 a	Joel	56 a
Jehoaddan	55 b	Jesaiah	65 b	Joelah	57 a

Joezer	57	a	Kallai			Kohathites	110 a
Jogbethah	51	b	Kanah	111	b	Kolaiah	110 b
Jogli	51	b	Kareah	111	b	Korah	111 b
Joha	56	b	Karkaa	112	b	Korahites	111 b
Johanan	55	a	Karkor	112	b	Korathites	111 b
Johanan	56	b	Karnaim, see Ash-			Kore	110 b
Joiada	56	b	taroth Karnaim	101	a	"Kore, sons of"	111 b
Joiakim	56	b	Kartah	112	b	Korhites	111 b
Joiarib	56	b	Kartan	112	b	Koz	37 b
Jokdeam	62	a	Kattath	110	b	Koz	110 b
Jokim	57	a	Kazin, see Ittah-kazin	101	b	Kushaiah	110 b
Jokmeam	62	b	Kedar	110	a		
Jokneam	62	b	Kedemah	109	b	Laadah	72 a
Jokshan	62	b	Kedemoth	109	b	Laadan	72 a
Joktan	62	a	Kedesh	110	a	Laban	70 b
Joktheel	62	b	Kehalathah	110	a	Lachish	72 a
Jonadab	56	b	Keilah	111	b	Lael	70 b
Jonadab	55	a	Kelaiah	111	a	Lahad	71 a
Jonah	57	a	Kelita	111	b	"Lahai-roi, the well"	19 a
Jonathan	57	a	Kemuel	111	b	Lahmam	71 b
Jonathan	55	a	Kenan	111	a	Lahmi	71 b
Joppa	61	b	Kenath	111	b	Laish	71 b
Jorah	57	b	Kenaz	111	b	Laish	71 b
Jorai	57	b	Kenezite	111	b	Lakum	72 a
Joram	57	b	Kenite	111	a	Lamech	72 a
Joram	55	a	Kenite	111	a	"language, Jews'"	53 a
Jordan	63	a	Kenizzites	111	b	Lapidoth	72 a
Jorkeam	64	a	Keren-happuch	112	a	Lasha	72 a
Josedech	55	b	Kerioth	112	a	Leah	70 b
Joseph	57	a	Keros	111	a	Lebanah	70 b
Joseph	55	a	Keturah	110	b	Lebanah	70 b
Joshah	57	b	Kezia	111	b	Lebanon	70 b
Joshaphat	57	b	"Keziz, the valley of"	98	a	Lebaoth	70 b
Joshaviah	57	b	Kibroth-hattaavah	109	b	Lebaoth, see Beth-le-baoth	22 a
Joshbekashah	65	a	Kibzaim	109	b		
Joshua	55	b	Kidron	110	a	Lebonah	70 b
Josiah	50	b	Kinah	111	b	Lecah	71 b
Josiah	50	b	"king's dale, the"	98	a	Lehabim	71 a
Josiah	50	b	Kir	111	a	Lehi	71 b
Josibiah	57	b	Kir-haraseth	111	a	Lehi, see Ramath-lehi	114 b
Josiphiah	57	a	Kir-hareseth	111	a	Lemuel	72 a
Jotbah	59	a	Kir-haresh	111	a	Leshem	72 a
Jotbath	59	a	Kir-heres	111	a	Letushim	71 b
Jotbathah	59	a	Kiriathaim	112	a	Leummim	70 b
Jotham	57	b	Kiriathaim, see Sha-veh Kiriathaim	119	a	Levi	71 b
Jozabad	56	b				Levite	71 b
Jozachar	56	b	Kirioth	112	a	Levites	71 b
Jozadak	57	a	Kirjath-arba	112	a	Libnah	70 b
Jubal	56	b	Kirjath-arim	112	a	Libni	71 a
Juchal	56	b	Kirjath-baal	112	a	Libnites	71 a
Judah	53	a	Kirjath-huzoth	112	a	Libya	102 a
Judah	53	a	Kirjath-jearim	112	a	Libyans	70 b
"Judah, men of"	53	a	Kirjath-sannah	112	a	Libyans	102 a
Judea	53	a	Kirjath-sepher	112	a	Likhi	72 a
Judith	53	a	Kirjathaim	112	a	Lo-ammi	70 b
Jushab-hesed	57	b	Kish	111	a	Lo-debar	70 b
Juttah	56	b	Kishi	111	a	Lo-debar	71 a
Juttah	59	a	Kishion	112	b	Lo-ruhamah	70 b
			Kishon	111	a	Lod	71 a
Kabzeel	109	b	Kishon	112	b	"Lord, the"	5 a
Kadesh	110	a	Kithlish	70	b	"Lord, the"	53 b
Kadesh-barnea	110	a	Kitron	110	b	Lot	71 b
Kadmiel	109	b	Kittim	70	a	Lotan	71 b
Kadmonites	110	a	Kohath	110	a	Lubim	71 a

Lubims	71 a	Maktesh	77 a	Meholah, *see* Abel-meholah	3 b
Lud	71 a	Malachi	77 a		
Ludim	71 a	Malcham	78 a	Meholathite	75 a
Luhith	71 a	Malchi-shua	78 a	Mehujael	74 b
Luz	71 a	Malchiah	77 b	Mehujael	75 a
Lydia	71 a	Malchiah	77 b	Mehuman	73 b
Lydians	71 a	Malchiel	77 b	Mehunim	79 a
		Malchielites	77 b	Mehunims	79 a
Maachah	79 a	Malchijah	77 b	Mekonah	77 a
Maachah, *see* Beth-maachah	22 b	Malchiram	78 a	Melah, *see* Tel-melah	128 a
		Mallothi	77 b	Melatiah	77 b
Maachathite	79 a	Malluch	77 b	Melchi-shua	78 a
Maachathites	79 a	Mamre	78 a	Melchizedek	77 b
Maadai	78 b	Manahath	78 a	Melech	77 b
Maadiah	79 a	"Manahethites, half of the"	46. b	Melech, *see* Ebed-melech	91 a
Maai	79 a				
Maaleh-accrabbim	79 a	"Manahethites, half the"	46 b	Melech, *see* Nathan-melech	87 b
Maarath	79 b				
Maaseiah	75 a	Manasseh	78 b	Melech, *see* Regem-melech	113 b
Maaseiah	79 b	"Manasseh, of"	78 b		
Maaseiah	79 b	Manassites	78 b	Melicu	77 b
Maasiai	79 b	Manoah	78 a	Melicu	77 b
Maaz	79 b	Maoch	79 a	Memphis	79 b
Maaziah	79 a	Maon	79 a	Memucan	74 a
Maaziah	79 a	Maonites	79 a	Memucan	78 a
Machbanai	76 b	Mara	80 b	"men of Judah"	53 a
Machbenah	76 b	Marah	81 b	"men of Tyre"	109 a
Machi	76 b	Maralah	81 b	Menahem	78 a
Machir	76 b	Maresha	80 b	Meon, *see* Baal-meon	26 a
"Machir, of"	76 b	Mareshah	81 b	Meon, *see* Beth-baal-meon	21 a
Machnadebai	77 a	Maroth	81 b		
Machpelah	77 a	Marsena	81 b	Meon, *see* Beth-meon	22 b
Madai	73 a	Mash	82 a	Meonothai	79 a
Madmannah	73 b	Mashal	82 b	Mephaath	74 b
Madmen	73 b	Masrekah	82 a	Mephaath	76 a
Madmenah	73 b	Massa	82 a	Mephibosheth	79 b
Madon	73 a	Massah	78 b	Merab	80 b
Magbish	72 b	Matred	75 b	Meraiah	81 b
Magdiel	72 b	Matri	75 b	Meraioth	81 b
Magog	73 a	Mattan	83 b	Merari	81 b
Magor-missabib	73 a	Mattanah	83 b	Merarites	81 b
Magpiash	73 a	Mattaniah	83 b	Merathaim	81 b
Mahalaleel	73 b	Mattaniah	83 b	"mercy, not obtained"	70 b
Mahalath	75 a	Mattathah	83 b	Mered	80 b
Mahali	75 a	Mattenai	83 b	Meremoth	81 b
Mahanaim	75 a	Mattithiah	83 b	Meres	81 b
Mahaneh-dan	75 a	Me-jarkon	75 b	Merib-baal	81 b
Maharai	73 b	Meah	72 b	Merib-baal	81 b
Mahath	75 b	Mearah	79 b	Meribah	76 b
Mahavite	74 b	Mebunnai	72 b	Merodach	80 b
Mahazioth	75 a	Mecherathite	77 a	Merodach, *see* Evil-merodach	6 a
Maher-shalal-hash-baz	74 a	Medad	75 b		
		Medan	73 b	Merodach-baladan	80 b
Mahlah	75 a	Mede	73 a	Merom	81 b
Mahli	75 a	Medeba	75 b	Meron, *see* Shimron-meron	123 b
Mahlites	75 a	Medes	73 a		
Mahlon	75 a	Media	73 a	Meronothite	81 b
Mahol	74 b	Median	73 a	Meroz	81 b
Maim, *see* Abel-maim	3 b	Megiddo	72 b	Mesha	76 b
Maim, *see* Misrephoth-maim	82 a	Megiddon	72 b	Mesha	76 b
		Mehetabeel	73 b	Mesha	82 a
Makaz	80 b	Mehetabel	73 b	Meshach	76 b
Makheloth	80 b	Mehida	75 a	Meshech	82 b
Makkedah	80 a	Mehir	75 a	Meshelemiah	82 b

Meshelemiah	82	b	Mispereth	78	b	Naioth	85	a
Meshezabeel	82	b	Misrephoth-maim	82	a	Naioth	86	a
Meshillemith	83	a	Mithcah	83	b	Naomi	86	b
Meshillemoth	82	b	Mithnite	83	b	Naphish	87	a
Meshobab	82	b	Mithredath	83	b	Naphtali	87	a
Meshullam	82	b	Mizpah	80	a	Naphtuhim	87	a
Meshullemeth	83	a	Mizpeh	80	a	Nathan	87	b
Mesobaite	80	a	Mizpeh, see Ramath-mizpeh	114	b	Nathan-melech	87	b
Mesopotamia	16	b				Neah	86	b
Mesopotamia	16	b	Mizraim	80	a	Neariah	87	a
Metheg-ammah	83	a	Mizraim, see Abel-mizraim	3	b	Nebai	84	b
Methusael	83	a				Nebai	86	a
Methuselah	83	a	Mizzah	74	b	Nebaioth	84	b
Meunim	79	a	Moab	74	a	Nebajoth	84	b
Mezahab	75	b	Moab, see Pahath-moab	102	b	Neballat	84	b
Miamin	76	a	"Moab, of"	74	a	Nebat	84	b
Mibhar	72	b	"Moab, women of"	74	a	Nebo	84	a
Mibsam	72	b	Moabite	74	a	Nebo, see Samgar-nebo	89	b
Mibzar	72	b	Moabitess	74	a	Nebuchadnezzar	84	a
Micah	76	a	Moabitish	74	a	Nebuchadrezzar	84	a
Micah	76	a	Moadiah	74	a	Nebushasban	84	a
Micah	76	a	Moladah	74	a	Nebuzaradan	84	a
Micaiah	76	a	Molech	77	b	Necho	86	a
Micha	75	a	Molid	74	a	Necho, see Pharaoh-necho	105	a
Michael	75	a	Morasthite	74	b			
Michaiah	76	a	Mordecai	81	a	Nedabiah	84	b
Michaiah	76	a	Moreh	74	b	Nego, see Abed-nego	91	a
Michaiah	76	a	Moresheth-gath	74	b	Nehelamite	85	b
Michal	76	a	Moriah	App.		Nehemiah	85	b
Michmas	76	b	Mosera	74	a	Nehum	85	a
Michmash	76	b	Moseroth	78	b	Nehushta	85	b
Michmethah	77	a	Moses	82	a	Nehushtan	85	b
Michri	77	a	Moza	74	b	Neiel	86	b
Middin	73	a	Mozah	80	a	Nekeb	87	b
Midian	73	a	Muppim	79	b	Nekodah	87	b
Midianite	73	a	Mushi	74	b	Nemuel	86	a
Midianite	73	b	Mushites	74	b	Nemuelites	86	a
Midianites	73	b				Nepheg	87	a
Migdal-el	72	b	Naam	86	b	Nephishesim	App.	
Migdal-gad	72	b	Naamah	86	b	Nephishesim	App.	
Migdol	72	b	Naaman	86	b	Nephtoah, waters of	76	b
Migron	73	a	Naamathite	86	b	Nephusim	87	a
Mijamin	76	a	Naamites	86	b	Nephusim	87	a
Mikloth	80	b	Naarah	86	b	Ner	87	b
Mikneiah	80	b	Naarai	87	a	Nergal	87	b
Milalai	78	a	Naaran	87	a	Nergal-sharezer	87	b
Milcah	77	b	Naashon	85	b	Neriah	87	b
Milcom	78	a	Nabal	84	b	Neriah	87	b
Millo	77	a	Naboth	84	a	Nethaneel	87	b
Miniamin	78	b	Nachon	86	a	Nethaniah	88	a
Minni	78	b	Nadab	84	b	Nethaniah	88	a
Minnith	78	b	Nahalal	84	b	Netophah	App.	
Miriam	81	b	Nahaliel	85	a	Netophathite	App.	
Mirma	81	b	Nahalol	84	b	Neziah	87	b
Misgab	82	b	Naham	85	b	Nezib	87	a
Mishael	76	b	Nahamani	85	b	Nibhaz	84	b
Mishal	82	a	Nahari	85	b	Nibshan	84	b
Misham	83	a	Nahash	85	b	Nimrah	86	a
Mishma	83	a	Nahash, see Ir-nahash	96	a	Nimrah, see Beth-nimrah	22	b
Mishmannah	83	a	Nahath	85	b			
Mishpat, see En-mishpat	95	a	Nahbi	85	a	Nimrim	86	a
			Nahor	85	a	Nimrod	86	a
Mishraites	83	a	Nahshon	85	b	Nimshi	86	b
Mispar	78	b	Nahum	85	a	Nineveh	86	a

NIS (234) RAB

Nisroch	86 b	Palestine	103 b	Peulthai	104 b
No	83 b	Palet, see Beth-palet	23 a	Phaltiel	103 b
Noadiah	85 a	Pallu	103 a	Pharaoh	105 a
Noah	85 a	Palluites	103 a	Pharaoh-hophra	105 a
Noah	86 b	Palti	103 b	Pharaoh-nechoh	105 a
Nob	84 a	Paltiel	103 b	Pharez	105 b
Nobah	84 b	Paltite	103 b	Pharphar	105 b
Nod	85 a	Parah	104 b	Pharzites	105 b
Nodab	85 a	Paran	101 b	Phaseah	104 a
Nogah	84 b	Paran, see El-paran	9 b	Phelet, see Beth-phelet	23 a
Nohah	85 a	Parez, see Rimmon-parez	114 b	Phichol	102 b
Non	85 a			Philistia	103 ?b
Noph	87 a	Parmashta	105 a	Philistine	103 b
Nophah	87 a	Parnach	105 a	Philistines	103 b
"not obtained mercy"	70 b	Parosh	105 b	Phinehas	103 a
"number, that"	78 b	Parshandatha	105 b	Phurah	104 b
Nun	85 a	Paruah	104 b	Phut	102 a
		Parvaim	104 b	Phuvah	102 a
Obadiah	91 a	Pas-dammim	104 a	Pi-beseth	102 b
Obadiah	91 a	Pasach	104 a	Pi-hahiroth	102 b
Obal	92 b	Paseah	104 a	Pildash	103 a
Obed	92 b	Pashur	105 b	Pileha	103 b
Obed-edom	90 b	"passages, the"	91 a	Pileser, see Tiglath-pileser	126 a
Obil	6 a	Pathros	106 a		
Oboth	4 a	Pathrusim	106 a	Pilneser, see Tilgath-pilneser	127 b
Ocran	96 b	Pau	104 a		
Oded	92 b	Pazzez, see Beth-pazzez	23 a	Piltai	103 b
Og	92 b	Pedahel	101 b	Pinon	103 a
Ohad	5 b	Pedahzur	101 b	Piram	104 b
Ohel	5 b	Pedaiah	102 a	Pirathon	105 b
Omar	6 a	Pedaiah	102 a	Pirathonite	105 b
Omri	98 b	Pekah	104 b	Pisgah	104 a
On	6 a	Pekahiah	104 b	Pison	103 a
On	14 a	Pekod	104 b	Pispah	104 a
Onam	6 a	Pelaiah	103 a	Pithom	106 a
Onan	6 a	Pelaiah	103 b	Pithon	103 a
Ono	6 a	Pelaliah	103 b	"place, fruitful"	69 b
Ophel	99 b	Pelatiah	103 b	"places, besieged"	80 a
Ophir	6 a	Pelatiah	103 b	"plain of the vineyards"	3 b
Ophni	99 b	Peleg	103 a		
Ophrah	99 b	Pelet	103 b	"plentiful field"	69 b
Oreb	App.	Peleth	104 a	"Pochereth of Zebaim"	103 a
Oregim, see Jaare-oregim	61 a	Pelonite	103 a	"populous"	83 b
		Peniel	104 a	Poratha	102 b
Oren	17 a	Peninnah	104 a	Potiphar	102 a
Ornan	17 a	Penuel	104 a	Potiphera	102 a
Orpah	100 b	Peor	104 a	"preacher"	110 a
Oshea	37 a	Peor, see Baal-peor	26 a	"privily" (marg. to Tormah)	129 a
Othni	101 b	Peor, see Beth-peor	23 a		
Othniel	101 b	Perazim, see Baal-perazim	26 a	Pua	102 a
Ozem	15 b			Puah	102 a
Oznites	7 a	Peresh	105 b	Puah	102 b
		Perez	105 b	Puhites	102 b
Paaneah, see Zaphnath-paaneah	108 b	Perez-uzzah	105 b	Pul	102 a
		Perida	105 a	Punites	102 a
Paarai	104 b	Perizzites	104 b	Punon	102 b
Padan	102 a	Persia	105 a	Put	102 a
Padan-aram	102 a	Persian	105 a	Putiel	102 a
Padon	102 a	Persian	105 a		
Pagiel	101 b	Persians	105 a	Raamah	115 a
Pahath Moab	102 b	Peruda	104 b	Raamiah	115 a
Pai	104 a	Pethahiah	106 a	Raamses	115 a
Palal	103 b	Pethor	106 a	Rabbah	113 a
Palestina	103 b	Pethuel	105 b	Rabbath	115 a

Rabbim, see Bath-rabbim	28 b	Reubenites	112 b	Sansannah	90 a
		Reuel	115 a	Saph	90 a
Rabbith	113 a	Reumah	113 a	Saphir	124 b
Rabshakeh	113 a	Rezeph	116 a	Sarah	117 a
Rachal	114 a	Rezia	116 a	Sarah	117 a
Rachel	114 a	Rezin	116 a	Sarai	117 a
Raddai	113 b	Rezon	113 b	Saraph	117 b
Raguel	115 a	Ribai	114 a	Sardites	90 b
Rahab	113 b	Riblah	113 a	Sargon	90 b
Rahab	113 b	Rimmon	114 b	Sarid	117 a
Raham	114 a	Rimmon, see En-rimmon	95 b	Sarsechim	117 b
Rahel	114 a			"sat in the seat, that"	64 b
Rakkath	116 a	Rimmon, see Gath-rimmon	33 a	Saul	117 a
Rakkon	116 a			"Sea, Red"	88 b
Ram	114 a	Rimmon-parez	114 b	Seba	88 a
Ramah	114 b	Rinnah	115 a	Sacacah	89 a
Ramath	113 a	Riphath (marg. Diphath)	34 b	Sechu	116 b
Ramath-lehi	114 b			Segub	116 a
Ramath-mizpeh	114 b	Riphath	114 a	Seir	117 a
Ramathaim-zophim	114 b	Rissah	115 a	"Seirath, unto"	App.
Ramathite	114 b	Rithmah	116 a	Sela	89 b
Rameses	115 a	Rizpah	116 a	Sela-hammalekoth	89 b
Ramiah	114 b	Rogel, see En-rogel	95 b	Selah	89 b
Ramoth	113 a	Rogelim	113 a	Seled	89 a
Ramoth	114 b	Rohgah	113 b	Semachiah	89 b
Rapha	115 b	Romamti-ezer	113 b	Senaah	89 b
Rapha	115 b	Rosh	113 b	Seneh	89 b
Raphu	115 b	Ruhamah, see Loruhamah	70 b	Senir	117 a
Reaia	113 a			Sennacherib	89 b
Reaiah	113 a	Rumah	113 b	Senuah	37 b
Reba	113 a	Ruth	113 b	Senuah	89 b
Rebekah	113 a			Seorim	117 a
Rechab	114 a	Sabeans	88 a	"Sephar, to"	90 a
Rechabites	114 a	Sabeans	118 a	Sepharad	90 a
Rechah	114 a	Sabeans	118 a	Sepharvaim	90 a
"Red sea"	88 b	Sabta	88 a	Sepharvaim	90 a
Reelaiah	115 a	Sabtah	88 a	Sepharvites	90 a
Regem	113 b	Sabtechah	88 a	Sepher, see Kirjath-sepher	112 a
Regem-melech	113 b	Sacar	116 b		
Rehabiah	114 a	Sahadutha, see Jegar-sahadutha	52 a	Serah	117 a
Rehabiah	114 a			Serah, see Timnath-serah	128 a
Rehob	114 a	Salah	121 a		
Rehob, see Beth-rehob	23 a	Salathiel	118 a	Seraiah	117 a
Rehoboam	114 a	Salcah	89 a	Seraiah	117 b
Rehoboth	113 b	Salem	121 a	Sered	90 a
Rehum	114 a	Sallai	89 a	Serug	117 a
Rei	115 a	Sallu	89 a	Seth	125 b
Rekem	116 a	Sallu	89 a	Sether	90 b
Remaliah	114 b	Salma	116 b	Shaalabbin	124 b
Remeth	114 b	Salmon	107 b	Shaalbim	124 a
Remmon	114 b	Salmon	116 b	Shaalbonite	124 a
Rephael	115 b	Salmon	116 b	Shaaph	124 a
Rephah	115 b	"salt, city of"	96 a	Shaaraim	124 a
Rephaiah	115 b	Salu	89 a	Shaashgaz	124 b
Rephaim	115 b	Samaria	123 a	Shabbethai	118 b
"Rephaim, the valley of"	98 a	Samaria	123 b	Shachia	118 a
		Samaritans	123 b	Shadrach	118 b
Rephaims	115 b	Samgar-nebo	89 b	Shage	118 b
Rephidim	115 b	Samlah	117 a	Shahar, see Zareth-shahar	109 b
Resen	115 a	Samson	123 a		
Resheph	116 a	Samuel	122 a	Shaharaim	120 a
Reu	115 a	Sanballat	89 b	Shahazimah	120 a
Reuben	112 b	Sannah, see Kirjath-sannah	112 a	Shalem	121 a
"Reuben, children of"	112 b			Shalim	124 a

Shalisha	122 a	Shechem	120 b	Shilhim	121 a
Shalisha, see Baal-shalisha	26 b	Shechem	120 b	Shillem	121 a
		Shechemites	120 b	Shillemites	121 b
Shallecheth	121 a	Shedeur	118 b	Shiloah	121 a
Shallum	121 a	Shehariah	120 a	Shiloh	120 b
Shallum	121 a	Shelah	120 b	Shiloh, see Taanath-shiloh	126 a
Shalmai	116 b	Shelah	121 a		
Shalmai	121 b	Shelanites	121 b	Shiloni	120 b
Shalmai	122 b	Shelemiah	121 b	Shilonite	120 b
Shalman	121 b	Shelemiah	121 b	Shilshah	122 b
Shalmaneser	121 b	Sheleph	121 b	Shimea	123 a
Shama	122 b	Shelesh	121 b	Shimeah	122 a
Shamer	123 a	Shelomi	121 b	Shimeah	123 a
Shamgar	122 a	Shelomith	121 b	Shimeah	123 a
Shamhuth	122 a	Shelomoth	121 a	Shimeam	122 a
Shamir	122 b	Shelumiel	121 b	Shimeath	123 a
Shamir	122 b	Shem	122 a	Shimeathites	123 a
Shamma	122 a	Shema	122 b	Shimei	123 a
Shammah	122 a	Shemaah	38 a	Shimei	123 a
Shammai	122 b	Shemaah	123 a	"Shimei, of"	123 a
Shammoth	122 b	Shemaiah	123 a	Shimites	123 a
Shammua	122 b	Shemaiah	123 a	Shimma	123 a
Shamsherai	123 b	Shemariah	123 b	Shimon	120 b
Shan, see Beth-shan	23 a	Shemariah	123 b	Shimrath	123 b
Shapham	124 b	Shemeber	122 a	Shimri	123 b
Shaphan	125 a	Shemer	123 a	Shimrith	123 b
Shaphat	124 b	Shemesh, see Beth-shemesh	23 a	Shimrom	123 b
Shapher	125 a			Shimron	123 b
Sharai	125 b	Shemesh, see En-shemesh	95 b	Shimron-meron	123 b
Sharar	125 b			Shimronites	123 b
Sharezer	125 a	Shemesh, see Ir-shemesh	96 a	Shimshai	123 b
Sharezer, see Nergal-sharezer	87 b			Shinab	124 a
		Shemida	122 b	Shinar	124 a
Sharon	125 a	Shemidah	122 b	Shiphi	125 a
Sharonite	125 a	Shemidaites	122 b	Shiphmite	125 a
Sharuhen	125 a	Shemiramoth	122 b	Shiphrah	125 a
Shashai	125 b	Shemuel	122 a	Shiphtan	124 b
Shashak	125 b	Shen	124 a	Shisha	120 b
Shaul	117 b	Shenazar	124 a	Shishak	120 b
Shaulites	118 a	Shenir	124 a	Shishak	120 b
Shaveh	119 a	Shepham	124 b	Shitrai	120 a
Shaveh Kiriathaim	119 a	Shephatiah	124 b	Shittah, see Beth-shittah	22 a
Shavsha	119 b	Shephatiah	124 b		
Sheal	118 a	Shephi	124 b	Shittim	120 a
Shealtiel	118 a	Shepho	124 b	Shiza	120 a
Shealtiel	122 a	Shephuphan	124 b	Shobab	119 a
Shean, see Beth-shean	23 a	Sherah	118 a	Shobach	119 a
Shear-jashub	118 a	Sherah, see Uzzen-sherah	6 b	Shobai	118 a
Sheariah	124 a			Shobal	119 a
"shearing house"	22 b	Sherebiah	125 a	Shobek	119 a
"shearing house"	22 b	Sheresh	125 b	Shobi	118 a
Sheba	118 a	Sheshach	125 b	Shocho	116 b
Sheba	118 b	Sheshai	125 b	Shochoh	116 b
Sheba, see Bath-sheba	29 a	Sheshan	125 b	Shoham	119 a
Shebah	118 b	Sheshbazzar	125 b	Shomer	119 b
Shebam	116 a	Sheth	125 b	Shophach	119 b
Shebaniah	118 b	Shethar	126 a	Shophan, see Atroth-Shophan	94 b
Shebaniah	118 b	Shethar-boznai	126 a		
Shebarim	118 b	Sheva	119 a	Shua	119 b
Sheber	118 b	Shibmah	116 a	Shua	119 b
Shebna	118 b	"Shicron, to"	120 b	Shua, see Bath-shua	29 a
Shebuel	118 a	Shihon	120 b	"Shua, daughter of"	29 a
Shechaniah	120 b	Shihor	120 b	Shuah	119 a
Shechaniah	120 b	Shilhi	121 a	Shuah	119 b

Name	Page	Name	Page	Name	Page
Shual	119 b	Suah	88 b	Tebah	49 b
Shual, see Hazar-shual	47 b	Succoth	89 a	Tebaliah	50 a
Shubael	119 a	Succoth-benoth	89 a	Tebeth	50 a
Shuham	119 a	Suchathites	116 b	Tehaphnehes	127 a
Shuhamites	119 b	Sukkiims	89 a	Tehinnah	127 a
Shuhite	119 a	Susah, see Hazar-susah	47 b	Tekoa	128 b
"Shulamite, the"	119 b	Susanchites	49 a	Tekoah	128 b
Shumathites	123 b	Susi	88 b	"Tekoah, of"	128 b
Shunamite	119 b	Susim, see Hazar-susim	47 b	Tekoite	128 b
Shunem	119 b			Tel-abib	127 b
Shuni	119 b	Syene	88 b	Tel-haresha	127 b
Shunites	119 b	Syria	16 b	Tel-harsa	127 b
Shupham	124 b	Syrian	16 b	Tel-mela	128 a
Shuphamites	119 b	Syrians	16 b	Telah	127 b
Shuppim	124 b	Syrians	16 b	Telaim	50 a
Shur	119 b	Syrians	114 b	Telassar	127 b
Shushan	119 b			Telem	50 a
Shuthalhites	126 a	Taanach	123 b	Tema	127 a
Shuthelah	120 a	Taanath-shiloh	126 a	Teman	127 a
Sia	88 b	Tabbaoth	50 a	Temani	127 b
Siaha	88 b	Tabbath	50 a	Temanite	127 b
Sibbechai	88 a	Tabeal	49 b	Temeni	127 b
Sibmah	116 a	Tabeel	49 b	Tera	129 a
Sibraim	88 a	Taberah	126 a	Teresh	129 a
Siddim	116 b	Tabor	126 a	Thahash	127 a
Sidon	107 a	Tabor, see Aznoth-tabor	7 a	Thamah	128 a
Sidonians	107 a			Tharshish	129 b
Sihon	88 b	Tabor, see Chisloth-tabor	69 a	Thebez	126 b
Sihor	120 b			Tibhath	50 a
Silla	89 a	Tabrimmon	50 a	Tibni	126 a
Siloah	121 a	Tachmonite	127 a	Tidal	126 b
Simeon	123 a	Tadmor	126 b	Tiglath-pileser	126 a
"Simeon, tribe of"	123 a	Tahan	127 a	Tikvah	128 b
Simeonites	123 a	Tahanites	127 a	Tikvath	127 a
Simri	123 b	Tahapanes	127 a	Tikvath	128 b
Sin	88 b	Tahath	127 a	Tilgath-pilneser	127 b
Sinai	88 b	Tahpanhes	127 a	Tilon	126 b
Sinim	88 b	Tahpenes	127 a	Tilon	127 b
Sinite	88 b	Tahtim-hodshi	42 a	Timna	128 a
Sion	116 b	Talmai	128 a	Timnah	128 a
Siphmoth	117 a	Talmon	50 a	Timnah	128 a
Sippai	90 a	Tamar	128 a	Timnath	128 a
Sirah	90 b	Tamar, see Baal-tamar	26 b	Timnath-heres	128 a
Sirion	125 b	Tamar, see Hazazon-tamar	47 a	Timnath-serah	128 a
Sirion	117 b			Timnite	128 a
Sisamai	90 a	Tammuz	128 a	Tiphsah	App.
Sisera	88 b	Tanach	128 b	Tiras	127 b
Sitnah	116 b	Tanhumeth	128 b	Tirathites	129 a
So	88 a	Taphath	50 a	Tirhakah	129 a
Socho	116 b	Tappuah	128 b	Tirhanah	129 a
Sochoh	116 b	Tappuah, see Beth-tappuah	23 a	Tiria	127 b
Socoh	116 b			Tirshatha	129 b
Sodi	88 a	Tappuah, see En-tappuah	95 b	Tirzah	129 a
Sodom	88 a			Tishbite	129 b
Solomon	121 a	Tarah	129 a	Tizite	127 b
"son of Geber, the"	24 b	Taralah	128 b	Toah	126 b
"sons of Gershon"	32 b	Tarea	126 a	Tob	50 a
"sons of Kore"	111 b	Tarea	127 a	Tob-adonijah	50 a
Sophereth	37 b	Tarpelites	50 a	Tobiah	50 a
Sophereth	90 b	Tarshish	129 b	Tobijah	50 a
Sorek	117 b	Tartak	129 b	Tochen	127 b
Sotai	88 b	Tartan	129 b	Togarmah	126 b
"spies"	18 b	Tatnai	129 b	Tohu	127 a

Toi	128	b	Zaanannim	108	b	Zephi	108	b
Tola	126	b	Zaavan	40	b	Zepho	108	b
Tolad	126	b	Zabad	39	a	Zephon	108	b
Tolaites	126	b	Zabbai	39	a	Zephon, see Baal-zephon	26	a
Tophel	App.		Zabbud	39	a			
Tou	128	b	Zabdi	39	a	Zephonites	108	b
"tower of Edar"	73	a	Zabdiel	39	a	Zer	109	a
"tower of the flock"	73	a	Zabud	39	a	Zeradatha	109	a
"troop, that"	29	b	Zaccai	40	a	Zerah	40	b
Tubal	126	b	Zaccur	40	a	Zerahiah	40	b
Tubal-cain	126	b	Zachariah	40	a	Zered	40	b
Tyre	107	a	Zachariah	40	a	Zereda	109	a
"Tyre, men of"	109	a	Zacher	App.		Zererath	109	b
"Tyre, of"	109	a	Zadok	106	b	Zeresh	40	b
Tyrus	107	a	Zaham	39	b	Zereth	109	b
			Zair	108	a	Zeri	109	a
Ucal	10	b	Zalaph	108	a	Zeror	109	a
Uel	6	a	Zalmon	107	b	Zeruah	109	a
Ulai	6	a	Zalmunna	107	b	Zerubbabel	40	b
Ulam	6	a	Zamzummims	40	b	Zeruiah	109	a
Ulla	96	b	Zanoah	40	b	Zetham	41	a
Ummah	96	b	Zaphnath-paaneah	108	b	Zethan	40	b
Unni	98	b	Zaphon	108	b	Zethar	41	a
Uphaz	6	b	Zarah	40	b	Zia	40	a
Ur	6	b	Zareathites	109	a	Ziba	107	a
Uri	6	b	Zared	40	b	Zibeon	106	b
Uriah	6	b	Zarephath	109	a	Zibia	106	a
Uriel	6	b	Zaretan	109	b	Zibiah	106	a
Urijah	6	b	Zareth-shahar	109	b	Zichri	40	a
Uthai	92	b	Zarhites	40	b	Ziddim	106	b
Uz	92	b	Zartanah	109	b	Zidkijah	106	b
Uzai	6	a	Zarthan	109	b	Zidon	107	a
Uzal	6	a	Zattu	41	a	"Zidon, them of"	107	a
Uzza	92	b	Zaza	39	b	Zidonians	106	b
Uzza	92	b	Zebadiah	39	a	Zidonians	107	a
Uzzah	92	a	Zebah	39	b	Ziha	107	a
Uzzah, see Perez-uzzah	105	b	Zebaim, see Pochereth of Zebaim	103	a	Ziklag	107	b
Uzzen-sherah	6	b				Zillah	107	b
Uzzi	92	a	Zebina	39	b	Zilpah	40	a
Uzzia	92	a	Zeboiim	106	b	Zilthai	108	a
Uzziah	92	b	Zeboim	106	a	Zimmah	40	a
Uzziah	92	b	Zeboim	106	b	Zimran	40	b
Uzziel	92	b	Zebudah	39	a	Zimri	40	b
Uzzielites	92	b	Zebul	39	a	Zin	108	a
			Zebulonite	39	a	Zina	39	b
Vajezatha	38	b	Zebulun	39	a	Zion	107	a
"valley of Achor"	98	a	Zechariah	40	a	Zior	107	b
"valley of Berachah"	98	a	Zechariah	40	a	Ziph	40	a
"valley of the giants"	98	a	Zedad	106	b	Ziphah	40	a
"valley of Keziz"	98	a	Zedekiah	106	a	Ziphims	40	a
"valley of Rephaim"	98	a	Zeeb	39	b	Ziphion	108	b
Vaniah	38	b	Zelah	107	b	Ziphites	40	a
Vashni	38	b	Zelek	108	a	"Ziphron, to"	40	b
Vashti	38	b	Zelophehad	108	a	Zippor	108	b
"vineyards, plain of the"	3	b	Zelzah	108	a	Zipporah	109	a
			Zemaraim	108	a	Zithri	90	b
Vophsi	38	b	Zemarite	108	a	Ziz	107	b
			Zemirah	40	b	Ziza	39	b
"what he did" (marg.) Vaheb	38	b	Zenan	108	a	Zizah	39	b
			Zephaniah	108	b	Zoan	108	a
Zaanaim	108	a	Zephaniah	108	b	Zoar	106	b
Zaanan	106	a	Zephath	109	a	Zoba	106	b
						Zobah	106	b

Zobebah	106 a	Zophar	107 a	Zuph	106 b
Zohar	107 a	Zophim	108 b	Zuph	107 b
Zoheleth	39 b	Zophim, see Rama- thaim-zophim	114 b	Zur	107 a
Zoheth	39 b			Zur, see Beth-zur	23 a
Zoheth, see Ben-zo-heth	24 b	Zorah	109 a	Zuriel	107 a
		Zorathites	109 a	Zurishaddai	107 a
Zopha	106 b	Zorites	109 a	Zuzims	39 b
Zophai	106 b	Zuar	106 b		

APPENDIX TO PROPER NAMES.

The following words, omitted in the List, are here supplied as an Appendix.

הִנֹּם, הִנֹּום [hinnōhm'], Hinnom; lamentation. From חנן, Arabic to groan (S.).

זֶכֶר [zĕ'hkher], Zacher (taken from the word in pause, זָכֵר 1 Chron. viii. 31); remembrance. Compare Appellatives.

חֹרֵב, חוֹרֵב [khōhrēhv'], Horeb; dry, arid, desert. From חָרֵב to be dry.

מוֹרִיָּה, מֹרִיָּה [mōhriy-yāh'], Moriah; chosen of God, for מֻרְאַי יָהּ = מַרְאֵה יָהּ, Hophal part. of רָאָה to see. Comp. Gen. xxii. 8, 14.

נְטוֹפָתִי [n'tōhphāhthēe'], Netophathite; gentile noun of נְטֹפָה q. v.

נְטֹפָה [n'tōhphāh'], Netophah; distillation. From נָטַף to drop, distil.

נְפוּשְׁסִים [n'phush'sēem'], Cheth. נְפִישְׁסִים [n'phēesh'sēem'], Keri, Nepheshesim; this word, Neh. vii. 52, seems to be an error of the transcribers, standing for נְפוּסִים or נְפִיסִים Ezr. ii. 50.

עוֹרֵב [ngōhrēhv'], Oreb; raven. Comp. Appellative עֹרֵב.

תִּפְסַח [tiphsakh'], Tiphsah; passage. From פָּסַח to pass over.

תֹּפֶל [tōh'phel], Tophel; murmuring; from תָּפֵל Arab. to spit out, despise, resist (S.). Or, lime, cement, from its insipidity (G.).

HEBREW PROPER NAMES.

The following attempt at a brief Dictionary of the Proper Names found in the Old Testament, does not pretend to any originality as to the explanation. It is chiefly a compilation from the Onomasticon Simonis, and the Thesaurus and Manuale of Gesenius. The meanings given by the former are marked thus (S.), those by the latter writer (G.). It will hardly be needful to notice the use of the following abbreviations—'comp.' for 'compare;' 'cont.' for 'contraction;' 'constr.' for 'construct;' 'Heb.' for 'Hebrew,' &c. &c.—Observe, the pronunciation of the Hebrew is given immediately after the word, and then follows the name found in the English Bible.

א

אֲבַגְתָא [ăvagthāh'], Abagtha, the same as בִּגְתָא, of doubtful derivation: *great* (S.); *fortunate*, or *cunning* (G.).

אֲבִגַיִל defective, and
אֲבִיגַיִל Kethib, from the Aramean dialect, where אָב takes י before the affix (S.), for אֲבִיגַיִל.

אֲבִי [ăvee'], Abi, abbreviated from אֲבִיָּה.

אֲבִי, or contracted אָב, אַב, requires special notice in relation to the Hebrew proper names, in which it is frequently found compounded with other words.

It affects the interpretation according as we consider it; First, as the construct of אָב, not in its primitive signification of *father**, but in the sense of בַּעַל *possessor*, as in the Arabic and Ethiopic (Gesenius' Thesaurus). In this view of it, it will refer to the *bearer* of the name, as אֲבִיאֵל (here compounded with אֵל *strength*,) *possessor of strength*, i.e. *strong one*.

* We do not set up ourselves as *arbiters* of the question, yet we *do* use this signification generally, leaving the decision with the competent reader.

But, secondly, finding the same also compounded with some proper names of *women*, as אֲבִיָּה, 2 Chron. ii. 24; אֲבִיחַיִל, ii. 18; אֲבִימַל, 2 Sam. iii. 4; we are forced sometimes to consider it in the primitive signification of *father*, in which case אֲבִי is not to be taken in the common sense of its construct state, *father of*, but, *of whom the father*, or *whose father* (compare Simonis Onomasticon, p. 448, אֲבִיגַיִל *patris gaudium*; Gesenius' Manuale, *cujus pater exultatio*); thus, אֲבִיָּה *whose father [is] the Lord*.

Thirdly, אֲבִי from אָבָה *to will* or *desire*, as אֲבִיָּה *will* or *desire of the Lord*, &c.

Or, fourthly, אֲבִי may be considered sometimes not as a construct, but י as a mere conjunction between the two words; comp. אֲבִידָן (S.).

This analogy is also in a great measure connected with other compounds, as אָח, אֵל, &c., to which the reader would do well to attend.

אֲבִיאֵל [ăvee-ēhl'], Abiel, *father of strength*, i. e. *strong one* (G. and S.), or, *the father's strength* (S.), from אָב

and אֵל; but perhaps *whose father [is] God*. Comp. note.

אֲבִיאָסָף [*ăvee-āh-sāph'*], Abiasaph, *he* [God] *took away* [his] *father* (S.); *father of gathering, i.e. gatherer, collector* (G.), from אָב and אָסַף *to gather, take away*.

אֲבִיגַיִל [*ăveegāh'yil*], Abigail; *the father's joy* (S.); comp. id. and גִיל *to rejoice*.

אֲבִיגַל [*ăveegal'*], marg. Abigal, contraction of the same.

אֲבִידָן [*ăveedāhn'*], Abidan; *whose father He* [God] *judged* (S.); *father of the judge* (G.), comp. id. and דִין *to judge*.

אֲבִידָע [*ăveedāhng'*], Abidah; *the father's prayer*, i. e. a son obtained by *the father's prayer* (S.); *father of knowledge, i. e. wise* (G.). Comp. id. and Arab. דעא *to invoke*, or Heb. יָדַע *to know*.

אֲבִיָּה [*ăviy-yāh'*], Abijah; *desire of the Lord* (S.); *whose father* [is] *the Lord* (G.), comp. id. or אָבָה *to will* or *desire*, and יָהּ *Jah*.

אֲבִיָּהוּ [*ăviy-yāh'hoo*], Abijah; the same as אֲבִיָּה, with יָהּ *more fully written* of יְהֹוָה.

אֲבִיהוּא [*ăveehooh'*], Abihu; *whose father* [is] *He*, i.e. *God*. Comp. אָב *father*, and הוּא *he*.

אֲבִיהוּד [*ăveehood'*], Abihud; *father of glory*, comp. id. and הוּד, i. q. הוֹד *glory*, (S.).

אֲבִי הָעֶזְרִי [*ăvee-hāh-ezree'*], Abiezrite, patronymic of אֲבִיעֶזֶר which see.

אֲבִיחַיִל [*ăveekhāh'yil*], Abihail; *the father's strength*, or, *father of strength*, i. e. *a strong one*; from אָב *father*, and חַיִל *strength* or *valour*.

אֲבִיטוּב [*ăveetoov'*], Abitub; *the father's goodness* (S.); *father of goodness*, i. e. *a good one*; comp. id. and טוּב *goodness*.

אֲבִיטָל [*ăveetal'*], Abital; *the father's dew* or *protection*; comp. id. and טָל *dew* or *protection*, from טָלַל *to cover* (S.).

אֲבִיָּם [*ăviy-yāhm*], Abijam; *great* desire (S.); *father of the sea* (G.); comp. id. or אָבָה *to will*, and יָם *sea*.

אֲבִימָאֵל [*ăveemāh-ēhl'*], Abimael; *father of fatness*; comp. id. Arab. מאל *to be fat* (S.). According to others, *Mael*, the name of an Arabian nation.

אֲבִימֶלֶךְ [*ăveemeh'lekh*], Abimelech; *father of the king*, or *whose father* [is] *king*; comp. id. and מֶלֶךְ *king*.

אֲבִינָדָב [*ăveenāhdāhv'*], Abinadab; *father of the noble*, or *whose father* [is] *noble* or *liberal*; comp. id. and נָדַב *to be liberal*.

אֲבִינֹעַם [*ăveenōh'ngam*], Abinoam; *the father's pleasantness*; comp. id. and נֹעַם *pleasantness*.

אֲבִינֵר [*ăveenēhr'*], marg. Abiner; *the father's light*, comp. id. and נֵר *light* (S.); but, perhaps, *whose father* [is] *Ner*. See 1 Sam. xiv. 50.

* ם and ן preceded by (ָ) and (וֹ) has been considered by philologers as a formative, signifying *augmentation* and *intensity*; comp. Sim. Onomast. p. 357.

אֲבִיאָסָף [ev-yāhsāph'], Ebiasaph; contracted from אֲבִיאָסָף q. v.

אֲבִיעֶזֶר [ăvee-ngēh'zer], Abiezer; *the father's help*, or *father of help*; comp. אָב and עֶזֶר *help*.

אֲבִי עַלְבוֹן [ăvee-ngalvōhn'], Abialbon; *the father's strength*, or *father of strength*; comp. id. and עַלְבוֹן *strength*.

אֲבִירָם [ăveerāhm'], Abiram; *the lifted up* or *high father*, or *father of exaltation*, or *the father's exaltation*; comp. id. and רָם as a participle or noun of רוּם *to be high*.

אֲבִישַׁג [ăveeshag'], Abishag; *the father's delight* or *error*; comp. id. and שָׁגָה *to delight one's self* (S.), or שָׁגַג *to err* (G.).

אֲבִישׁוּעַ [ăveeshoo'ang], Abishua; *the father's* or *father of deliverance*, comp. id. and שׁוּעַ, for יֵשׁוּעַ *help*.

אֲבִישׁוּר [ăveeshoor'], Abishur; *the father's wall*, comp. id. and שׁוּר *wall*.

אֲבִישַׁי [ăveeshāy'], Abishai; *the father's present*; comp. id. and שַׁי *gift*, *present*.

אֲבִישָׁלוֹם [ăveeshāhlōhm'], Abishalom; *the father's*, or *father of peace*; comp. id. and שָׁלוֹם *peace*.

אֲבִיָתָר [ev-yāhthāhr'], Abiathar; *whose father was left*, i. e. after his mother's death (S.); *the father of abundance* (G.), or *the father's abundance*; comp. id. and יָתַר *to be left*.

אָבֵל [āhvēhl'], Abel (different from הֶבֶל *Abel*, the son of Adam); *mourning*, the name of a place, from the comparison with Gen. l. 11; but, from the Arabic, *moist*, *watered*, *a meadow* (S.) and (G.).

אָבֵל בֵּית־מַעֲכָה [āhvēhl' bēhth-magnăkhāh'], Abel-beth-maachah; *meadow of*, i. e. near בֵּית מַ'.

אָבֵל הַשִּׁטִּים [āhvēhl' hashshitteem'], Abel-Shittim; *meadow of*, *acacia trees*, the name of a place.

אָבֵל כְּרָמִים [āhvēhl-k'rāhmeem'], marg. *Abel of the vineyards*, from כֶּרֶם *a vineyard*, id.

אָבֵל מְחוֹלָה [āhvēhl' m'khōlāh'], Abel-meholah; *meadow of dancing*; from חוּל *to dance*.

אָבֵל מַיִם [āhvēhl' mah'yim], Abel-maim; *meadow of water*.

אָבֵל מִצְרַיִם [āhvēhl mitsrah'yim], Abel-Mizraim; marg. *mourning of*, others, *meadow of the Egyptians*.

אֶבֶן הָאָזֶל [eh'ven hāh-eh'zel], the stone Ezel; marg. *that sheweth the way*; *stone of departure* (S.); from אָזַל *to go away*.

אֶבֶן הַזֹּחֶלֶת [eh'ven hazzōhkheh'leth], the stone of Zoheleth, i. e. *smooth*; זְחַל Chaldee, *to shine* (S).

אֶבֶן הָעֶזֶר also הָעֶזֶר [eh'ven hāh-ngēh'zer], Eben-ezer; *stone of help*, from עָזַר *to help*.

אֲבָנָה [avāhnāh'], Abana; marg. Amana; Kethib, probably by permutation of the labials, for אֲמָנָה Keri.

אַבְנֵר [avnēhr'], Abner; cont. from אֲבִינֵר q. v.

אָבֵץ [ēh'vets], Abez; *tin* (G).

אִבְצָן [ivtsāhn'], Ibzan; the same as אִיבְצָן Chaldee, *labour*, or *great labour* (S.); comp. note to אֲבִיָּם.

אַבְרָהָם [avrāhāhm'], Abraham; *father of a great multitude*, contracted from אָבִי *father of*, רַב for רָב *great*, הָם *multitude*, from הָמָה *to make a tumultuous noise;* comp. מְהֻמְהָם Eze. vii. 11. Lest the sense might be limited to one peculiar multitude or nation, the Lord gives immediately his own blessed and fuller exposition. Gen. xvii. 4. thus: אָב { רַב הָם / הֲמוֹן גּוֹיִם } *a father of a multitude* (see marg.) *of nations*.

אַבְרָם [avrāhm'], Abram: comp. אֲבִירָם.

אֲבִישַׁי [avshay'], Abishai; contracted from אֲבִישַׁי.

אַבְשָׁלוֹם [avshāhlōhm'], Absalom; cont. from אֲבִישָׁלוֹם.

אֹבוֹת [ōhvōth'], Oboth; *skin bottles*, the name of a place where travellers used, and still are in habit, to fill their *bottles* (Hilleri Onomast).

אָגֵא [āgēh'], Agee; *fugitive*, from Arabic אגא *to flee* (S).

אֲגַג [ăgāhg] and אָגָג, Agag; *tall*, i.q. Arabic and Persic אוג *very high* (S.); Latin, *gigas*, a giant.

אֲגָגִי [ăgāhgee'], Agagite; either a gentile or patronymic noun of the same.

אָגוּר [āhgoor'], Agur; *collected*, participial of אָגַר *to gather*.

אֶגְלַיִם [eglah'yim], Eglaim; *two borders, two lakes* or *pools*, dual of אֶגֶל, from the Arabic, *to set a mark* (S.), or *a pool* (G.).

אַדְבְּאֵל [adb'ēhl'], Adbeel; *sorrow of God*, i.e. *great sorrow; miracle of God*, from אָדַב *sorrow* (S.), or from an Arabic derivation *wonder* (G.), and אֵל *God*.

אֲדַד [ădad'], Adad; by permutation, i. q. הֲדַד.

אִדּוֹ [iddōh'], Iddo; *affliction, sorrow*, from an Arabic root הדד (S.).

אֱדוֹם [ĕdōhm], Edom; *red*, from אָדַם *to be red*.

אֲדוֹמִי [ădōhmee'], Edomite; a gentile noun of the same.

אַדּוֹן [addōhn'], i. q. אִדּוֹ.

אֲדוֹרַיִם [ădōrah'yim], Adoraim; *two habitations* (S.); *two chiefs* or *princes* (G.); dual from דּוּר *to dwell*, or אָדוֹר i. q. אַדִּיר *magnificent, mighty*, from אָדַר.

אֲדַלְיָה [ădal-yāh'], Adaliah; *strong of heart*, collated from the Arabic.

אָדָם [āhdāhm'], Adam; *earth*, or *red*, from אֲדָמָה *earth* and אָדַם *to be red*.

אֱדוֹם for אֱדוֹם.

אַדְמָה [admāh'], *red*, from אָדַם.

אֲדָמָה [ădāhmāh'], Adamah; *earth, ground;* comp. Appellatives.

אֲדוֹמִי for אֲדוֹמִי.

אֲדָמִי [ădāhmee'], Adami; *human*, from אָדָם *man*.

אֲדֻמִּים [ădummeem'], Adummim; *red* (rocks), plural of אָדֹם adjective, *red*.

אֲדֹמִית feminine of אֲדֹמִי.

אַדְמָתָא [admāhthāh'], Admatha; *red*, from אָדַם *to be red*.

אַדָּן [addāhn'], Addan; i. q. אֲדוֹן and אִדּוֹ; compare also note under אֵבִים.

אֲדֹנָי [ădōhnāy'], the Lord; from אָדוֹן of the root דוּן *to judge*, with ־ָי formative.

אֲדֹנִי בֶזֶק [ădōnee vēh'zek], Adoni-bezek; *lord of Bezek*, from אָדוֹן *lord*, and בֶּזֶק the name of a city.

אֲדֹנִיָּה [ădōhniy-yāh'], Adonijah; *my lord [is] Jah*, contr. from אֲדֹנִי and יָה contr. from יְהֹוָה *Jehovah*.

אֲדֹנִיָּהוּ [ădōhniy-yāh'hoo], id.

אֲדֹנִי צֶדֶק [ădōhnee-tsēh'dek], Adoni-zedek; *lord of righteousness*, from אָדוֹן *lord*, and צֶדֶק *righteousness*, comp. Appellatives.

אֲדֹנִיקָם [ădōhneekāhm'], Adonikam; *the Lord has risen* (S.); *lord of foes* (G.), from אָדוֹן *lord*, and קָם preterite *or* participle of קוּם *to arise*.

אֲדֹנִירָם [ădōhneerāhm'], Adoniram; *the Lord was exalted*, or *lord of exaltation*, from אָדוֹן *lord*, and רָם pret. *or* noun of רוּם *to be high, lifted up*.

אַדָּר [addāhr'], Addar; *chief*, comp. אַדִּירִים.

אֲדֹרָם [ădōhrāhm'], Adoram; contracted from אֲדֹנִירָם.

אֲדְרַמֶּלֶךְ [ădrammēh'lekh], Adrammelech; *magnificence of the king*; others, *king of fire*, i. e. *of the sun*, compounded of אֶדֶר *magnificence, majesty*, or from a Persian root, *fire*, and מֶלֶךְ *king*.

אֶדְרֶעִי [edr'ngee'], Edrei; *plenty of pasture*; compounded of אֶדֶר *amplitude*, רְעִי *pasture*, from רָעָה *to feed* (S.); *arm*, i. q. אֶדְרָע Chaldee (G.).

אֹהַד [ōh'had], Ohad; *part, portion* (S.).

אֵהוּד [ēhood'], Ehood; id.

אַהֲוָא [ahăvāh'], Ahava; *continual defluxion*, from the Arabic הוי (S.).

אֹהֶל [ōh'hel], Ohel; *tent*, compare Appellatives.

אָהֳלָה [ōhŏlāh'], Aholah; *her tent*, from the same.

אָהֳלִיאָב [ōhŏleeāhv'], Aholiab; *tent of the father*, from the same, and אָב *father*.

אָהֳלִיבָה [ōhŏleevāh'], Aholibah; *my tent [is] in her*, from the same, and בָּהּ *in her*.

אָהֳלִיבָמָה [ōhŏleevāhmāh'], Aholibamah; *tent of the high place*, from the same and בָּמָה.

אַהֲרֹן [ahărōhn'], Aaron; *mountainous*, from הַר *mountain*; or, perhaps, diminutive, *little mountain*, with א prosthetic. (It may possibly signify *progenitor*, from הָרָה with א prosthetic; the verb is used in this sense, Gen. xlix. 26.)

אוּאֵל [oo-ēhl'], Uel; strength of God, contracted from אוּל strength, and אֵל God.

אוֹבִיל [ōhveel'], Obil; an overseer of camels, collated from the Arabic (G.).

אוּזַי [oozāy'], Uzai; of doubtful derivation; perhaps i.q. עוּזַי strong.

אוּזָל [oozāhl'], Uzal; progressing, from אָזַל to go, pass on.

אֵוִי [ĕvee], Evi; desire, from אָוָה to desire.

אֱוִיל מְרֹדַךְ [ĕveel-merōhdakh'], Evil-merodach; the chief [god is] merodach, collated from the Arabic (S.); if we consider אֱוִיל as a Hebrew word, fool, we are led to suppose it as a contemptuous expression applied, instead of some previous, dignified appellation, as wise or prudent, to Merodach, the name of a Babylonish idol.

אוּלַי [oolay'], Ulai; pure water, from the Persian (d'Anville by Gesenius); according to the Hebrew, strength, from אוּל with ־ִי formative; comp. also אַחְזַי.

אוּלָם [oolāhm'], Ulam; first of all, i. e. first-born, collated from the Arabic (S.); but rather strength, from the Hebrew אוּל, and also with the secondary meaning of first-born; comp. אוֹן (Gen. xlix. 3) and note under אֲבִים.

אוֹמָר [ōhmāhr'], Omar; high, from אָמַר; comp. אָמִיר height, summit (S.), eloquent (G.).

אוֹן [ōhn], On; pain or strength, comp. Appellatives; as the name of an Egyptian city; light, collated from the Egyptian (S.).

אוֹנוֹ [ōhnōh'], Ono; his strength or pain, comp. the preceding.

אוֹנָם [ōhnāhm'], Onam; their strength or pain, id., comp. also note to אֲבִים.

אוֹנָן [ōhnāhn], Onan; their strength, id.

אוּפָז [oophāhz'], Uphaz; isle of pure gold. (S.), compounded of אוּ i.q. אִי for אֱוִי an island, from אָוָה, and פָז fine gold.

אוֹפִיר [ōhpheer'], Ophir; fat, from the Arabic אפר to be fat (S).

אוּר [oor], Ur; light, compare Appellatives.

אוּרִי [ooree'], Uri; id. or my light.

אוּרִיאֵל [ooree-ēhl'], Uriel; light of God, compounded of אוּר light, and אֵל God.

אוּרִיָּה [ooriy-yāh'], Uriah; light of Jah, id. and יָהּ.

אוּרִיָּהוּ [ooriy-yāh'hoo], Uriah; light of Jehovah, apocopate of יְהוָה.

אוֹרְנָה [ōh'rnāh'], Kethib, i. q. אָרְן (S.).

אֶזְבַּי [ĕzbay'], Ezbai; perhaps a dwarf, collated from the Persian (G.).

אֶזֶל see אֶבֶן.

אֻזֵּן שֶׁאֱרָה [uzzēhn Shehĕrāh'], Uzzen Sherah; armoury of (from אֹזֶן

to arm) *Sherah*, see שְׁאֵרָה; or from אֹזֶן *ear* i. e. *arch, palace*.

אַזְנוֹת תָּבוֹר [*aznōhth' tāhvōhr'*], Aznoth-tabor; *ears* or *heights of Tabor* (Rabbi Solomon), from the same.

אָזְנִי [*oznee'*], Ozni; *having large ears* or *hearing well* (*auritus*), from אֹזֶן *ear*.

אֲזַנְיָה [*ăzan-yāh'*], Azaniah; *Jah gave ear*, from אָזַן *to give ear*, and יָה.

אֶזְרָחִי [*ezrāhkhee'*], Ezrahite; patronymic from זֶרַח.

אַחְאָב [*akhāhv'*], Ahab; *father's brother*, compounded of אָח *brother*, and אָב *father*.

אֶחָב [*ekhāhv'*], Ahab; contraction of the same.

אַחְבָּן [*akhbāhn'*], Ahban; *brother of understanding*, compounded of אָח *brother*, and בֵּן from בִּין *to understand*.

אֵחוּד [*ēhkhood'*], Ehud; *oneness*, from אֶחָד *one*.

אֲחוֹחַ [*akhōh'-akh*], Ahoah; evidently from אָחָה, but without a suitable sense for this name; in 1 Ch. viii. 7, אֲחִיָּה is put instead.

אֲחוֹחִי [*ăkhōhkhee'*], Ahohite; patronymic of the same.

אֲחוּמַי [*ăkhoomay'*], Ahumai; *brother of water*, i. e. *pusillanimous*, from אָחוּ for אָחִי *brother*; comp. אֲבוּ, and מֵי as if singular of מַיִם *water*.

אָחָז [*akhāhz'*], Ahaz; *possessor*, from אָחַז *to lay hold of*.

אַחְזַי [*akhzay'*], Ahazai; id. *a great possession*, with יִ formative.*

אֲחַזְיָה [*ăkhaz-yāh'*], Ahaziah; [*whom*] *Jah sustained*, from the same and יָה.

אֲחַזְיָהוּ [*ăkhaz-yāh'hoo*], Ahaziah; [*whom*] *Jehovah sustained*, from the same and יְהֹוָה apocopated.

אֲחֻזָּם [*ăkhuzzāhm'*], Ahuzam; *their possession*, comp. אָחַז; or *a large possession*, comp. note under אָבִים.

אֲחֻזַּת [*ăkhuzzath'*], Ahuzzath; *possession*; ת a termination found annexed to Philistine, Idumæan, and Egyptian names: as, גְּנֻבַת, גָּלְיָת, אָסְנַת, &c.

אֵחִי [*ēhkhee'*], Ehi; a Syriac formation for אָחִי or אֲחִי which see.

אֲחִי [*ăkhee'*], Ahi; *brother*: comp. אָח Appellatives.

אֲחִיאָם [*ăkheeāhm'*], Ahiam; *brotherhood*, id. for the formative ם, see note under אָבִים, and א inserted may find *some* analogy in פְּתִי and פְּתָאִים.

אֲחִיָּה [*ăkhiy-yāh'*], Ahiah; *brother*, (i. e. *friend*) *of Jah*, from אָח *brother*, and יָה.

אֲחִיָּהוּ [*ăkhiy-yāhoo'*], id. from אָח and יְהֹוָה apocopated.

* This formative יִ or יַ has been considered by philologers as an abbreviation from יְהֹוָה *Jehovah*, for הִי (qui est), comp. Sim. Onomast. p. 350; thus אַחְזַי *possession of Jehovah* or *the Lord*, hence also *great possession*.

אֲחִיהוּד [ăkheehood'], Ahihud; *brother of glory,* comp. אֲבִיהוּד.

אַחְיוֹ [akh-yōh'], Ahio; *brotherly, kinsman,* i. q. Syriac אֲחִיוֹן (G.).

אֲחִיחָד [ăkheekhood'], Ahihud.; *brother of conjunction* or *unity,* for אֲחִי *brother,* and יָחַד *conjunction,* from יָחַד *to be joined, united.*

אֲחִיטוּב [ăkheetoov'], Ahitub; *brother of goodness,* from אָח *brother,* and טוּב *goodness.*

אֲחִילוּד [ăkheelood'], Ahilud; *brother of* [the one] *born,* for אֲחִי יָלוּד of יָלַד *to bear,* participle passive.

אֲחִימוֹת [ăkheemōhth'], Ahimoth; *brother of death* or *the brother's death,* from אָח and מוּת *to die.*

אֲחִימֶלֶךְ [ăkheemeh'lekh], Ahimelech; *brother, associate,* or *friend of the king,* from אָח *brother,* and מֶלֶךְ *king.*

אֲחִימָן [ăkheeman'], Ahiman; *the brother's image,* compound id. and מִן (comp. תְּמוּנָה) *a likeness,* from מוּן and מִין *a species, kind.*

אֲחִימַעַץ [ăkheemang'ats], Ahimaaz; *brother of wrath,* compounded of the same, and מַעַץ; according to the Arabic, *wrath* (G.).

אֲחִיָן [akhyāhn'], Ahian; i. q. אַחְיוֹ.

אֲחִינָדָב [akheenāhdāhv'], Ahinadab; *brother of the noble,* compounded of אָח *brother,* and נָדַב *to be liberal.*

אֲחִינֹעַם [ăkheenōh'ngam], Ahinoam; *brother of pleasantness,* comp. id. and נֹעַם *pleasantness.*

אֲחִיסָמָךְ [ăkheesāhmāhkh'], Ahisamach; *brother of support,* compound id. and סָמַךְ *to support.*

אֲחִיעֶזֶר [ăkhee-ngeh'zer], Ahiezer; *brother of help,* comp. id. and עָזַר *help.*

אֲחִיקָם [ăkheekāhm'], Ahikam; *the brother has risen,* i. e. *succeeded, followed* (S.); *brother of the rising* [one] (G.); comp. id. and קָם pret. or part. of קוּם *to rise.*

אֲחִירָם [ăkheerāhm'], Ahiram; *brother of the high, exalted,* or *exaltation,* comp. id. and רָם part. or subst. of רוּם *to be high.*

אֲחִירָמִי [ăkheerāh'mee], Ahiramite; patronymic of the same.

אֲחִירַע [ăkheerang'], Ahira; *brother of the evil, wicked,* comp. id. and רַע adj. *evil.*

אֲחִישַׁחַר [ăkheeshah'khar], Ahishahar; *brother of the morning star,* comp. id. and שַׁחַר *the morning star.*

אֲחִישָׁר [ăkheeshāhr'], Ahishar; *brother of the singer* (G.), or, perhaps, *brother* or *friend of the upright,* compound of the same, and שָׁר participle of שִׁיר *to sing;* or a contraction for אֲחִי יָשָׁר.

אֲחִיתֹפֶל [ăkheetōh'phel], Ahithophel; *brother of insipidness, foolishness,* compare id. and תֹּפֶל *insipidness.*

אַחְלָב [akhlāhv'], Ahlab; *fat,* from חֵלֶב.

אַחְלַי [akhlay'], Ahlai; *O that! would God!* see אַחֲלֵי Appellatives.

אַחְמְתָא [akhm'thăh'], Achmetha, marg. Ecbatana, or in a coffer; supposed to be compounded of אַח, i. q. Persian ak, lord, and מָתָא Chaldee, city; thus, the lord's, i. e. the king's, city or residence: see Sim. Onomast. p. 578.

אֲחַסְבַּי [ăkhasbay'], Ahasbai; I [the father] will confide in the Lord (S.), of חָסָה future of חָסָה; בְּ in; ־ִי; see note to אֲחֻזַי.

אַחֵר [akhēhr'], Aher; another [son]; comp. Appellatives.

אַחְרַח [akhrakh'], Aharah; after the brother, for אַחַר אָח.

אֲחַרְחֵל [akharkhēhl'], Aharhel; behind the pomarium, i.e. the space about the wall of a city (G.); compounded of אַחַר after, and חֵל; see חֵיל Appellative.

אֲחַשְׁוֵרוֹשׁ [ăkhashvēhrōhsh'], Ahasuerus; excellency or majesty of the prince; according to Persian אחש excellence, and ורוש for ברוש prince (S.).

אֲחַשְׁרֹשׁ Kethib for the same.

אֲחַשְׁתָּרִי [ăkhashtāhree'], Haahashtari; perhaps a muleteer (G.); compare אֲחַשְׁתְּרָנִים mules.

אָטֵר [āhtēhr'], Ater; closed or impeded, i. e. in one's right hand, left-handed, comp. אָטַר Appellative.

אַיָּה [ay-yāh'], Ajah; falcon, compare Appellatives.

אִיּוֹב [iy-yōhv'], Job; treated with hostility, from אָיַב to hate, be an enemy to; for the form of which comp. יִלּוֹד.

אִיזֶבֶל [eezēh'vel], Jezebel; no habitation; compounded of אִי not, and זְבֻל habitation.

אִי כָבוֹד [ee-khāh-vōhd'], I-chabod (marg. where is the glory?); no glory, i.e. inglorious.

אַיָּלוֹן [ay-yāh-lōhn'], Ajalon; (cervinus) of a stag (G.); but, perhaps, diminutive, a little stag, comp. אַיָּל Appellative.

אֵילוֹן [ēhlōhn'], Elon; an oak, or terebinth, comp. אַיִל Appellative.

אֵילוֹת [ēhlōhth'], Eloth; oaks, or terebinths, pl. of אֵילָה.

אֵילִם [ēhleem'], Elim; id. plural of אַיִל.

אֵיל פָּארָן [ēhl-pāhrāhn'], El-paran; the oak or terebinth of Paran; see also פָּארָן.

אֵילַת [ēhlath'], Elath, for אֵילָה, comp. אֲחֻזַּת; i. q. pl. אֵילוֹת.

אֵימִים [ēhmeem'], Emims; terrors from אָיֹם.

אִיעֶזֶר [ee-ngēh'zer], Jeezer; contracted from אֲבִי עֶזֶר.

אִיעֶזְרִי [ee-ngezree'], Jeezrite; contracted from אֲבִי הָעֶזְרִי.

אִישׁ־בֹּשֶׁת [eesh-bōh'sheth], Ish-bosheth; man of shame, compounded of אִישׁ man, and בֹּשֶׁת shame, from בּוֹשׁ to be ashamed.

c

אִישׁהוֹד [eesh-hōhd'], Ishhod; *man of glory*, compounded of id. and הוֹד *glory*.

אִישׁ־טוֹב [eesh-tōhv'], Ish-tob; marg. *man of Tob*; אִישׁ is here commonly received as an Appellative, compare טוֹב.

אִישַׁי [eeshay'], Ishai; for יִשַׁי with א prosthetic.

אִיתַי [eethay'], Ithai; although this word may easily be explained by אִית Chaldee, *there is*, and ־י the termination for הִי, comp. אַחְזַי, yet since this name is elsewhere always written אִתַּי it is more likely to signify the same when written fully.

אִיתִיאֵל [eethee-ēhl'] Ithiel; *there is a God*, or *God* [is] *with me*, either for אִיתִי Chaldee, *there is*, or for אִתִּי *with me*, from אֵת (compare the preceding), compounded with אֵל *God*.

אִיתָמָר [eethāhmāhr'], Ithamar; *desire of palm-tree*, i. e. *a desirable palm-tree; island of palm-trees* (G.), compounded of אִי (for אַוִי, from אָוָה *to desire*, or אִי *an island*,) and תָּמָר *a palm-tree*.

אֵיתָן [eethāhn'], Ethan; *constant, never-failing,* (perennis), or *strong;* comp. Appellatives.

אַכַּד [akkad'], Accad; *band*, from the Arabic اكد, comp. the Chaldee אֲגַד *to bind*, or *tie fast* (S.).

אַכְזִיב [akhzeev'], Achzib; *lying, failing;* comp. כָּזַב *to lie.*

אָכִישׁ [āh-kheesh'], Achish; *feared, reverenced,* from the Arabic (S.).

אוּכָל [ookkāhl'], Ucal; *I shall prevail*, for אוּכַל fut. from יָכֹל *to prevail.*

אַכְשָׁף [akhshāhph'], Achshaph; *bewitching*, comp. כָּשַׁף.

אֵלָא [ēhlāh'], Elah; for אֵלָה q. v.

אֵל אֱלֹהֵי יִשְׂרָאֵל [ēhl-ĕlōhēh-yisrāh-ēhl'], El-elohe-Israel; marg. *God the God of Israel.*

אֵל בֵּית־אֵל [ēhl-bēhth-ēhl], El-beth-el; marg. *the God of Bethel,* comp. בֵּית־אֵל.

אֶלְדָּד [eldāhd'], Eldad; contracted for אֱלִידָד q. v.

אֶלְדָּעָה [eldāh-ngāh'], Eldaah; [whom] *God has called*, from אֵל *God*, and Arabic دَعَا *to call* (S.).

אֵלָה [ēhlāh'], Elah; *an oak* or *terebinth*, for אֵילָה from אוּל or אֵיל *to be strong.*

אַלּוֹן [allōhn'], Allon; *an oak,* from אָלַל *to be strong.*

אֵלוֹן [ēhlōhn'], Elon; id. from אוּל or אֵיל *to be strong.*

אַלּוֹן בָּכוּת [allōhn bāh-khooth'], Allon-bachuth; *oak of weeping,* בָּכוּת from בָּכָה *to weep.*

אָלוּשׁ [āh-loosh'], Alush; *a troop* or *company*, from לוּשׁ *knead, make compact.*

אֶלְזָבָד [elzāhbāhd'], Elzabad; [whom] *God has given,* from אֵל *God,* and זָבַד *to present.*

אלח (11) אלי

אֱלְחָנָן [elkhāhnāhn'], Elhanan; [whom] God has favoured, or graciously given, compounded of id. and חָנַן to favour or give graciously.

אֱלִיאָב [ĕlee-āhv'], Eliab; [to whom] God was a father, from אֵל God, and אָב father.

אֱלִיאֵל [ĕlee-ēhl'], Eliel: [to whom] God [was] God.

אֱלִיאָתָה [ĕlceāh'thāh], Eliathah; [to whom] God came, compounded of id. and אָתָה to come (G.), great lamentation, from אָלָה to lament, with ה intensive (S.), which the accent on the penultimate confirms.

אֱלִידָד [ĕleedāhd'], Elidad; [whom] God loved, compounded id. and דָּד preterite of דּוּד to love.

אֶלְיָדָע [el-yāhdāhng'], Eliada; [whom] God knew, compounded of id. and יָדַע to know.

אֵלִיָּה [ēh-liy-yāh'], Elijah; [whose] God [is] Jah, compounded of id. and יָהּ Jah.

אֵלִיָּהוּ [ēh-liy-yāh'hoo], Elijah; compounded of id. and יהוה apocopated.

אֱלִיהוּא & אֱלִיהוּ [ĕleehoo'], Elihu; [whose] God he is, compounded of id. and הוּא he.

אֶלְיְהוֹעֵינַי [el-y'hōh-ngēh-nay'], Elihoenai; unto Jehovah [are] mine eyes, comp. אֶל to, יהוה Jehovah, עֵינַי mine eyes, from עַיִן.

אֶלְיוֹעֵינַי [el-yōh-ngēh-nay'], Elioenai; contracted from the same.

אֱלִיוֹעֵנַי id.

אֱלִיַחְבָּא [el-yakh-bāh'], Eliahba; [whom] God will hide, i. e. protect, compounded of אֵל God, and future of חָבָא to hide.

אֱלִיחֹרֶף [ĕleekhōh'reph], Elihoreph; [to whom] God [is] recompense, compounded of the same, and חֹרֶף from the Arabic, to recompense (S.).

אֱלִימֶלֶךְ [ĕleemeh'lekh], Elimelech; [to whom] God [is] king, compounded of id. and מֶלֶךְ king.

אֶלְיָסָף [el-yāhsāph'], Eliasaph; [whom] God added, compounded of id. and יָסַף to add.

אֱלִיעֶזֶר [ĕlee-ngeh'zer], Eliezer; [to whom] God [is] help, compounded of id and עֶזֶר help.

אֱלִיעֵינַי [ĕlee-ngēh-nay'], Elienai; contr. of אֱלִיהוֹעֵינַי.

אֱלִיעָם [ĕlee-ngāhm'], Eliam; God's people, compounded of id. and עָם people.

אֱלִיפַז [ĕleephaz'], Eliphaz; [to whom] God [is] exultation (S.), compounded of id. and פָּז from פָּזַז to leap nimbly.

אֱלִיפָל [ĕleephāhl'], Eliphal; [whom] God has judged, compounded of id. and פָּל from פָּלַל to judge.

אֱלִיפְלֵהוּ [ĕlee-ph'lēh'hoo], Elipheleh; God shall distinguish him, for אֵל God, יַפְלְהוּ Hiphil future, from פָּלָה to be separate.

אֱלִיפֶלֶט [ĕleepheh'let], Eliphelet; [to whom] God [is] deliverance, compounded of פֶּלֶט from פָּלַט to escape.

אֱלִיצוּר [ĕlee-tsoor'], Elizur; [whose] God [is] *a rock*, compounded of id. and צוּר *a rock*.

אֱלִיצָפָן [ĕlee-tsāhphāhn'], Elizaphan; [whom] *God has hidden, protected*, compounded of id. and צָפַן *to hide*.

אֱלִיקָא [ĕleekāh'] Elika; *God's congregation*, compounded of id. and קָהָ, contr. from קְהָא Chaldee, *to congregate*.

אֱלִיָקִים [el-yāhkeem'], Eliakim; [whom] *God shall establish*, compounded of id. and יָקִים Hiphil future, from קוּם *to arise*.

אֱלִישֶׁבַע [ĕlee-sheh'vang], Elisheba; *God's oath*; [to whom] *God [is] the oath*, i. e. *who swears by, worships God* (G.), compounded of id. and שֶׁבַע.

אֱלִישָׁה [ĕleeshāh'], Elishah; of doubtful derivation: *a tight band* (S.), from an Arabic root: comp. also אֱלוּשׁ *a troop*, from the same root, or the Hebrew לוּשׁ *to make compact, knead*.

אֱלִישׁוּעַ [ĕleeshoo'ang], Elishua; *to whom God [is] salvation*, compounded of id. and שׁוּעַ for יָשׁוּעַ *salvation*, from יָשַׁע.

אֱלִיָשִׁיב [el-yāhsheev'], Eliashib; [whom] *God shall restore*, compounded of id. and יָשִׁיב Hiphil future of שׁוּב *to return*.

אֱלִישָׁמָע [ĕleeshāhmāhng'], Elishama; [whom] *God has heard*, compounded of id. and שָׁמַע *to hear*.

אֱלִישָׁע [ĕleeshāhng'], Elisha; *to whom God [is] salvation*, for אֱלִי יֵשַׁע

אֱלִישָׁפָט [ĕleeshāhphāht'], Elishaphat; [whom] *God has judged*, compounded of id. and שָׁפַט *to judge*.

אֱלִיָתָה [ĕliy-yāh'thāh], Eliathah; i. q. אֱלִיאָתָה (G.); *great lamentation*, from אָלָה *to lament*, with ה intensitive (S.); of which אֱלִיאָתָה q. v. is the less regular form.

אַלְמוֹדָד [almōhdāhd'], Almodad; *immeasurable, immense*, from אַל *not*, and מָדַד *to measure*.

אַלַּמֶּלֶךְ [allammeh'lekh], Alamelech; *oak of the king*, compounded of אֵל i.q. אַלָּה *an oak*, and מֶלֶךְ *king* (G.).

אֵלֹנִי [ēhlōhnee'], Elonite; patronymic from אֵלוֹן.

אֶלְנַעַם [elnah'ngam], Elnaam; [to whom] *God [is] pleasantness, delight*, compounded of אֵל *God*, and נַעַם *pleasantness*.

אֶלְנָתָן [elnāhthāhn'], Elnathan; [whom] *God has given*, compounded of id. and נָתַן *to give*.

אֶלָּסָר [ĕllāhsāhr'], Ellasar; of uncertain derivation.

אֶלְעָד [el-ngāhd], Elad; [whom] *God has acknowledged*, compounded of אֵל *God*, and עָד, from עוּד *to testify*.

אֶלְעָדָה [el-ngāhdāh'], Eladah; [whom] *God adorned*, compounded of id. and עָדָה *to adorn*.

אֶלְעוּזַי [el-ngoozay'], Eluzai; *God [is] my strength*, compounded of id. and עוּז i.q. עוֹז *strength* or *praise*; compare also note to אֲחֻזִי.

אֶלְעָזָר [el-ngāhzāhr'], Elazar; [whom] God has helped, compounded of id. and עָזַר to help.

אֶלְעָלֵה & אֶלְעָלֶא [el-ngāhlēh'], Elealeh, *towards the ascent*; compounded of אֶל *to*, עָלֵא and עָלָה *an ascent*; comp. the Arabic עלא, and Hebrew עָלָה *to go up* (S.).

אֶלְעָשָׂה [el-ngāhsāh'], Elasah; *God has done* [it], compounded of אֵל *God*, and עָשָׂה *to do, make*.

אֶלֶף [ēh'leph], Eleph; *thousand*; compare Appellatives.

אֶלְפֶּלֶט [elpeh'let], Elipalet; contraction of אֱלִיפֶלֶט.

אֶלְפַּעַל [elpah'ngal], Elpaal; *God's work* or *reward*, compounded of אֵל *God*, and פַּעַל; compare פֹּעַל.

אֶלְצָפָן [el-tsāhphāhn'], Elzaphan; contraction of אֱלִיצָפָן.

אֶלְקָנָה [elkāhnāh'], Elkanah; [whom] *God hath taken into possession*, compounded of אֵל *God*, and קָנָה *to buy, take into possession*.

אֶלְקֹשִׁי [elkōshee'], Elkoshite; gentile noun from אֶלְקֹשׁ.

אֶלְתּוֹלַד [eltōhlad'], Eltolad; *God's generation*, compounded of אֵל *God*, and תּוֹלַד i. q. תּוֹלְדָה *a generation*, from יָלַד *to bear*.

אֶלְתְּקֵא [el-t'kēh'], Eltekeh; *to which God* [is the object of] *fear*, compounded of id. and תְּקֵא *fear*, from the Arabic (S).

אֶלְתְּקֵה id.

אֶלְתְּקוֹן [el-t'kōhn'], Eltekon; *to which God* [is] *the foundation*, compounded of id. and תְּכוֹן; compare תָּכַן.

אַמָּה [ammāh'], Ammah; *cubit*, compare Appellatives.

אָמוֹן [ahmōhn'], Amon; *artificer*, compare Appellatives.

אָמוֹץ [ahmōts'], Amoz; *strong*, from אָמַץ *to be strong*.

אָמִי [ahmee'], Ami; found once instead of אָמוֹן, the analogy of which is obscure.

אֵמִים i. q. אֵימִים.

אֲמִינוֹן [ămeenōhn'], Amnon, (margin, Aminon); *faithful*, for אַמְנוֹן, of which some consider it to be a diminutive; root אָמַן *to be firm*.

אֲמָם [ămāhm'], Amam; *mother*, i. q. אֵם from אָמַם obsolete.

אָמוֹן see אָמוֹן.

אֲמָנָה [ămāhnāh'], Amana; *constancy*, from אָמַן *to be firm, true*.

אַמְנוֹן [amnōhn'], Amnon; *faithful*, id.

אַמְצִי [am-tsee'], Amzi; *strong*, from אָמַץ *to be strong*.

אֲמַצְיָה [ămats-yāh'], Amaziah; [whom] *Jah has strengthened*, compounded of id. and יָה.

אֲמַצְיָהוּ [ămats-yāh'hoo], id. with יהוה apocopated.

אִמֵּר [immēhr'], Immer; *word* or *promise*, from אָמַר *to say.*

אֱמֹרִי [ĕmōhree'], Amorite; *mountainous* (S.).

אִמְרִי [imree'], Imri; *word* or *promise*, i. q. אָמַר with the termination ־ִי, from אָמַר *to say.*

אֲמַרְיָה [ămar-yāh'], Amariah; [whom] *Jah has promised*, compare id. and יָה.

אֲמַרְיָהוּ [ămar-yāh'hoo], id. and יהוה.

אַמְרָפֶל [amrāhphel'], Amraphel; of obscure analogy; supposed to be compounded of אָמַר *word* or *command*, אָפֵל *failure*, from an Arabic verb, obsolete in the Hebrew.

אֲמִתַּי [ămittay'], Amittai; *truth*, from אֱמֶת with the termination ־ִי, (compare אַחְזַי) from אָמַן *to be firm.*

אֹן [ōhn], On; see אוֹן.

אֱנוֹשׁ [ĕnōhsh'], Enos; marg. Enosh; *man*, compare Appellatives.

אֲנָחֲרַת [ănāhkhărath'], Anaharath; *a snorting*, comp. נַחֲרָה Appellative.

אֲנִיעָם [ănee-ngāhm'], Aniam; *mourning of the people*, compounded of אֲנִי, from אָנָה *to mourn*, and עָם *people.*

אָסָא [āhsāh'], Asa; *physician*, from the Chaldee אָסָא *to heal.*

אַסִּיר [aseer'], Assir; *prisoner*, compare Appellatives, from אָסַר *to bind.*

אַסְנָה [asnāh'], Asnah; *thorn, bush*, compare Chaldee אַסְנָה and Hebrew סְנֶה (S).

אָסְנַפַּר [osnappar'], Asnapper; *very quick* or *ready*, compounded of אָס, synonymous with the Arabic *very*, and נפר Syriac and Arabic *to hasten* (S.).

אָסְנַת [āhs'nath'], Asenath; *beauty*, according to the Ethiopic (S.).

אָסָף [āhsāhph'], Asaph; *gatherer, collector*, from אָסַף *to gather.*

אַסְפָּתָא [aspāhthāh'], Aspatha; *a young horse*, from the Persian (S.).

אַסִּיר see אָסִיר.

אֵסַר־חַדֹּון [ēhsar-khaddōhn'], Esarhaddon; *prince of power*, חַדּוֹן (probably for אֲחַדּוֹן) from Chaldee אחד *to hold*, and Syriac *to have dominion*, (S.), אֲסַר probably from אָסַר *to bind, imprison*; hence, *a governor, prince.* Compare also אָסַר in פִּלְאֶסֶר and שַׁלְמַנְאֶסֶר.

אֶסְתֵּר [estēhr'], Esther; *star*, (Targum); compare *sitareh* Persic, ἀστήρ, English, *star* (G.).

אֵפֹד [ēh-phōhd'], Ephod; *the sacerdotal robe*; comp. אֵפוֹד Appellative.

אֲפִיַּח [ăphee'akh], Aphiah; *refreshed, recreated* (G.), from פּוּחַ *to blow, breath.*

אַפַּיִם [appah'yim], Appaim; *face* or *a double portion*, compare אַף from אָנַף.

אֲפִיק [ăphee'k], Aphik; *strong*, from אָפַק.

אֲפַלָל [ephlāhl'], Ephlal; *justice*, from פָּלַל *to judge*.

אֶפֶס דַּמִּים [ehphes'-dammeem'], Ephes-dammim; *margin, the coast of Dammim; ceasing of blood or bloodshed;* comp. Appellatives for both.

אֲפֵק [ăphēhk], Aphek; *strong, firm*, from אָפַק·

אֲפֵקָה [ăphēhkāh'], Aphek, id.

אֶפְרַיִם [ephrah'yim], Ephraim; *double fruit* (S.), *double earth* or *ground* (G.), dual of אֶפֶר, from פָּרָה *to be fruitful*, or comp. Appellatives.

אֲפָרְסָיֵא [ăphārsāh-yēh'], Apharsites, and—

אֲפַרְסְכָיֵא [ăphars'khāh-yēh'], Apharsachites, and—

אֲפַרְסַתְכָיֵא [ăphursathkhāh-yēh'], Apharsatchites, names of unknown nations; yet they also seem to have פרס Persia in their analogy.

אֶפְרָת [ephrāhth'], Ephrath; and with ה paragogic.

אֶפְרָתָה [ephrāh'thāh], id.; *fruitfulness, fertility*, from פָּרָה *to be fruitful*.

אֶפְרָתִי [ephrāhthee'], Ephrathite; or *Ephraimite*, gentile noun of אֶפְרַיִם·

אֶצְבּוֹן [etsbōhn'], Ezbon; probably *ornament* (G.).

אָצֵל [āhtsēhl'], Azel; in pause אָצַל Azal; *separate, distinguished, noble,* comp. Appellatives, and אָצִיל from אָצַל (S.).

אֲצַלְיָהוּ [ătsal-yāh'hoo], Azaliah; [whom] *Jehovah separated* or *re-

served*, compounded of id. and יהוּ for יהוה·

אֹצֶם [ōh'tsem], Ozem; *strength*, i. q. אֹמֶץ Appellative.

אֵצֶר [ēh'tser], Ezer; *treasure*, from אָצַר *to lay up*.

אֲרָא [ărāh'], Ara; probably i. q. אֲרִי *lion*, q. v.

אַרְאֵלִי [arēhlee], Areli; *heroic*, from אֲרִיאֵל *lion of God*; also patronymic *Arelite*.

אֲרָב [ărāhv'], Arab; *lurking-place*, from אָרַב *to lay in wait*.

בֵּית אר׳ see אַרְבְּאֵל·

אֲרֻבּוֹת [ăroobbōhth'], Aruboth; *lattices* or *windows*, comp. אֲרֻבָּה Appellative.

אַרְבִּי [arbee'], Arbite; see אָרַב·

אַרְבַּע [arbang'], Arba; *squared, well set* or *made* (comp. Latin *quadratus*), i. e. *giant*, compare Appellative אַרְבַּע *four*, from רָבַע, participle passive, Ex. xxvii. 1. *four-square*.

אַרְגֹּב [argōhv'], Argob; *lion's den*, for אֲרִי גֹּב *lion and den* (S.); *heap of stones*, רָגַב kindred with רָגַם *to heap up stones* (G.).

אַרְדְּ [ard], Ard; *excellent*, for אֶדֶר (S.); *mushroom*, i. q. Chaldee אַרְדָּא (G.).

אַרְדּוֹן [ardōhn'], Ardon; from the same, וֹן formative.

אַרְדִּי [ardee'] Ardite; see אַרְדְּ·

אֲרוּ (16) אֲרָם

אַרְוָךְ [arvāhd'], Arvad; for רָוָד with א prosthetic, *a straying*, i. e. *a place for fugitives*, from רוּד *to wander* (G.).

אֲרוֹד [ărōhd'], Arod; perhaps i. q. עָרוֹד *a wild ass* (G.); but comp. also אַרְדְּ.

אַרְוָדִי [arvāhdee'], Arvadite; see אַרְוָד.

אֲרוֹדִי [ărōhdee'], Arodite; see אֲרוֹד.

אֲרוּמָה [ăroomāh'], Arumah; i. q. רוּמָה *a high place*.

אֲרַוְנָה [ăravnăh'], Araunah: of obscure derivation.

אֲרַח [āhrakh'], Arah; for אֹרֵחַ *departing* (G.), comp. Appellatives.

אֲרִי see אוּרִי.

אַרְיֵה [ar-yēh'], Arieh; *lion*, comp. Appellatives.

אֲרִידַי [ăreeday']. Aridai; *great* (S.), *strong* (G.), from the Persian.

אֲרִידָתָא [areedāhthāh'], Aridatha; id.

אֲרִיאֵל [ăree-ēhl'], Ariel; *lion of God*, compounded of אֲרִי *lion*, and אֵל *God* or *strength*.

אַרְיוֹךְ [ar-yōhkh'], Arioch; *great lion*, from אֲרִי *lion*, and the Assyrio-Chaldean ךְ augmentative (S.).

אֲרִיסַי [ăreesay'], Arisai; *lion-like*, collated from the Hebrew and Persian (Hiller), comp. the preceding.

אֶרֶךְ [ēh'rekh], Erech; *length*, *longitude*, comp. Appellatives.

אַרְכְּוָיֵא [ark'vāh-yēh'], Archevites; Chaldee, see the preceding.

אַרְכִּי [arkee'], Archite; see אֶרֶךְ.

אֲרָם [ărāhm'], Aram, Syria, Syrians; *high*, from רוּם *to be high*, or אָרַם id. (S.).

אֲרַם בֵּית רְחוֹב [ăram bēhth rēhkhōhv'], Syrians of Bethrehob; *Syria of* בֵּית רְחוֹב q. v.

אֲרַם דַּמֶּשֶׂק [ăram dammeh'sek], Syrians of Damascus; *Syria of* דַּמֶּשֶׂק q. v.

אֲרַם דַּרְמֶשֶׂק [ăram darmeh'sek], Syrians of Damascus (marg. Darmesek); *Syria of* דַּרְמֶשֶׂק.

אֲרַמִּי [ăramee'], Syrian; see אֲרָם.

אֲרַמִּיָּה [arammiy-yāh'], Aramitess; fem. of the same.

אֲרַמִּים [ărammeem'], Syrians; pl. masc. of the same.

אֲרַם מַעֲכָה [ăram mah-ngăkhāh'], Syria-maachah; *Syria of* מַעֲכָה q. v.

אַרְמֹנִי [armōhnee'], Armoni; *belonging to the palace* (Palatinus), from אַרְמוֹן *a palace*.

אֲרַם נַהֲרַיִם [ăram nahărāh'yim], Aram-naharaim, Mesopotamia; *Syria of the two rivers*, dual of נָהָר *a river*.

אֲרַם צוֹבָא and אֲרַם צוֹבָה [ăram tsōhvāh], Syrians of Zoba; *Syria of Zoba*, q. v.

אָרָן [ărāhn'], Aran; *wild goat*, as in the Syriac (S.).

אֹרֶן [ōh'ren] Oren; *ash* or *pine-tree*, comp. Appellatives.

אַרְנוֹן [arnōhn'], Arnon; *noisy*, from רָנַן.

אֲרוֹנְיָה Kethib for אֲרַנְיָה.

אׇרְנָן [ornāhn'], Ornan; i. q. אֹרֶן *ash* or *pine-tree*, with ־ָן formative.

אַרְנָן [arnāhn'], Arnan; *brisk*, from the Arabic אָרַן *to be brisk* (S.).

אַרְפָּד [arpāhd'], Arpad; *couch* or *bed*, from רָפַד *to spread over*.

אַרְפַּכְשַׁד [arpakh-shad'], Arphaxad; of obscure derivation.

אַרְצָא [artsāh'], Arza; *earth*, i. q. אֶרֶץ.

אֲרָרָט [ărāhrāht'], Ararat; of obscure derivation.

אֲרָרִי [ărāhree'], Hararite; for הֲרָרִי q. v.

אַרְתַּחְשַׁשְׂתְּא [artakh-shasht'], אַרְתַּחְשַׁשְׂתָּא [artakh-shashtāh'], אַרְתַּחְשַׂסְתְּא [artakh-shast'], Artaxerxes; *strong* or *mighty king*, collated with the Persian.

אֲשַׂרְאֵל [ăsarēhl'], Asareel; [whom] *God has bound* [*by a vow*], for אֲסַרְאֵל, compounded of אָסַר *to bind*, and אֵל *God*.

אַשְׂרְאֵלִי [asree-ēhlee'], Asrielite; patronymic from the following.

אַשְׂרִיאֵל [asree-ēhl'], Asriel; *vow of God*, from אֱסָר *a vow*, and אֵל *God*.

אַשְׁבֵּל [ashbēhl'], Ashbel; *reproof of God*, for אַשְׁבְּאֵל compounded of אשב Arabic, *to rebuke*, אֵל *God* (G.).

אַשְׁבֵּלִי [ashbēhlee'], Ashbelite; patronymic of the same.

אֶשְׁבָּן [eshbāhn'], Eshban; *reproof*, compare אַשְׁבֵּל.

אַשְׁבֵּעַ [ashbēh'ang], Ashbea; *I will adjure*, comp. Hiphil Future of שָׁבַע.

אֶשְׁבַּעַל [eshbah'ngal], Eshbaal; *fire of Baal*, compounded of אֵשׁ *fire*, and בַּעַל.

אַשְׁדּוֹד [ashdōhd'], Ashdod; *strong, fortified place*, for שָׁדוֹד from שָׁדַד *to be mighty*, comp. שַׁדַּי *the Almighty*.

אַשְׁדּוֹדִי [ashdōhdee'], Ashdodite.

אַשְׁדּוֹדִיּוֹת [ashdōhdiy-yōth'], Kethib for אַשְׁדֳּדִיּוֹת [ashdŏdiy-yōth'], Keri, of Ashdod; fem. of the same.

אַשְׁדּוֹדִים [ashdōhdeem'], Ashdodites; masculine plural of the same.

אַשְׁדּוֹדִית [ashdōhdeeth'], in the speech of Ashdod. Compare the preceding.

אַשּׁוּר [ashshoor'], Ashur and Assyria; *step*, comp. Appellatives.

אֲשׁוּרִי [ashooree'], Ashurite; gentile name, as if from אָשׁוּר *step*.

אֲשׁוּרִים [ash-shooreem'], Ashurim; plural of the same.

אַשְׁחוּר [ashkhoor'], Ashhur; *blackness, black*, from שָׁחַר *to be black*.

אֲשִׁימָה [ăshee-māh"], Ashimah; *lion*, as a symbol of the sun, compared with the Arabic (Hiller); *heaven*, compared with the Persian (G).

אֶשְׁכּוֹל [eshkōhl'], Eshcol; *cluster, grape*, compare Appellatives.

אַשְׁכְּנַז [ashk'naz'], Ashkenaz; of uncertain derivation.

אַשְׁנָה [ashnāh'], Ashnah; *strong, firm, mighty*, from the Arabic (S.).

אֶשְׁעָן [esh-gnāhn'], Eshan; *a prop, couch, bed*, from שָׁעַן *to lean, rest*.

אַשְׁפְּנַז [ashp'naz'], Ashpenaz; *quick assistance*, compounded of אֶשֶׁף Syriac, *aid*, and נוז Arabic, *to run swiftly*, (S.).

אַשְׁקְלוֹן [ashk'lōhn'], Askelon; *emigration*, from שקל Syriac, *to emigrate* (S.).

אֶשְׁקְלוֹנִי [eshk'lōhnee'], Eshkalonite.

אָשֵׁר [āh-shēhr'], Asher; *happy, blessed*, compare Appellatives.

אַשּׁוּר see אַשּׁוּר.

אֲשֵׁרִי [āhshēhree'], Asherite.

אֲשַׂרְאֵלָה [ăsharēh'lāh], Asarelah; *upright towards God*, compounded of אָשַׁר i. q. יָשַׁר *to be straight*, and אֵל *God*, with ה local, accent penultimate.

אֶשְׁתָּאוֹל [eshtāh-ōhl'], Eshtaol; *petition*, an infinitive form of Hithpael, from שָׁאַל *to ask*, imitating the Arabic (G.).

אֶשְׁתָּאֻלִי [eshtāh-oolee'], Eshtaulite.

אֶשְׁתּוֹן [eshtōhn'], Eshton; *effeminate*, from אֶשֶׁת *a woman* (G.).

אֶשְׁתְּמֹה [esht'mōh'], Eshtemoh; probably for

אֶשְׁתְּמוֹעַ [esht'mōh'ăng], Eshtemoa; *obedience*, from שָׁמַע *to hear*, an infinitive form of the Hithpael; compare אֶשְׁתָּאוֹל.

אֶתְבַּעַל [ethbah'ngal], Ethbaal; *with Baal*, compounded of אֵת *with*, and בַּעַל.

אִתַּי [ittay'], Ittai; *with the Lord*, from אֵת *with*, compare אָחֻזִּי (S.); *neighbour*, from אֵת *neighbourhood*, with the termination ִ (G.).

אֵתָם [ethāhm'], Etham; compared with the Egyptian it is supposed to mean *end* or *border* (terminus) *of the sea*.

אֶתְנִי [ethnee'], Ethni; *liberal*, from אֶתְנָה *a gift*, root תָּנָה *to give*.

אֶתְנָן [ethnāhn'], Ethnan; *gift*, or *wages*; root תָּנָה *to give*.

אֲתָרִים [ăthāhreem'], spies; plural of אֲתָר i. q. Chaldee אֲתַר *place*.

ב

בְּאֵר [b'ēhr'], Beer; *a well*, compare Appellatives.

בְּאֵרָא [b'ēhrāh'], Beera; id.

בְּאֵר אֵלִים [b'ēhr-ēhleem'], Beer-elim; *well of the mighty heroes*, or *oaks*, compare בְּאֵר, and Appellatives אֵל or אַיִל.

בְּאֵרָה [b'ēhrāh'], Beerah; i. q. בְּאֵרָא.

בְּאֵרוֹת [b'ēhrōth'], Beeroth; *wells*, plural of בְּאֵר.

בְּאֵרִי [b'ēhree'], Beeri ; (*fontanus*) *of a spring*, compare בְּאֵר.

בְּאֵר לַחַי רֹאִי [b'ēhr lahkhāy rōh-ee'], Beer-lahai-roi; margin, *the well of him that liveth and seeth me*, compare Gen. xvi. 14; and the note*.

בְּאֵר שֶׁבַע [b'ēhr sheh'vang], Beer-sheba ; *well of oath*, compare בְּאֵר; for שֶׁבַע *oath*, compare Gen. xxi. 31.

בְּאֵרֹת בְּנֵי יַעֲקָן [b'ēhrōth' b'nēh yangăkāhn], Beeroth of (compare the same above) *the children of* (בְּנֵי) *Jaakan*, compare יַעֲקָן.

בְּאֵרֹתִי [b'ēhrōthee'], Beerothite; gentile noun of בְּאֵרוֹת.

בֵּבַי [bēhvay'], Bebai ; supposed to be a contraction from בְּאֲבִי *with desire of the Lord*, i. e. *with great desire*, בְּ *in*, אֲבָה *desire*, compare Appellatives; for י ֖ see אַחְוַי; in pause בֵּבָי.

בָּבֶל [bāhvel'], Babel, Babylon; *confusion*, for בַּלְבֵּל, from בָּלַל *to confuse* :—*confusion is come* (Aben Ezra); *in her* (is) *confusion* (Hiller) ; contraction of בָּא from בּוֹא *to come*, or בָּהּ *in her*, and בֵּל *confusion*, for the form of which compare חֵן from חָנַן, קֵץ from קָצַץ.

בַּבְלָיֵא [bavlāhyēh'], Babylonians ; Chaldaic gentile noun of the same.

בִּגְוַי [bigvay'], Bigvai ; *with exultation*, from בְּ *with*, and גֵּוִי *exultation*, then, after the analogy of חֲלִי—חָלְיִי and אָהֳלִי—אָיַי, it should have been רָאִי (rō-ŭyee). By this, however correct in itself, some (see especially Gesenius) have been led to consider רֹאִי of the second clause of this verse also as a substantive, and that, in pause of רָאִי. But against this, the accent proves, which ought in this case to have been on the penultimate (רֳאִי) instead of the ultimate syllable. Compare 1 Sam. xvi. 12., Neh. iii. 6., Job xxxiii. 21., where רָאִי occurs in pause. In this second clause then, and in the proper name before us, we should either take it with our translators as a participle, or as a substantive רֹאֶה *a vision*, with suffix, compare Gesenius under חֹזֶה *a seer* and *vision*. This clause might then be rendered thus, *have I even here seen* (i e. have I the sense of sight preserved) *after my vision?* Hence the proper name in question, *the well of life of* (i. e. after) *my vision*.

---

* Others, *the well of the life of vision*, i e. where after the *vision* of God, *life* has notwithstanding been preserved. Taking חַי, not as an adjective *living*, but as a substantive *life*, and רֹאִי in pause from רָאִי. Although this translation may be admitted, as will be seen hereafter, yet not upon the stated, but upon other grounds, which we will give here on account of its close connexion with the preceding verse 13, it affords an opportunity of examining the right rendering of the latter.

" Thou, God, *seest me*." The word רֳאִי the translators evidently took as a participle with suffix for רֹאִי, from רֹאֶה. But since no other instance can be produced where וֹ of the participle is *pure* or changeable, we must at once admit it to be a substantive of לִ״ה (after the form חֲלִי, in pause חָלְיִי from חָלָה), *vision*, hence, " thou art the God of *vision* or *revelation*." Not *my*; for root בָּאָה, compare also Hebrew גָּנָה Job xxii. 29. *husbandman, gardener,* from the Chaldaic בָּנָא *field*, and the Syriac *garden* (G.).

בִּגְתָא [*bigthah'*], Bigtha and
בִּגְתָן [*bigthāhn'*], Bigthan and
בִּגְתָנָא [*bigthāhnāh'*], Bigthana; supposed to be of the same analogy with אֲבַגְתָא.

בְּדַד [*b'dad*], Bedad; *separate* or *separation,* from בָּדַד *to be separate.*

בְּדְיָה [*bēh-d'yāh'*], Bediah; *by the power of Jah,* for בְּ, בְּאַד יָה *in,* according to the Arabic *strength*, and יָה *Jah,* for Jehovah (S.), *under a calamity from the Lord;* compare Appellatives.

בְּדָן [*b'dāhn'*], Bedan; *stout, strong,* from the Arabic בדן *to be stout, corpulent* (S.), for בֶּן־דָן *a Danite* (G.).

בִּדְקַר [*bidkar'*], Bidkar; *son of thrusting through, i. e. he who thrusts through,* for בֶּן דָּקַר (G.), compare Appellatives.

בֹּהַן [*bōh'han*], Bohan; *thumb,* i.q. Appellative בֹּהֶן.

בּוּז [*booz'*], Buz; *contempt,* compare Appellatives.

בּוּזִי [*boozee'*], Buzi or Buzite; id. or patronymic of the same.

בַּוַּי [*bavvay'*], Bavai; perhaps of Persian origin (G.).

בּוּנָה [*boonāh'*], Bunah; *understanding, prudence,* from בּוּן *to understand.*

בֻּנִּי i. q. בָּנִי.

בֹּוצֵץ [*bōhtsēhts'*], Bozez; *shining,* from the Arabic בצץ *to shine* (S.).

בִּזְיוֹתְיָה [*bizyōthyāh'*], Bizjothjah; *contempt of Jah,* compounded of בִּזְיוֹת plural of בִּזְיָה *contempt,* root בָּזָה *to despise,* and יָה *Jah,* Jehovah.

בֶּזֶק [*beh'zek*], Bezek; *lightning,* i. q. Appellative בָּזָק and בָּרָק.

בִּזְתָא [*bizthāh'*], Biztha; *bound,* namely, in a member, i. e. *castrated, a eunuch,* collated with the Persian (G.).

בַּחוּרִים [*bahkhooreem'*], Bahurim; *youths,* compare Appellatives.

בַּחֲרוּמִי [*bakhăroomee'*], Baharumite; gentile noun of the same.

בֶּטַח [*beh'takh*], Betah; *confidence, security,* compare Appellatives.

בֶּטֶן [*beh'ten*], Beten; *belly,* compare Appellative.

בְּטֹנִים [*b'tōneem'*], Betonim; *pistachio nuts,* i. q. Appellative בָּטְנִים.

בַּיִת [*bah'yith*], Bajith; *house, temple,* compare Appellative; only Isa. xv. 2. supposed to be the same with בֵּית מְעוֹן, but according to others an Appellative.

בֵּית אָוֶן [*bēhth āh'ven*], Beth-aven; *house of vanity,* בֵּית *house of,* construct of בַּיִת and אָוֶן *vanity,* by paronomasia for בֵּית אֵל (house of God); compare Appellative אָוֶן.

בֵּית אֵל [bēhth-ehl'], Beth-el; *house of God*, compare Appellatives.

בֵּית אַרְבֵּאל [bēth arbēhl'], Beth-arbel; *house of the snares of God*, compounded of בֵּית *house of*, אֲרָב *snares* (insidiæ), and אֵל *God*.

בֵּית בַּעַל מְעוֹן [bēhth bah'-ngal m'ngōhn], Beth-baal-meon; *house or place of Baal's habitation*, for בֵּית מְעוֹן בַּעַל, בֵּית *house of*, מָעוֹן const. of מָעוֹן *habitation*, בַּעַל *Baal*.

בֵּית בִּרְאִי [bēhth bir-ee'], Beth-birei; *house of my* (own) *making*, בֵּית *house of*, and בְּרָא *a creating*, from בָּרָא.

בֵּית בָּרָה [bēhth bāhrāh'], Beth-barah; *house or place of passage*, for בֵּית עֲבָרָה, compare Βηθαβαρά, John i. 28. (S.).

בֵּית גָּדֵר [bēhth gāhdēhr'], Beth-gader; *house of the wall*, compare Appellatives.

בֵּית גָּמוּל [bēhth gāhmool'], Beth-gamul; *house of the weaned child*, בֵּית *house of*, גָּמוּל participle passive of גָּמַל *to wean*:—or *house of* (perhaps builded by) *Gamul*, compare גָּמוּל.

בֵּית דִּבְלָתַיִם [bēhth diblāhthah'-yim], Beth-diblathaim; *house of two fig-cakes*, בֵּית *house of*, דִּבְלָתַיִם dual of דְּבֵלָה *a round cake of dried figs*.

בֵּית דָּגוֹן [bēhth dāhgōhn']; Beth-dagon; *house or temple of Dagon*, compare דָּגוֹן.

בֵּית הָאֱלִי [bēhth hāh-ĕlee'], Beth-elite; gentile noun of בֵּית אֵל.

בֵּית הָאֵצֶל [bēhth hāh-ēh'tzel], Beth-ezel; margin, *a place near, house or place of the neighbourhood*, compare Appellative אֵצֶל.

בֵּית הַגִּלְגָּל [bēhth haggilgāhl'], *house of Gilgal; house or place of rolling*, compare גִּלְגָּל.

בֵּית הַיְשִׁימוֹת [bēhth hah-y'shee-mōh'th], Beth-jeshimoth; *house or place of the desert*, יְשִׁימוֹת i.q. יְשִׁימוֹן *desert*, compare Appellatives.

בֵּית הַכֶּרֶם [bēhth hakkeh'rem], Beth-haccerem; *house or place of the vineyard*, compare Appellative כֶּרֶם.

בֵּית הַלַּחְמִי [bēhth hallakhmee'], the Bethlehemite; a gentile noun of בֵּית לֶחֶם.

בֵּית מַעֲכָה see בֵּית הַמַּעֲכָה.

בֵּית מַרְכָּבוֹת see בֵּית הַמַּרְכָּבוֹת.

בֵּית הָעֵמֶק [bēth hāh-ngēh'mek], Bethemek; *house or place of the valley*, compare Appellative עֵמֶק.

בֵּית הָעֲרָבָה [bēhth hāh-ngărāh-vāh'], Beth-arabah; *house or place of the plain or desert*, compare עֲרָבָה.

בֵּית הָרָם [bēhth hāhrāhm'], Beth-haram; *house or place of Haram* (S.); *house of height, high place*, בֵּית *house of*, and הָרָם either 'the name of a person or *a height*, from הָרַם according to the Arabic *to be high*. Comp. Gesenius under הָרַם.

בֵּית הָרָן [bēhth hāhrāhn'], Beth-haran; *house or place of Haran* (S);

בית (22) בית

comp הָרָן. But this seems evidently to be the same as the preceding, and ם and ן merely interchanged, compare Num. xxxii. 36. with Josh. xiii. 27.

בֵּית הַשִּׁטָּה [bēhth hashshittāh'], Bethshittah; *house of the acacia*, compare Appellative שִׁטָּה.

בֵּית הַשִּׁמְשִׁי [bēhth hashshimshee'], Beth-shemite; gentile noun of בֵּית שֶׁמֶשׁ.

בֵּית חָגְלָה [bēhth khoglāh'], Beth-hoglah; *house* or *place of Hoglah*, or *partridges*, compare חָגְלָה.

בֵּית חוֹרוֹן [bēhth khōrōhn'], Beth-horon; *house* or *place of the cave*, compare Appellative חוֹר *hole, cave*.

בֵּית חָנָן [bēhth khāhnāhn'], Elon-beth-hanan; *house* or *place of Hanan* or *grace*, compare חָנָן.

בֵּית כַּר [bēhth kar'], Beth-car; *house of pasture* or *lamb*, compare Appellative כַּר.

בֵּית לְבָאוֹת [bēhth l'vāh-ōhth'], Beth-lebaoth; *house* or *place of lionesses*, בֵּית *house of*, and לְבָאוֹת plural of לְבִי *a lion*.

בֵּית לֶחֶם [bēhth leh'khem], Bethlehem; *house of bread*, i. e. *fruitfulness*, compounded of the same and לֶחֶם *bread*.

בֵּית לְעַפְרָה [bēhth l'aphrāh'], house of Aphrah; *house of dust*, compare margin; *house of the hind* (G.), compounded of the same and עַפְרָה *dust*, or the same as עָפְרָה *hind*.

בֵּית מִלֹּא [bēhth millōh'], house of Millo; and in 2 Kings xii. 20 (21), margin, Beth-millo, comp. מִלּוֹא.

בֵּית מְעוֹן [bēhth m'ngōhn'], Beth-meon; *house of habitation*, the same as בַּעַל מְעוֹן and בֵּית בַּעַל מְעוֹן.

בֵּית מַעֲכָה [bēhth māh-gnăkhāh'], Beth-maachah; *house of Maachah*, compare מַעֲכָה.

בֵּית מַרְכָּבוֹת [bēhth markāhvōhth'], Beth-mercaboth; *house* or *place of chariots*, compare Appellative מֶרְכָּבָה *chariot*, from רָכַב *to ride*.

בֵּית נִמְרָה [bēhth nimrāh'], Beth-nimrah; *house* or *place of clear waters*, the same as נִמְרָה, from the Arabic נמר *to find clear and wholesome water*. (S.).

בֵּית עֵדֶן [bēhth ngeh'den], house of Eden, margin, Beth-eden; *house* or *place of pleasure* or *loveliness*, compare עֵדֶן.

בֵּית עַזְמָוֶת [bēhth gnazmāh'veth], Beth-azmaveth; *house of Azmaveth*, the same as עַזְמָוֶת alone, which latter is also the name of a person, which compare.

בֵּית עֲנוֹת [bēhth gnănōhth'], Beth-anoth; *house* or *place of answers*, i. e. *echos*, compare עָנָה *to answer*.

בֵּית עֲנָת [bēhth gnănāhth'], Beth-anath; the same, or *house of Anath*, compare עֲנָת.

בֵּית עֵקֶד [bēhth gnēh'ked], shearing-house; and

בֵּית עֵקֶד הָרֹעִים [bēhth gnēhked hāh-rōh-ngeem'], shearing-house; marg. *house of shepherds binding* (sheep), lit. *house of the binding of the shepherds*, comp. עָקַד *to bind*, and רָעָה *to feed; farm-house of the shepherds* (G.), collated from the Arabic.

בֵּית פֶּלֶט [bēhth peh'let], found only in pause, פָּלֵט, Beth-palet; *house of escape*, compare פָּלַט *to escape*.

בֵּית פְּעוֹר [bēhth p'ngōhr'], Beth-peor; *house or temple of Peor*, comp. פְּעוֹר *the name of a mount*, and בַּעַל פְּעוֹר *the name of an idol*.

בֵּית פַּצֵּץ [bēhth patstsēhts'], Beth-pazzez; *house or place of dispersion*, from an obsolete root פָּצַץ (i. q. פּוּץ and נָפַץ) *to scatter, disperse*.

בֵּית צוּר [bēhth tsoor'], Beth-zur; *house of rock or refuge*, compare Appellative צוּר.

בֵּית רְחוֹב [bēhth r'khōhv'], Beth-rehob; *house or place of streets*, compare Appellative רְחוֹב.

בֵּית שְׁאָן [bēhth sh'āhn'], Beth-shean; *house or place of quietness or ease:* compare verb שָׁאַן.

בֵּית שֶׁמֶשׁ [bēhth sheh'mesh], Beth-shemesh; *house or temple of the sun*, compare Appellative שֶׁמֶשׁ.

בֵּית שָׁן & שָׁן [bēhth shāhn & shan], Beth-shan; contracted from שְׁאָן.

בֵּית תַּפּוּחַ [bēhth tappoo'akh], Beth-tappuah; *house or place of apple-trees*, compare Appellative תַּפּוּחַ.

בְּכוֹרַת [b'khōhrath'], Bechorath; *of primogeniture*, i. e. *first-born*, construct of בְּכוֹרָה; compare Appellatives.

בֹּכִים [bōhkheem'], Bochim; *weeping*, or *weepers*, i. e. *place of the weepers*, participle of בָּכָה *to weep*.

בֶּכֶר [bekher'], Becher; *first-born* (S.), *a young camel* (G.), compare Piel of the verb בָּכַר and בֶּכֶר Appellative.

בֹּכְרוּ [bōhkh'roo'], Bocheru; contracted from בְּכֹר הוּא *he (is) the first-born*, compare the preceding.

בִּכְרִי [bikhree'], Bichri; *first-born* (S.), *youthful* (G.), compare בֶּכֶר.

בַּכְרִי [bakhri'], Bachrite; *gentile noun of* בֶּכֶר.

בֵּל [bēhl], Bel; commonly considered as a contraction of בַּעַל for בַּעַל (Baal), according to the Syrian mode of expelling the gutturals ה and ע (Drusius by Simonis). But this being the name of a Babylonian divinity, no matter how much the mythological accounts or historical analogies may favour the view stated above, *sacred* history would lead us to trace its origin to the confusion of tongues. Hence *confusion*, as a concrete, *author of confusion*, from בָּלַל *to mingle*, like חֵן from חָנַן, compare also בָּבֶל for בַּלְבֶּל.

בַּלְאֲדָן [balădāhn'], Baladan; *of of whom Bel (is) lord*, or *whose lord (is) Bel*, (comp. note under אֲבִי) i. e. *worshipper of Bel*, compounded of the preceding בֵּל and אֲדָן for אָדוֹן *lord*.

בֵּלְשַׁאצַּר see בֵּלְאשַׁאצַּר.

בִּלְגָּה [bilgāh'], Bilgah; *recreation*, from בָּלַג.

בִּלְגַי [bilgay'], Bilgai; id. comp. אֲחָזַי.

בִּלְדַּד [bildad'], Bildad; probably contracted from בֶּן לָדָד son of strife, from the Arabic לדד to debate (G.).

בָּלָה [bāhlāh'], Balah; probably contracted from

בִּלְהָה [bilhāh'], Bilhah; terror (S.), bashfulness (G.), from the root בָּלַה.

בִּלְהָן [bilhāhn'], Bilhan; terror, (S.), bashful (G.), root בָּלַה.

בֵּלְטְשַׁאצַּר [bēhlt'shatstsar'], Belteshazzar; Bel's prince, i. e. prince whom Bel favours, compounded of בֵּל Bel, מְשָׁא Zendic, genitive of צַר prince (G.).

בֶּלַע [bēh'lang], Bela; a devouring, destruction, from בָּלַע to swallow.

בַּלְעִי [bal-ngee'], Belaite; gentile noun of the same.

בִּלְעָם [bil-ngāhm'], Balaam; a devouring or destruction of the people, contracted from בֶּלַע עָם, or for בַּל not, עָם people, i. e. stranger (G.).

בָּלָק [bāhlāhk'], Balak; empty (G.).

בֵּלְאשַׁצַּר [bēhlshatstsar'], Belshazzar; probably a contraction of בֵּלְטְשַׁאצַּר once.

בִּלְשָׁן [bilshāhn'], Bilshan; contracted for בֶּן לָשׁוֹן son of tongue, i.e. eloquent (G.); for the form לְשָׁן compare בִּלְאֲדָן.

בִּמְהָל [bimhāhl'], Bimhal; in quietness, from the Arabic מהל to do quietly (S.); contracted for בֶּן מְהָל

son of circumcision, i. e. circumcised, i. q. מוּל to circumcise.

בָּמוֹת [bāhmōhth'], Bamoth; high places, plural of בָּמָה. More fully written

בָּמוֹת בַּעַל [bāhmōhth bah'ngal], Bamoth-baal; margin, high places of Baal, see also בַּעַל.

בֵּן [bēhn'], Ben; son, compare Appellatives.

בֶּן אוֹנִי [ben ōhnee'], Ben-oni; son of my sorrow, from בֶּן son of, and אָוֶן sorrow.

בֶּן־גֶּבֶר [ben geh'ver], son of Geber margin, Bengeber; son of strength, compare the verb גָּבַר.

בֶּן־הֲדַד [ben hădad'], Ben-hadad; son, i. e. worshipper, of Hadad, a Syrian idol (Adodus), comp. הֲדַד.

בִּנּוּי [binnooy'], Binnui; a building, from בָּנָה to build.

בֶּן־זוֹחֵת [ben zōkhēhth'], Benzoheth; only 1 Chron. iv. 20. probably son of Zoheth, grandson of Ishi, and not, as it would appear from our English version, brother of Zoheth.

בֶּן־חַיִל [ben khah'yil], Ben-hail; son of valour, compare Appellatives.

בֶּן־חָנָן [ben khāhnāhn'], Benhanan; son of grace, compare חָנַן to be gracious.

בָּנִי [bāhnee'], Bani; built up, from בָּנָה to build.

בֻּנִּי [boonnee'], Bunni; built up, of the form Pual from בָּנָה to build.

בְּנֵי־בְרָק [b'nēh b'rak'], Bene-berak; *sons of Berak,* the name of a town; בָּרָק the same as בָּרָק *lightning.*

בְּנָיָה [b'nāh-yāh'], Benaiah; [whom] *the Lord builded up,* compounded of בָּנָה *to build,* and יָהּ *Jah.*

בְּנָיָהוּ [b'nāhyāh'hoo], id.; but more fully of יהוה.

בְּנֵי יַעֲקָן [b'nēh yahngăkāhn'], Bene-jaakan; *sons of Jaakan,* the name of a place; יַעֲקָן *he shall surround like a necklace,* i. e. *he shall be the glory* [of his parents] by transposition, i. q. עָנָק.

בִּנְיָמִין, בִּנְיָמִין [binyāh-meen'] Benjamin; *son of the right hand,* i. e. *support of the father;* or, *son of days,* i. e. *of the father's old age,* compare Gen. xxxvii. 3; compounded of בֶּן *son of,* and יָמִין *the right hand,* or plural of יוֹם *day,* compare Appellatives.

בְּנְיָמִינִי once in Kethib, and בֶּן־יְמִינִי [ben y'meenee'], Benjamite; *gentile noun of the same.*

בְּנִינוּ [b'neenoo'], Beninu; *our son* (G.).

בִּנְעָה, בִּנְעָא [bin-ngāh'], Binea; i. q. נִבְעָה *a spring, source,* from נָבַע *to spring, flow* (S.).

בֶּן־עַמִּי [ben ngammee'], Ben-ammi; *son of my people,* compounded of בֶּן *son of,* and עָם *people,* with suffix.

בְּסוֹדְיָה [b'sōhd'yāh'], Besodiah; *in the counsel* or *secret of the Lord,* בְּ *in,* סוֹד *counsel,* יָהּ *Jah.*

בֵּסַי [bēhsay'], Besai; *contempt,* or *contemner,* בָּסַס or בּוּס *to tread under foot,* with formative ־ִי perhaps of intensity, compare אֲחָזִי.

בְּעוֹר [b'ngōhr'], Beor; *torch, lamp,* from בָּעַר *to burn* (G.).

בֹּעַז [boh'ngaz], Boaz; contracted from בּוֹ עַז *in him* [is] *strength* (S.); *readiness,* from the Arabic, בעז *to be swift* (G.).

בַּעַל* [bah'ngal], Baal; *lord, possessor,* compare Appellatives.

בַּעַל בְּרִית [bah-ngal b'reeth'], Baal-berith; *lord of covenant,* compare Appellatives.

בַּעַל גָּד [bahngal gad'], Baal-gad; *lord* or *possessor of fortune,* or *Gad,* the name of a divinity worshipped in that place, compare גָּד proper name, and גָּד Appellative.

בַּעֲלָה [bah-ngălāh'], Baalah; *mistress,* the name of a town, fem. of בַּעַל.

בַּעַל הָמוֹן [bah-ngal hāhmōhn'], Baal-hamon; *possessor of,* or *possessing a multitude,* compare Appellatives.

בְּעָלוֹת [b'ngāhlōhth'], Bealoth; *mistresses,* fem. plural of בַּעַל.

בַּעַל זְבוּב [bah-ngal z'voov'], Baal-zebub; *lord,* or *Baal the fly,* compare Appellatives.

* Baal is the name of an idol: once (1 Chron. iv. 33) also the name of a town. In composition with other names of towns, it may have reference to the place itself in the sense of *possessor* or *having,* for the masculine מָקוֹם *place,* as also בַּעֲלָה and בַּעֲלַת for the feminine עִיר *city.*

בַּעַל חָנָן [bah-ngal khāhnāhn'], Baal-hanan; *lord of grace*, from חָנַן *to be gracious.*

בַּעַל חָצוֹר [ba-ngal khāhtsōhr'] Baal-hazor; *possessor of*, i. e. *having a villa*, חָצוֹר *a court, a villa* (G.); compare note under בַּעַל.

בַּעַל חֶרְמוֹן [bah-ngal khermōhn'], Baal-hermon; *having Hermon*, i. e. *situated near mount Hermon*, compare חֶרְמוֹן.

בְּעֶלְיָדָע [b'ngelyāhdāhng], Beeliada; [*whom*] *the Lord knows*, compounded of בְּעֵל a Syriac form for בַּעַל *Lord*, and יָדַע *to know.*

בְּעַלְיָה [b'ngalyāh'], Bealiah; [*whom*] *the Lord governs* (G.), from בַּעַל *to master*, יָהּ *Jah.*

בַּעֲלִיס [bah-ngălees'], Baalis; *with exultation* (S.); contracted from בֶּן עָלִים *son of exultation* (G.), עָלַס *to exult.*

בַּעַל מְעוֹן [bah-ngal m'ngōhn'], Baal-meon; *Baal's habitation* (S.); *place of habitation* (G.), compare note under בֵּית בַּעַל מְעוֹן & בַּעַל מְעוֹן & בֵּית מְעוֹן.

בַּעַל פְּעוֹר [bah-ngal p'ngōhr'], Baalpeor; *lord* or *Baal of* (mount) *Peor*, compare פְּעוֹר.

בַּעַל פְּרָצִים [bah-ngal p'rāhtseem'], Baal-perazim, marg. *plain of breaches; place of overthrow, defeat* (G.); comp. note under בַּעַל: פֶּרֶץ *a breach, overthrow*, plural פְּרָצִים.

בַּעַל צְפוֹן [bah-ngal ts'phōhn'], Baal-zephon; *place of Zephon*, i. e.

sacred to Zephon (Typhon), an idol (G.); צָפוֹן *a hiding, concealment, refuge* from צָפַן.

בַּעַל שָׁלִשָׁה [bah-ngal shāleeshāh'], Baal-shalishah; *Baal of*, i. e. situated in *Shalishah*, compare שָׁלִשָׁה the name of a country.

בַּעֲלָת [bah-ngălath']; Baalath; *mistress, the name of a town*; compare בַּעֲלָה.

בַּעֲלַת בְּאֵר [bah-ngălath b'ēhr'], Baalath-beer; *possessor of* or *having a well*, compare note under בַּעַל.

בַּעַל תָּמָר [bah-ngal tāhmāhr'], Baal-tamar; *possessor of* or *having palm-trees*, compare id. and Appellatives.

בְּעֹן [b'ngōhn'], Beon; contracted from בֵּית מְעוֹן (S.).

בַּעֲנָא [bah-ngănāh'], Baana; *in answer* (to prayer), i. e. *obtained by prayer* (S.); contracted from בֶּן עֲנָא *son of affliction* (G.), עֲנָא for עָנָה from עָנָה *to answer*, also *to suffer.*

בַּעֲנָה [bah-ngănāh'], Baanah; id.

בַּעֲרָא [bah-ngărāh], Baara; for בַּעֲרָה *fool* (G.), compare בַּעַר *stupid.*

בַּעֲשֵׂיָה [bah-ngăsēhyāh'], Baaseiah; for בְּמַעֲשֵׂה־יָהּ *through the work* or *operation of the Lord*, from עָשָׂה *to make* (S.).

בַּעְשָׁא [bangshāh'], Baasha; *wickedness*, בְּעֵשׁ Chaldee, i. q. בָּאַשׁ *to be evil.*

בְּעֶשְׁתְּרָה [b'ngesht'rāh'], Beeshterah; contracted for בֵּית עֶשְׁתְּרָה *house* or *temple of Eshterah* (Astarte), plural Ashtaróth, comp. בְּעוֹן (S.).

בֵּצַי [*bēhtsay'*], Bezai; *white*, compare Gesenius' Manuale on the root בּוּץ *to be white*, and בֵּיצָה *an egg*; for the formative ‾ִ compare אַחְזַי.

בְּצַלְאֵל [*b'tsal-ēhl'*], Bezaleel; compounded of בְּ צֵל אֵל *in the shadow of God*, compare Appellatives.

בַּצְלוּת [*batslooth'*], Bazluth; *nakedness*, from בָּצַל i. q. פָּצַל *to peel*, hence *to make bare* (G.). The same person is also called:

בַּצְלִית [*batsleeth'*], Bazlith.

בָּצְקַת [*botskath'*], Bozkhath; *a tumid* or *high place*, from בָּצֵק *to swell*.

בֶּצֶר [*beh'tser*], Bezer; *fortification* or *ore*, compare בָּצַר *to fortify*, and בֶּצֶר *gold* or *silver ore*.

בָּצְרָה [*botsrāh'*], Bozrah; *fortification*, from בָּצַר *to fortify*.

בַּקְבּוּק [*bakbook'*], Bakbuk; *bottle*, from בָּקַק *to pour* or *empty out*.

בַּקְבֻּקְיָה [*bakbookyāh'*], Bakbukiah; *effusion*, i. e. *devastation of the Lord*, from the same root.

בַּקְבַּקַּר [*bakbakkar'*], Bakbakkar; perhaps contracted from בְּקַב הַר *destruction of the mountain* (G.), of the same root.

בֻּקִּי [*bookkee'*], Bukki; abbreviated from

בֻּקִּיָּהוּ [*bukkiyyāh'hoo*], Bukkiah; *devastation* [come forth] *from the Lord* (G.), compounded of בֹּק infinitive form of בָּקַק *to empty out*, and יהוה *Lord*.

בְּרֹאדַךְ בַּלְאֲדָן [*b'rōhdakh balădāhn'*], Berodach-baladan; by permutation of מ into ב i. q. מְרֹאדַךְ בַּ'; Hiller considers it as a contraction for בַּר מְרֹאדַךְ בַּ' *son of Merodach-baladan*, compare בְּעוֹן (S.).

בְּרָאיָה [*b'rāh-yāh'*], Beraiah; [whom] *the Lord elected* (S.); *whom the Lord created* (G.), compounded of בָּרָא *to create*, or for בָּרָה i. q. בָּרַר *to choose*, and יָהּ *Jah*.

בֶּרֶד [*beh'red*], Bered; *hail*, i. q. בָּרָד Appellative.

בָּרוּךְ [*bāhrookh'*], Baruch; *blessed*, participle passive of בָּרַךְ *to bless*.

בֵּרוֹתָה [*bēhrōh'thāh*], Berothah; *a well* or *wells*, contracted for בְּאֵרוֹתָה or בְּאֵרוֹת with local ה.

בִּרְזוֹת Kethib [*birzōhth'*], Birzavith; *holes, wounds*, from the Chaldee and Talmudic בְּרַז *to thrust through* (G.), for which

בִּרְזַיִת Keri [*birzāh'yith*], Birzavith; *choice olive*, compounded of בָּרַר or בָּרָה *to choose*, and זַיִת *olive*.

בַּרְזִלַּי [*barzillay'*], Barzillai; *of iron*, [ferreus], from בַּרְזֶל *iron*, with the adjective ending ‾ִי.

בַּרְחֻמִי [*barkhoomee'*], Barhumite; a gentile noun, by transposition, and defective for בַּחֲרוּמִי *Baharumite*, compare 1 Chron. xi. 33.

בֵּרִי [*bēhree'*], Bere; contracted from בְּאֵרִי (*fontanus*) *of a spring* (S.).

בָּרִיחַ [bāhree'akh], Bariah; *fugitive*, compare Appellatives.

בְּרִים [bēhreem'], Berites; gentile noun of בְּרִי.

בְּרִיעָה [b'ree-ngāh'], Beriah; *in evil or calamity*, compare 1 Chron. vii. 23. But ב in this word, is generally considered radical, according to the Arabic برع *to give*, hence the name here; and בְּרָעָה in the passage mentioned, is rendered *gift, present*.

בְּרִיעִי [b'ree-ngee'], Beriite; patronymic of the same.

בְּרִית [b'reeth'], Berith; *covenant*, once Jud. ix. 46, for בַּעַל בְּרִית; compare Jud. vii. 33.

בַּרַכְאֵל [bahrakhēhl'], Barachel; [whom] *God has blessed*, compounded of בָּרַךְ *to bless*, and אֵל *God*.

בְּרָכָה [b'rāhkhāh'], Berachah; *blessing*, compare Appellative.

בֶּרֶכְיָה [behrekh-yāh'], Berechiah; [whom] *the Lord blessed*, contracted בָּרַךְ יָה.

בֶּרֶכְיָהוּ [behrekh-yāh'hoo], Berechiah; id.

בַּרְגַּע see קָדֵשׁ.

בֶּרַע [beh'rang], Bera; *gift, present*, according to the Arabic برع *to give* (S.).

בָּרָק [bāhrāhk'], Barak; *lightning*, compare Appellative.

בַּרְקוֹס [barkōhs'], Barkos; *painter*, contracted from בֶּן *son of*, and רְקוֹם according to the Arabic, *to paint with colours* (G.).

בִּרְשַׁע [birshāhng'], Birsha; *stout man*, collated with the Arabic (S.); a contraction from בֶּן רֶשַׁע *son of malice* (G.), compare Appellatives.

בֵּרֹתַי [bēhrōhthay'], Berothai; *my wells*, for בְּאֵרֹתַי, compare בְּאֵר and also note under אֲחַזַי.

בֵּרֹתִי [bēhrōthee'], Berothite; contracted from בְּאֵרֹתִי gentile noun of בְּאֵרוֹת.

בְּשׂוֹר [b'sōhr'], Besor; *cold*, collated with the Arabic (S.).

בָּשְׂמַת [bāhs'math'], Bashemath; *smelling sweetly*, from בָּשָׂם i. q. Chaldee בְּסַם *to smell sweetly*.

בִּשְׁלָם [bishlāhm'], Bishlam; contracted from בֶּן שָׁלָם *son of peace*, compare Chaldee שְׁלָם *peace*, also בְּעוֹן.

בָּשָׁן [bāhshāhn'], Bashan; *level soil*, collated with the Arabic (S.).

בְּתוּאֵל [b'thooēhl'], Bethuel; *separation, or separated of God*, i. e. *consecrated to God*, contracted from בְּתוּל *separation*, or as a participle passive of the obsolete בָּתַל *to separate*, and אֵל *God* (S.).

בְּתוּל [b'thool'], Bethul; a simple form of the same.

בִּתְיָה [bithyāh'], Bethiah; for בַּת יָה *daughter*, i. e. *worshipper of the Lord*.

בַּת־רַבִּים [bath rabbeem'], Bath-rabbim; *daughter of many*, compare Appellatives.

בִּתְרוֹן [bithrōhn'], Bithron; *dissection*, from בָּתַר *to cut asunder*.

בַּת שֶׁבַע [bath sheh'vang], Bathsheba; *daughter of oath*, from בַּת *daughter*, and שָׁבַע *to swear*.

בַּת שׁוּעַ [bath shoo'ang], Bathshua, margin Bath-sheba; id. contracted from בַּת שְׁבוּעָה, compare Appellatives.

ג

גְּאוּאֵל [g'oo-ēhl'], Geuel; *redeemed of God* (S.), *majesty of God* (G.). Either contracted from גָּאוּל participle passive of גָּאַל *to redeem*, and אֵל *God*, or גְּאוּ a Chaldee form of גָּאָה *to be exalted*.

גֹּב, גּוֹב [gōhv], Gob; *pit*, as in the Chaldee, from the obsolete גָּבַב *to be hollow*.

גַּבַּי [gabbay'], Gabbai; *tax-gatherer*, from the Syriac (G.).

גֵּבִים [gēh-veem'], Gebim; *cisterns or locusts*, plural of גֵּב, compare Appellatives.

גְּבַל [g'val'], Gebal; *bound, border* (S.), *mountain* (G.); either i. q. גְּבוּל *a border*, or collated with the Arabic.

גְּבָל [g'vāhl'], Gebal; i. q. גְּבַל (S.), *mountainous* (G.), compare the preceding.

גִּבְלִים [givleem'], "stone-squarers," marg. "Giblites," gentile noun of גְּבָל·

גֶּבַע [geh'vang], Geba; *hill*, i. q. Appellative גִּבְעָה·

גִּבְעָא [giv-ngāh'], Gibea; id.

גִּבְעָה [giv-ngāh'], Gibeah; id. compare Appellatives.

גִּבְעוֹן [giv-ngōhn'], Gibeon; *belonging to a hill*, i. e. *built upon a hill* (G.).

גִּבְעוֹנִי [giv-ngōhnee'], Gibeonite; gentile noun of גִּבְעוֹן·

גִּבְעַת [giv-ngath'], Gibeath; *of a hill*, construct of גִּבְעָה, compare note under אֲבִי·

גִּבְעַת הָעֲרָלוֹת [giv-ngath hāh-ngărāh-lōhth'], "hill of the foreskins," marg. Gibeah-haaraloth, compare the preceding, and Appellative עָרְלָה *foreskin*.

גִּבְעָתִי [giv-ngāh-thee'], Gibeathite; gentile noun of גִּבְעָה·

גֶּבֶר [geh'ver], Geber; *man*, compare Appellatives.

גִּבָּר [gibbāhr'], Gibbar, margin, Gibeon; as in the Chaldee, i. q. גִּבּוֹר *strong, mighty*.

גַּבְרִיאֵל [gavree-ēhl'], Gabriel; *man of God*, compounded of גֶּבֶר *man*, and אֵל *God*.

גִּבְּתוֹן [gibb'thōhn'], Gibbethon; *high place, declivity*, compare Chaldee גִּבְתָא (G.), root גָּבַב·

גָּד [gāhd], Gad; marg. (Gen. xxx. 11.) *troop* or *company*; *fortune* (fortuna) (G.).

גַּדְגָּד [goodgōhd'], Gudgod; *a well of much water*, collated with the Arabic (S.); *thunder*, i. q. גִּדְגָּד from the Ethiopic (G.).

גְּדוֹר [g'dōhr'], Gedor; *wall*, compare Appellatives גָּדֵר and גְּדֵר.

גָּדִי [gāhdee'], Gadee, Gadite; *fortunate*, from גָּד *fortune*. Also patronymic of the same.

גַּדִּי [gaddee'], Gaddi; *fortunate*, compare the preceding.

גַּדִּיאֵל [gaddee-ēhl'], Gaddiel; *troop, company*, or *fortune of God*, compare גָּד.

גִּדֵּל [giddēhl'], Giddel; *too great, a giant* (G.), an adjective form of Piel, from גָּדוֹל.

גְּדַלְיָה [g'dal-yāh'], Gedaliah; [whom] *the Lord has made great*, compounded of גָּדַל Piel of גָּדַל *to be great*, and יָה *Jah*.

גְּדַלְיָהוּ [g'dalyāh'-hoo], Gedaliah; id.

גִּדַּלְתִּי [giddaltee'], Giddalti; [whom] *I have brought up*, Piel of גָּדַל *to be great*.

גִּדְעוֹן [gid-ngōhn'], Gideon; *cutter*, from גָּדַע *to cut down*.

גִּדְעָם [gid-ngōhm'], Gideom; *a cutting down*, from גָּדַע *to cut down*.

גִּדְעֹנִי [gid-ngōhnee'], Gideoni; id.

גֶּדֶר [geh'-der], Geder; *a wall*, compare Appellative.

גְּדוֹר & גְּדֹר [g'dōhr'], Gedor; id.

גְּדֵרָה [g'dēhrāh'], Gederah; id.

גְּדֵרוֹת [g'dēhrōth'], Gederoth; *walls, or sheepcotes*, compare Appellative גְּדֵרָה.

גְּדֵרִי [g'dēhree'], Gederite; gentile noun of גְּדֵר.

גְּדֵרָתִי [g'dēhrāhthee'], Gederathite; gentile noun of גְּדֵרָה.

גְּדֵרֹתַיִם [g'dēhrōhthah'yim], Gederothaim; *two sheepcotes*, dual of גְּדֵרָה *wall or sheepcote*.

גּוֹב see גַּב.

גּוֹג [gōhg], Gog; of doubtful derivation; according to Simonis, from the Arabic גבב *to extend, spread out*, hence גּוֹב *extension*.

גּוֹזָן [gōhzāhn'], Gozan; *quarry*, from גָּזָה *to cut stones*, according to its derivative גָּזִית *hewn stone*.

גּוֹלָן [gōhlāhn'], Golan; *exile, captivity*, from גָּלָה *to emigrate*.

גּוּנִי [goonee'], Guni, Gunite; *form, or likeness* (S.), *painted with colours* (G.); collated with the Syriac.

גּוּר [goor], Gur; *dwelling*, from גּוּר *to dwell for a short time*, hence *an inn*.

גּוּר בַּעַל [goor bah'-ngal], Gurbaal; *dwelling* or *inn of Baal*, comp. the preceding and בַּעַל.

גִּזוֹנִי [geezōhnee'], Gizonite; gentile noun of the absolute גִּזוֹ *quarry* (G.), from גָּזָה comp. גָּזִית *hewn stone*.

גָּזַז [gāhzēhz'], Gasez; *shearer,* from גָּזַז *to shear.*

גַּזָּם [gazzāhm'], Gazzam; *devouring* (G.), from גָּזַם, of which גָּזָם *locust.*

גֶּזֶר [geh'zer], Gezer; *part, piece,* hence, *a detached, precipitous place,* from גָּזַר *to cut, divide.*

גִּזְרִי [gizree'], Gizrite; gentile noun of the same.

גֵּחֲזִי see גִּיחֲזִי.

גַּחַם [gah'kham], Gaham; *having large inflamed eyes* (S.), collated with the Arabic.

גַּחַר [gah'khar], Gahar; *red, having red hair* (rufus) collated with the Chaldee (S.), *shelter, retreat* (G.), according to the Arabic.

גִּיחַ [gee'-akh], Giah; *a bursting forth,* i. e. *of water,* from גּוּחַ or גִּיחַ *to burst forth.*

גִּיחוֹן [gee-khōhn'], Gihon; *stream* compare the preceding.

גֵּחֲזִי & גִּיחֲזִי [gēhkhăzee'], Gehazi ; *valley of vision,* compounded of גֵּי i.q. גַּיְא *valley,* and חֲזִי from חָזָה *to see.*

גִּילֹנִי [geelōhnee'], Gilonite; gentile noun of גִּלֹה.

גִּנַּת [geenath'], Ginath; *form, likeness* (S.), collated with the Syriac, *garden,* i. q. גִּנָּה (G.).

גֵּישָׁן [gēh-shāhn'], Geshan; *filthy,* collated with the Arabic (G.).

גִּלְבֹּעַ [gilbōh'ăng], Gilboa; *spring of bubbling,* i. e. *a bubbling spring,* compounded of גַּל *spring, source,* and בֹּעַ from בּוּעַ or for נְבֹעַ from נָבַע *to bubble.*

גִּלְגָּל [gilgāhl'] Gilgal; *circle or devolution,* from גָּלַל *to roll.*

גִּלֹה [geelōh'], Giloh; *exile, captivity,* from גָּלָה *to emigrate.*

גָּלִיל [gāhleel'], Galilee; *circuit, region,* from גָּלַל *to roll.*

גַּלִּים [galleem'], Gallim; *springs,* from the same.

גָּלְיָת [gol-yath'], Goliath; *great, corpulent, stout,* from the Arabic גלל (S.), with the Philistine, Egyptian, and Punic formation ת–, compare אָסְנַת; *captivity, captive* (G.), from גָּלָה *to emigrate.*

גָּלָל [gāhlāhl'], Galal; *weighty, worthy* (dignus) compare Appellative גָּלָל *a cause, circumstance, matter.*

גִּלֲלַי [geelălay'], Gilalai; *stercoracious,* compare גְּלָלִים *dung.*

גִּלֹנִי [geelōhnee'], Gilonite; gentile noun of גִּלֹה.

גִּלְעָד [gil-ngāhd'] Gilead; as the name of a person, *hard, rough,* collated with the Arabic (G.); as the name of a region, compare Gen. xxxi. 44, *heap of witness.*

גִּלְעָדִי [gil-ngāhdee'], Gileadite; patronymic of the same.

גַּמָּדִים [gammāhdeem'], Gammadims; commonly not taken as a proper name; according to the LXX φύλακες, guards, warriors, collated with the Arabic.

גָּמוּל [gāhmool'], Gamul; recompensed or weaned, participle passive of גָּמַל.

גִּמְזוֹ [gimzōh'], Gimzo; sycamore-tree (S.), collated with the Arabic.

גְּמַלִּי [g'mallee'], Gemalli; owner of camels, compare Appellative גָּמָל a camel.

גַּמְלִיאֵל [gamlee-ēhl'], Gamaliel; kindness of God, from גָּמַל to show kindness, and אֵל God.

גֹּמֶר [gōh'mer], Gomer; perfection or accomplishment, from גָּמַר to finish.

גְּמַרְיָה [g'mar-yāh'] Gemariah; [whom] the Lord perfected, from the same, and אֵל God.

גְּמַרְיָהוּ [g'mar-yāh'-hoo], Gemariah; id.

גְּנֻבַת [g'noovath'], Genubath; stolen, participle passive of גָּנַב to steal.

גִּנְּתוֹי [gin-n'thōhy'], Ginnetho; probably (compare margin of Neh. xii. 14) a corrupt reading for

גִּנְּתוֹן [gin-n'thōhn'], Ginnethon; gardener, compare גַּנָּה and Chaldee גִּנָּה garden.

גֹּעָה [gōh-ngāh'] Goath (better, Goah); bellowing, participle active feminine of גָּעָה to bellow.

גַּעַל [gah'ngal], Gaal; aversion, from גָּעַל to loath.

גַּעַשׁ [gah'-ngash], Gaash; a shaking, from גָּעַשׁ to shake.

גַּעְתָּם [gah-ng'tāhm'], Gatam; their touch, גַּעַת infinitive of נָגַע to touch, compare דַּעַת from יָדַע.

גֵּרָא [gēhrāh'], Gera; grain, i. q. גֵּרָה Gerah, a Hebrew coin.

גָּרֵב [gāhrēhv'], Gareb; scabby, compare Appellative גָּרָב scab.

גִּרְגָּשִׁי [girgāhshee'], Girgashite; gentile noun of the obsolete גִּרְגָּשׁ i.q. Chaldee גַּרְגִּשְׁתָּא clay, hence an inhabiter of the clay country.

גִּרְזִי or גֵּרְזִי [g'rizzee' or gir'zee'] Kethib: English, Gezrites, margin, Gerzites; gentile noun of גְּרָז a sterile soil (G.).

גְּרִזִּים [y'rizzeem'], Gerizim; preceded by הַר mountain of the Gerizites, compare the preceding.

גַּרְמִי [garmee'], Garmite (perhaps better, Garmi); bony, from גֶּרֶם a bone.

גְּרָר [g'rāhr'], Gerar; a sojourning, hence, a lodging, or an inn, from גָּרַר i. q. גּוּר (S.).

גֵּרְשֹׁם & גֵּרְשׁוֹם [gēhrshōhm'], Gershom; according to Ex. ii. 22, שָׁם גֵּר i. q. שָׁם גֵּר a stranger there, but perhaps also i. q.

גֵּרְשׁוֹן & גֵּרְשׁוֹן [gēhr'shōhn'], Gershon; expulsion, banishment, from one's own country, from גָּרַשׁ to drive out.

גֵּרְשֻׁנִּי [gēhr'shoonnee'], Gershonite; patronymic of the same.

גְּשׁוּר [g'shoor'], Geshur; *bridge* (G.), collated with the Arabic and Syriac.

גְּשׁוּרִי [g'shooree'], Geshurite; gentile noun of the same.

גֶּשֶׁם [geh'shem], Geshem; *rain*, compare Appellative.

גַּשְׁמוּ [gashmoo'], Gashmu, marg. Geshem, once for גֶּשֶׁם.

גֹּשֶׁן [gōh'shen], Goshen; as the name of a city, *coat of mail*, collated with the Arabic; as the name of a country in Egypt, *region of Hercules*, collated with the Coptic (Jablonski by Joh. Simonis).

גִּשְׁפָּא [gishpāh'], Gishpa; *flattery*, collated with the Syriac (S.).

גַּת [gath], Gath; *winepress;* compare Appellative.

גַּת־חֵפֶר [gath-khēh'pher], Gath-hepher; *wine-press of the pit*, from the same, and חָפָר from חָפַר *to dig*.

גִּתִּי [gittee'], Gittite; gentile noun of גַּת.

גִּתַּיִם [gittah'yim], Gittaim; *two wine-presses*, dual of גַּת.

גֶּתֶר [geh'ther], Gether; *dregs, sediment*, collated with the Syriac (G.).

גַּת־רִמּוֹן [gath-rimmōhn'], Gath-rimmon; *pomgranate-press*, compare גַּת and רִמּוֹן *pomegranate*.

דֹּאֵג [doh-ēhg'], Doeg; *timorous*, a participial form of דָּאַג *to be troubled about* any thing, *to fear*.

דֹּאר see דּוֹר.

דְּבוֹרָה [d'vōhrāh'], Deborah; *bee*, comp. Appellatives.

דְּבִיר [d'veer'], Debir; *recess*, a most sacred place of a temple (Adytum); compare Appellatives.

דְּבֵלָה [divlāh'], Diblath; *fig-cake*, a round cake of dried figs pressed together, i. q. דְּבֵלָה Appellative.

דִּבְלַיִם [divlah'yim], Diblaim; *two cakes*, dual of דְּבֵל, probably i q. דְּבֵלָה; comp. the preceding.

בֵּית דִּ' see דִּבְלָתָיִם.

דִּבְרִי [divree'], Dibri; *eloquent*, from דָּבַר *to speak*, comp. אִמְרִי.

דָּבְרַת [dovrath'] and דָּבְרַת [dāh-v'rath'], Doberath; *a pasture*, fem. of דָּבָר, from דָּבַר *to lead* or *drive* cattle upon the pastures; comp. also מִדְבָּר *a wilderness*, properly an uncultivated country, into which cattle are driven to feed.

דַּבֶּשֶׁת [dabbēh'sheth], Dabbasheth; *a bunch* or *protuberance* on the back of a camel, comp. Appellatives.

דָּגוֹן [dāhgōhn'], Dagon; *great fish*; compare דָּג Appellative, the syllable וֹן as intensive.

דּוֹדוֹ, כתיב דֹּדִי, see דֹּדִי.

דְּדָן [d'dāhn'], Dedan; *progress*, from דָּדָה *to move on*.

F

דֹּדָנִים [dōdāhneem'], Dodanim; gentile noun of an obsolete דֹּדָן, and of obscure origin, since in 1 Chron. i. 7, רוֹדָנִים is found instead.

דְּדָנִים [d'dāhneem'], Dedanim; gentile noun of דְּדָן.

דְּהָוֵא [dehāhvēh'], Kethib, דְּהָיֵא [dehāhyēh'], Keri, Dehavites; villagers, collated with the Persian (S.).

הוֹאָג see דֹּאֵג.

דּוֹדוֹ [dōhdōh'], Dodo; his beloved, comp. דּוֹד Appellative.

דּוֹדָוָהוּ [dōhdāhvāh'hu], Dodavah; beloved of the Lord, compound of the same and יְהוָֹה abbreviated.

דָּוִיד see דָּוִד below.

דּוֹדַי [dōhdahy'], Dodai; my love, lit. loves (amores); comp. the plural of דּוֹד Appellative. The termination ־ַי may also be here the ancient absolute plural form.

דּוֹיֵג Kethib for דֹּאֵג.

דָּוִד more frequently דָּוִיד [dāhveed'], David; beloved, a passive form of דּוּד=דָוּד to love, like מָשִׁיחַ anointed, from מָשַׁח, אָסִיר prisoner, from אָסַר.

דּוּמָה [doomāh'], Dumah; silence, comp. Appellatives.

דֻּמְשֶׂק an uncommon form for דַּרְמֶשֶׂק or דַּמֶּשֶׂק.

דּוֹר, דֹּאר [dōhr], Dor; a dwelling, compare Appellatives.

דּוּרָא [doorāh'], Dura; roundness, collated with the Arabic (S.).

דִּיבוֹן [deevōhn'], Dibon; consumption, decline, from דּוּב to waste away.

דִּי זָהָב [dee zāhāb], Dizahab; abounding with gold, from דִּי i. q. דַּי abundance, and זָהָב gold.

דִּימוֹן [deemōhn'], Dimon; silence, from דּוּם, stands for דִּיבוֹן.

דִּינָה [deenāh'], Dinah; judged, freed, from דִּין or דּוּן to judge.

דִּינָיֵא [deenāhyēh'], Dinaites; of doubtful signification.

דִּיפַת [deephath'], Riphath, marg. Diphath; of doubtful signification, the parallel passage Gen. x. 3, reads רִיפַת instead.

דִּישׁוֹן [deeshōhn'], Dishon; roebuck, comp. Appellatives

דִּישָׁן [deeshāhn'], Dishan; id.

דְּלָיָה [d'lāhyāh'], Delaiah; [whom] the Lord has delivered, from דָּלָה to draw up, out, and יָהּ Jah.

דְּלָיָהוּ [d'lāhyāh'hoo], id.

דְּלִילָה [d'leelāh'], Delilah; languishing, longing, a passive form of דָּלַל to hang down, be exhausted.

דִּלְעָן [dil-ngāhn'], Dilean; a field of gourds, comp. Chaldee דְּלַעַת a gourd.

דַּלְפוֹן [dalphōhn'], Dalphon; strenuous, collated with the Arabic (S.); but as the name of a son of

Haman we should expect it to be of Persic origin.

דִּמְנָה [dimnāh'], Dimnah; *dunghill*, compare Appellatives, דֹּמֶן *dung*, מַדְמֵנָה *dung-hill*.

דַּמֶּשֶׂק [dammeh'sek], Damascus; *activity*, perhaps for trade or merchandise; collated with the Arabic (G.).

דָּן [dāhn], Dan; *a judge*, a participial noun of דּוּן or דִּין *to judge*, comp. Gen. xlix. 16.

דָּנִיֵּאל see דְּנִיאֵל.

דַּנָּה [dannāh'], Dannah; *humble or low place*, from the Arabic דכן *to be pressed down* (S.).

דִּנְהָבָה [dinhāh'väh], Dinhabah; [a place] *yielding oil*, contracted from דְּהֵן; דהן הבה, Chaldee, *fat*, Arabic *oil*, and הָבָה from יָהַב *to give* (S.).

דָּנִי [dāhnee'], Danite; paronymic of דָּן.

דָּנִיֵּאל [dāhniy-yēhl'] and דָּנִאֵל [dāhnee-ēhl'], Daniel; *God [is] my judge*, compare דָּן, אֵל *God*.

דָּן יַעַן [dāhn yah'-ngan], Dan-jaan; *purpose or aim of Dan*, יַעַן from עָנָה *to answer*.

דְּעוּאֵל [d'ngoo-ēhl], Deuel; *invocation of God*, i. e. obtained by intreating God, from the Arabic דֶּעָה *to invoke* (S.); but perhaps, *know [ye] God*; דְּעוּ imperative plural of יָדַע, comp. הוֹדַוְיָה; or *known of God*, i. e cared for by God, contracted (and transposed) from יְדוּעֵאל.

דָּפְקָה [dophkāh'], Dophkah; *a pushing or driving on*, from דָּפַק *to push, drive on*.

דִּקְלָה [diklāh'], Diklah; *palm-tree*, i. q. Chaldee דִּקְלָא.

דֶּקֶר [dēh'ker], Dekar; *branch*, i. q. Chaldee דִּיקְרָן (S.), or *a piercing or thrusting through*, from דָּקַר *to pierce, thrust through*.

דַּרְדַּע [dardang'], Darda; *pearl of knowledge*, compounded of דַּר *a pearl*, compare Appellatives, and דֵּע *knowledge*, from יָדַע *to know*.

דָּרְיָוֶשׁ [dāhr'yāh'vesh], Darius; collated with the Persian, we are told that this word signifies *king*.

דַּרְיוֹשׁ [dar-yōhsh'], Darius; id.

דַּרְמֶשֶׂק [darmeh'sek], Damascus; a Syriac orthography for דַּמֶּשֶׂק q. v.

דָּרַע [dah'rang], Dara; a contraction from דַּרְדַּע.

דַּרְקוֹן [darkōhn'], Darkon; *scatterer*, i. e. liberal, from obsolete דָּרַק a Chaldee form, i. q. זָרַק *to scatter*.

דִּישׁוֹן see דִּשׁוֹן.

דֹּתַיִן [dōhthah'yin], Dothan; *two cisterns*, dual of דּוֹת as in the Chal. *a cistern*.

דֹּתָן [dōhthāhn'], Dothan; a contraction of the same.

דָּתָן [dāhthāhn'], Dathan; perhaps *of a fountain, fontanus*, from דֹּת=דָּת *cistern* (G.), comp. the preceding.

הבל (36) חוש

ה

הֶבֶל [heh'vel], Abel; *breath, vapour, vanity,* compare Appellatives.

הֵגֵא [hēhgeh'], Hege, and הֵגַי [hēhgay'], Hegai; *venerable,* collated with the Persic (S.).

הָגָר [hāhgāhr'], Hagar; *fugitive,* collated with the Arabic (G.).

הַגְרִי [hagree'], Haggri, Hagerite; *fugitive,* compare the preceding. In the plural הַגְרִיאִים and הַגְרִים Hagarites, as a gentile noun of הָגָר.

הֲדַד [hădad'], Hadad; *fear,* hence *object of fear* or *reverence,* collated with the Arabic (S.); it is besides the name of men, also the name of an Assyrian idol.

הֲדַדְעֶזֶר [hădad-ngeh'zer], Hadadezer; [whose] *help* [is] *Hadad,* compounded of הֲדַד q. v. and עֶזֶר *help,* compare Appellatives.

הֲדַדְרִמּוֹן [hădad-rimmōhn'], Hadadrimmon; the name of a place bearing the names of two Syrian idols, *Hadad* and *Rimmon;* see הֲדַד and רִמּוֹן.

הֹדוּ [hōhd'doo], India; contracted from הֹדוּ (G.) *India* or *Indus,* the river of that name; collated with the Arabic, it signifies *making a humming noise* (S.).

הֲדֹרָם [hădōhrāhm'], Hadoram; *ornament, glory,* from הָדַר *to adorn, honour,* or as a contraction from הֲדוֹר רָם *a great ornament,* compare רוּם *to be high.*

הִדַּי [hidday'], Hiddai; *great*

shouting or *joy,* compare הֵד Appellative, and note under אֲחָזַי (Hiller).

הֲדַסָּה [hădassāh'], Hadassah; *myrtle,* compare Appellatives.

הֲדַר [hădar'], Hadar; *ornament, glory,* compare הֲדוֹרָם.

הֲדַרְעֶזֶר [hădar-ngeh'zer], Hadarezer; *glory of help,* i. e. *a glorious help,* compare the preceding; this frequently stands for הֲדַדְעֶזֶר q. v.

הוֹד [hōhd], Hod; *glory,* compare Appellatives.

הוֹדְיָה Kethib for הוֹדַוְיָה.

הוֹדַוְיָה [hōhdav-yāh'], Hodaviah; *praise* [ye] *the Lord,* contracted from הוֹדוּ יָה Hiph. of יָדָה *to praise,* and יָה *Jah,* compare דְעוּאֵל.

הוֹדַוְיָהוּ Keri [hōhdav-yāh'hoo], Hodaviah; id.

הוֹדְיָה Keri [hōhd-yāh'], Hodevah; marg. Hodiah; *glory of the Lord,* compare הוֹד and יָה.

הוֹדִיָּה [hōhdiy-yāh'], Hodijah; id.

הוֹדַוְיָהוּ Kethib for הוֹדְיָהוּ.

הוֹהָם [hōh-hāhm'], Hoham; *multitude of multitude,* i. e. *a great multitude* (Hiller); or [whom] *the Lord confounded,* contracted either from הוֹם הָם *multitude,* or from יְהוֹ הָם, הָם preterite of הוּם *to confound.*

הוֹמָם [hōhmāhm'], Homam; *destruction,* from הָמַם *to confound, destroy.*

הוֹשָׁמָע [hōhshāhmāh'], Hoshama; [whom] *the Lord has heard, answered,* for יְהוֹשֻׁעַ‎, יְהוָֹה‎ and Kal preterite of שָׁמַע‎ to hear, comp. also הוֹתָם‎ and דְּעוּאֵל‎.

הוֹשֵׁעַ‎ [hōhshēh'ang], Hoshea; *help, deliverance,* infinitive noun of the Hiph. of יָשַׁע‎.

הוֹשַׁעְיָה‎ [hōhshangyāh'], Hoshaiah; [whom] *the Lord has holpen,* Hiph. preterite of יָשַׁע‎, compare the preceding, and יָהּ‎ *Jah*.

הוֹתִיר‎ [hōhtheer'], Hothir; [whom] *he* [*the Lord*] *has preserved,* Hiph. preterite of יָתַר‎ *to remain*.

הֵימָם‎ [hēhmāhm'], Hemam; only found once (Gen xxxvi. 22), instead of which we find in the parallel passage (1 Chron. i. 39) הוֹמָם‎ q. v.

הֵימָן‎ [hēhmāhn'], Heman; *faithful,* from מְהֵימָן‎ *faithful;* a Chaldaic participle of אָמַן‎ *to confide in,* in the Hebrew, *to be true,* compare Dan. ii. 45, and vi. 5.

הַלּוֹחֵשׁ‎ [hallōh-khēhsh'], Holohesh; *the enchanter,* participial of לָחַשׁ‎ *to conjure,* with the article ה‎ prefixed.

הִלֵּל‎ [hillēhl'], Hillel; *praise,* from הָלַל‎ *to shine,* in Piel *to praise*.

הֶלֶם‎ [hēh'lem], Helem; *a stroke,* from הָלַם‎ *to strike*.

הָם‎ [hāhm], Ham; *multitude,* compare Appellatives.

הַמְּדָתָא‎ [hamm'dāh'thāh], Hammedatha; with the article ה‎ prefixed, doubtless of Persian, but obscure derivation; *of twins* (S.).

הֲמוֹנָה‎ [hămōhnāh'], Hamonah; *multitude,* i. q. הָמוֹן‎ comp. Appellatives.

הַמֹּלֶכֶת‎ [hammōhleh'kheth], Hammolekheth; *the queen,* participial of מָלַךְ‎ *to rule, reign,* with the article ה‎ prefixed.

הָמָן‎ [hāhmāhn'], Haman; *only, alone,* i. e. born alone, in contradistinction to his father, who was Hammedatha [born] *of twins,* collated with the Persian (S.).

הֵנַע‎ [hēh'nang], Hena; *a shaking,* from the Hiph. of נוּעַ‎ *to shake*.

הַסְּנֻאָה‎ & הַסְּנוּאָה‎ [hass'noo-āh'], Senuah; *the hated,* participle passive of סָנָא‎ i. q. שָׂנֵא‎ *to hate,* with the article ה‎ prefixed.

הַסֹּפֶרֶת‎ [hassōhpheh'reth], Sophereth; *the scribe,* viz. female scribe, participial סָפַר‎ *to write,* with the article ה‎ prefixed.

הַפִּצֵץ‎ [happits-tsēhts'], Aphses; *the dispersion,* from an obsolete פָּצַץ‎ i. q. פּוּץ‎ *to scatter,* with the article ה‎ prefixed.

הַצְלֶלְפּוֹנִי‎ [hats-ts'lelpōhnee'], Hazelelponi; *the shadow looks upon me,* of צְלֵל‎ i. q. צֵל‎ *shadow,* with the article ה‎ prefixed פָּנָה‎ participle of פָּנָה‎ *to turn, look,* with suffix.

הַקּוֹץ‎ [hakkōhts'], Koz; *the thorn,* compare Appellatives.

הַקָּטָן‎ [hakkāhtāhn'], Hakkatan; *the little* or *younger,* comp. Appellatives.

הֹר‎ [hōhr], Hor; *mountain,* i. q. Appellative הַר‎.

הָרָא [hāhrāh'], Hara; mountainous, denominative of הַר a mountain.

הָרֹאֶה [hāhrōh-eh'], Haroeh; upon [whom] He [the Lord] looketh, a participle of רָאָה to see, with the article ה prefixed, found only once (1 Chron. v. 5) instead of the usual רְאָיָה upon [whom] the Lord has looked.

הֲרוֹרִי [hărōhree'], Harorite, marg. Harodite; only once found (1 Chron. xi. 27) instead of הֲרֹדִי, its signification is evidently mountaineer, but its reading very spurious.

הֹרָם [hōhrāhm'], Horam; height or mountainous, either from an obsolete הָרַם i. q. רוּם [to be high] according to the form of עוֹלָם from עָלַם, or from הַר with the termination ם, (G.).

הָרֻם [hāhrum'], Harum; high, exalted, participle passive of הָרַם compare the preceding.

הָרָן [hāhrāhn'], Haran; mountainous, denominative of הַר mountain.

הֲרָרִי [hărāhree'], Hararite; mountaineer, denominative from הָרָר mountain; but it may in all the passages of its occurrence be taken as an Appellative.

הָשֵׁם [hāhshēhm'], Hashem; fat, i. q. חָשֵׁם fat (G.).

הַשִּׁמְעָה [hash-sh'māhngāh'], Shemaah, marg. Hasmaah; report, from שָׁמַע.

הֲתָךְ [hăthāhkh'], Hatach; gift, collated with the Persian (S.); truth (Bohlen by Gesenius).

ו

וְדָן [v'dāhn], and Dan; the ו beginning this word in the occurrence of Eze. xxvii. 19, as the name of a place, is by some considered radical and not a prefix.

וָהֵב [vāhhēhv'], "What he did," marg. "Vaheb;" gift, from יָהַב i. q. יָתַב to give, which Clericus supposes to be the same with מַתָּנָה gift (the name of a place). The translators, according to their translation as an Appellative, seem to have supposed an understood אֲשֶׁר in the text, *אֶת אֲשֶׁר וָהֵב (Num. xxi. 14.)

וַיְזָתָא [vah-y'zāh'thāh], Vajezatha; white, pure, collated with Persic (S.).

וַנְיָה [van-yāh'], Vaniah; oppression, for יַנְיָה from יָנָה to oppress.

וָפְסִי [vophsee'], Vophsi; my addition; וֹפֶס by transposition for יֹסֶף from יָסַף to add, with a personal suffix.

וַשְׁנִי [vashnee'], Vashni; my gift, וֶשֶׁן according to Simonis, from a collation with the Arabic, a gift, with the personal suffix.

וַשְׁתִּי [vashtee'], Vashti; beauty, collated with the Persic (S).

* If we read וְאֶתוָהֵב in one word, with some MSS. found by Kimchi, this Aram. Hith. may be rendered and it happened. The Kal to give, and the Hithp. to give itself, for it happened, finds a striking analogy in the German geben to give, and ſich (se) begeben to happen, Begebenheit an event.

ז

זְאֵב [z'ēhv'], Zeeb; *wolf,* compare Appellatives.

זָבָד [zāhvāhd'], Zabad; *gift,* i. q. Appellative זֶבֶד from זָבַד *to present.*

זַבְדִּי [zavdee'], Zabdi; *my gift,* from זֶבֶד with suffix, compare the preceding, unless it be an abbreviation from זְבַדְיָה, and י standing for יָה.*

זַבְדִּיאֵל [zavdee-ēhl'], Zabdiel; *gift of God* or *God* [is] *my gift,* comp. the preceding, and אֵל *God.*†

זְבַדְיָה [z'vad-yāh'], Zebadiah; *gift of the Lord,* compare the same, and יָה *Jah.*

זָבוּד [zāhvood'], Zabud; *given, presented,* participial of זָבַד *to present.*

זַבּוּד [zabbood'], Zabbud; id.

זְבוּדָה [z'vood-dāh'], Zebudah; *given, presented,* participial passive form of זָבַד *to present.*

זְבוּל only defective זְבֻל [z'vool'], Zebul; *a dwelling,* from זָבַל *to dwell.*

זְבוּלֻן, זְבוּלוּן, זְבֻלוּן [z'vooloon'], Zebulun; id.

זְבוּלֹנִי [zevoolōhnee'], Zebulonite; gentile noun of the same.

* This would in a great measure confirm the supposition given in the note under אֲחֹזַי.

† The י between two words need not necessarily be taken as a suffix of the first, but as a mere conjunction.

זֶבַח [zēh'vakh], Zebah; *sacrifice,* compare Appellatives.

זַבַּי [zabbay'], Zabbai; of uncertain signification, it evidently stands for זַכַּי; but by collation with the Arabic (S.) *just* (justus).

זְבִידָה Kethib for זְבוּדָה.

זְבִינָה [z'veenāh'], Zebinah; *a purchase,* from זבן in the Chaldee, *to buy, purchase.*

זְבֻל see זְבוּל.

זְבֻלוּן see זְבוּלוּן.

זָהַם [zah'ham], Zaham; *aversion,* from זָהַם *to loathe.*

זוּזִים [zoozeem'], Zuzims; a gentile noun from obsolete זוּז *to move one's self.* Hence according to Clericus *a wandering nation.*

זוֹחֵת [zōh-khēhth'], Zoheth; of obscure signification.

זָזָא [zāhzāh'], Zaza; *motion, life,* or *abundance,* from זוּז *to move one's self,* compare זִיזָא.

זֹחֶלֶת [zōh-kheh'leth], Zoheleth; *serpent,* participle from זָחַל *to creep,* comp. the Latin *serpens,* from *serpere.*

זִיזָא [zeezāh'], Ziza; *motion, life* or *abundance,* from זוּז, see זָזָא. According to others *splendour,* from the same root *to shine;* comp. Appellative זִיז Ps. l. 11 and Isa. lx. 11.

זִיזָה [zeezāh'], Zizah; id.

זִינָא [zeenāh'], Zinah; *splendour,*

ornament, collated with the Arabic (S.), stands (1 Chron. xxiii. 10), for זִיזָה (v. 11), comp. זִיזָא.

זִיעַ [*zee'-ang*], Zia; *commotion*, from זוּעַ *to move one's self.*

זִיף [*zeeph*], Ziph; *loan*, from the Chaldee זוּף *to lend.*

זִיפָה [*zeephāh'*], Ziphah; id.

זִיפִים [*zeepheem'*], Ziphites, Ziphims; gentile noun of the same.

זֵיתָן [*zēthāhn'*], Zethan; *olive-tree*, from זַיִת *olive-tree*, to which ן forms the personification like the English *er*, compare the English name *Oliver.*

זַכּוּר [*zakkoor'*], Zaccur: *mindful* or *grateful*, from זָכַר *to remember.*

זַכַּי [*zakkay'*], Zaccai; *innocent*, from זָכָה *to be pure.*

זִכְרִי [*zikhree'*], Zichri; *celebrated*, from זָכַר *to remember;* or *my memorial*, comp. Appellative זֵכֶר.

זְכַרְיָה [*z'khar-yāh'*], Zechariah; [whom] *the Lord remembered*, from זָכַר and יָה *Jah.*

זְכַרְיָהוּ [*z'khar-yāh'hoo*], Zechariah; id.

זִלְפָּה [*zilpāh'*], Zilpah; *a drop*, from זָלַף Chaldee, i. q. Hebrew דָּלַף *to drop.*

זִמָּה [*zimmāh'*], Zimmah; *a purpose*, compare Appellatives.

זַמְזֻמִּים [*zamzoommeem'*], Zam-

zummims; *noisy ones*, from זָמַם collated with the Arabic *to hum* (G.).

זְמִירָה [*z'meerāh'*], Zemirah; *song*, זָמַר *to sing.*

זִמְרִי [*zimree'*], Zimri; *praised*, from זָמַר *to sing, praise;* or *my song*, comp. Appellative זֶמֶר *song*, suffixed.

זִמְרָן [*zimrāhn'*], Zimran; *praised*, compare the preceding.

זָנוֹחַ [*zānōh'akh*], Zanoah; perhaps *fen, moor*, from זָנַח *to stink, be rancid* (G.).

זַעֲוָן [*zah-ngăvāhn'*], Zaavan; *restless*, from זוּעַ *to move one's self.*

זִפְרוֹן [*ziphrōhn'*], Ziphron; *pleasant smell*, collated with the Arabic (S.).

זְרֻבָּבֶל [*z'rubbāh'vel*], Zerubbabel; *sown* [i. e. begotten], *in Babylon*, contracted for זְרוּעַ בָּבֶל, from זָרַע *to sow.*

זֶרֶד [*zeh'red*], Zered; *a pruning of trees*, i. e. abounding with trees; collated with the Arabic (S.).

זֶרַח [*zeh'rakh*], Zerah; *a rising* (of the son), comp. Appellatives.

זַרְחִי [*zarkhee'*], Zarhite; patronymic of the same.

זְרַחְיָה [*z'rakh-yāh'*], Zeraiah; *a rising of the Lord*, i. e. whom the Lord caused to shine forth; compare the preceding.

זֶרֶשׁ [*ze'resh*], Zeresh; *gold* (G.), collated with the Persic.

זַתּוּא [zattoo'], Zattu; *ornament* (S.), collated with the Arabic.

זֵתָם [zēhthăhm'], Zetham; *olive*, probably personified by the ending ם, (comp. the English *Oliver*), from זַיִת *an olive.*

זֵתַר [zēhthar'], Zethar; perhaps i. q. שְׁתַר *a star* (G.).

ח

חֹבָב [khōhvāhv'], Hobab; *beloved*, from חָבַב *to love.*

חֻבָּה [khoobbāh'], Jechubbah (reading according to the כתיב); *love* (as a noun) from חָבַב *to love.*

חָבוֹר [khāhvōhr'], Habor; *joining*, from חָבַר *to join.*

חֲבָיָה [khăvay-yāh'], and חֹבָיָה [khŏvāh-yāh'], Habaiah; (whom) *the Lord has hidden* i. e. *protected.* But according to the second, passive form, *the Lord has hidden* or *hid himself*, of which latter reflexive sense, the passive forms often admit, compound of חָבָה *to hide, protect* and יָה *jah.*

חֲבַצִּנְיָה [khăvats-tsin-yāh'], Habaziniah; [whom] *the Lord covered with* [his] *shield*, contracted for בְּצִן חָבָה יָה (S.), comp. the preceding, and צֵן i. q. צִנָּה Appellative; but Gesenius compares it with the Chaldee בּוֹצִינָא, taking ח as a prepositive; hence *light* or *lamp of the Lord.*

חֲבַקּוּק [khăbakkook'], Habakkuk; *an embrace*, from חָבַק *to embrace*, after the form of שַׁעֲרוּר (G.),

חֶבֶר and חָבֵר [khēh'ver], Heber; *a joining, company*, compare Appellatives.

חֶבְרוֹן [khevrōhn'], Hebron; id.

חֶבְרוֹנִי [khevrōhnee'], Hebronite; patronymic of the same.

חֶבְרִי [khevree'], Heberite; patronymic of חֶבֶר.

חָגָב [khāhgāhv'], Hagab; *locust*, comp. Appellatives.

חֲגָבָה & חֲגָבָא [khăgāhvāh'], Hagaba; id.

חַגַּי [khaggay'], Haggai; *festive, pleasant*, from חַג *a feast*, personified by the termination ־ִי; but, comp. note under אֲחִי.

חַגִּי [khaggee'], Haggi; id.

חַגִּיָּה [khaggiy-yah'], Haggiah; *feast of the Lord*, comp. חַגַּי.

חַגִּית [khaggeeth'], Haggith; *festive, pleasant*, as a feminine of חַגַּי (*festiva*).

חָגְלָה [khoglāh'], Hoglah; *partridge*, so in the Syriac and Arabic (S.),

חֲדַד [khădad'], Hadad; *sharpness* from חָדַד *to be sharp.*

חָדִיד [khāhdeed'], Hadid; *sharp, acute*, from the same.

חַדְלַי [khadlay'], Hadlai; *forsaken, rejected of the Lord*, comp. Appellative חָדֵל, and the note under אֲחִי.

חִדֶּקֶל [khiddehkel'], Hiddekel;

swift and *light*; according to the Jewish interpreters, on account of the rapidity with which the water of that river (the Tigris) flows, from חַד *sharp swift*, and קַל *light, swift*. But, saith Gesenius (Thesaur. in rad. חדק), the Hebrews appear to have been ignorant, that, the simple word דקל means *swift*, and then the Hebrew חַד is put before it.

חֲדַר [*khădar'*], Hadar; only according to some copies (Gen. 25:15), where others read חֲדַד [Hadad], see above; which latter reading is confirmed by the parallel passage (1 Chr. 1:50).

חַדְרָךְ [*khadrāhkh'*], Hadrach; *roundness, round*, collated with the Syriac חדר, with formative ךְ (S.).

חֹדֶשׁ [*khōh'desh*], Hodesh; *new-moon* or *month*, comp. Appellatives.

חֲדָשָׁה [*khădāhshāh'*], Hadashah; *new*, feminine of חָדָשׁ. compare Appellatives.

חָדְשִׁי [*khodshee'*], Hodshi; metronymic of חֹדֶשׁ.

חֹבָה [*khōhvāh'*], Hobah; *hiding-place*, from חָבָה *to hide*.

חַוָּה [*khavvah'*], Eve; *life*, from an obsolete חָוָה *to live*, i.q. חָיָה from which חַיָּה *life* is derived, comp. הָוָה and הָיָה.

חִוִּי [*khivvee'*], Hivite; *villager*, from חַוָּה *a village*, comp. Appellatives.

חֲוִילָה [*khăveelāh'*], Havilah; *terror fear*, from חוּל *to tremble, fear*.

חוּל [*khool'*], Hul; id.

חוּפָם [*khoophāhm'*], Hupham; prob. *covering*, with ־ם formative from obsolete חוּף i. q. חָפָף *to cover*. It occurs only once (Num. 26:39) in this form for חֻפִּים q. v.

חוּפָמִי [*khoophāhmee'*], Huphamite; patronymic of the same.

חוּקֹק [*khookāhk'*], Hukak; i. q. חֻקֹק q. v.

חוּר [*khoor'*], Hur; *freeborn, noble*, from חוּר i. q. חרר *to be free, noble*, comp. Eccl. 10:17.

חוֹרֵב see חֹרֵב.

חוֹרִי more frequently חֹרִי [*khohree'*], Hori, Horite, *freeborn, noble*, from חוּר or חרר (compare חוּר above) as the name of a man, but as the name of a people, perhaps *inhabitant of caves*, compare Appellative חוֹר *a hole*.

חוּרִי [*khooree'*], Huri; i. q. חוּר; from חוּר *linen*, or according to Gesenius, *linendraper*.

חוּרַי [*khooray'*], Hurai; only once (1 Chr. 11:32.) for חֲדַי (2 Sam. 23:30.) Prob. i. q. חוּרִי *linendraper*.

חוּרָם [*khoorahm'*], Huram; *noble* or *most noble*, if the formative ־ם expresses intensity, comp. חוּר.

חַוְרָן [*khavrāhn'*], Havran; *white* or *very white*, if ־ן expresses intensity, from חָוַר *to be white*.

חוּשָׁה [*khooshah'*], Hushah; *haste*, from הוּשׁ *to make haste*.

חוֹשַׁי [khooshay'], Hushai; *making haste, hastening,* participial of חוּשׁ *to make haste,* personified by formative ־ַ.

חוּשִׁים and חֻשִׁים [khoosheem'], Hushim; *hastening, haste,* comp. the preceding.

חוּשָׁם and חֻשָׁם [khooshāhm'], Husham; *haste,* see the preceding articles.

חַוֺּת יָאִיר [khavvohth-yāh-eer'], Havoth-jair; *towns of Jair, villages of Jair,* the first word signifying *villages,* may, in all its occurrences, be taken as an Appellative.

חוֹתָם [khōhthāhm'], Hotham; *seal-ring,* comp. Appellatives.

חֲזָאֵל and sometimes plenè חֲזָהאֵל [khăzāh-ēhl'], Hazael; *upon* [whom] *God has looked from* חָזָה *to see,* and אֵל *God.*

חֲזוֺ [khăzōh'], Hazo; *vision,* from the same.

חֲזִיאֵל [khazee-ēhl'], Haziel; *seen of,* i. e. *looked upon by God,* from חֲזִי a passive form, corresponding with Chaldee participle P'il, of חָזָה *to see,* and אֵל *God.*

חֲזָיָה [khăzāh-yāh'], Hazaiah; *upon* [whom] *the Lord has looked,* from the same, and יָהּ *Jah.*

חֶזְיוֺן [khez-yōhn'], Hezion; *vision,* from חָזָה *to see,* comp. Appellatives.

חֵזִיר [khēhzeer'], Hezir; *returned, converted,* from obsolete חָזַר i. q. Chaldee חֲזַר *to return.*

חִזְקִי [khizkee'], Hezki; *strength,* from חָזַק *to be strong.*

חִזְקִיָּה [khizkiy-yāh', Hezekiah; *strength of the Lord,* from the same, and יָהּ *Jah.*

חִזְקִיָּהוּ [khizkhy-yāh'hoo], Hezekiah; id.

חַטּוּשׁ [khattoosh'], Hattush; *congregated,* collated with the Arabic (G.).

חֲטִיטָא [khăteetāh'], Hatita; *a digging* from חָטַט, collated with the Syriac *to dig* (G.).

חַטִּיל [khatteel'], Hattil; *shaking,* from חָטַל, collated with the Arabic (G.).

חֲטִיפָא [khāteephāh'], Hatipha; *seizure, captivity,* from חָטַף *to seize.*

חִיאֵל [khee-ēhl'], Hiel; an abbreviation of יְחִיאֵל q. v.

חֵילָם [khēhlāhm'], Helam; *great army,* from חַיִל *host,* and the intensitive termination ־ָם (S.).

חִילֵן [kheelēhn'], Hilen; only once (1 Chr. vi. 58). for חֹלוֹן and חִלֵּן q. v.

חִירָה [kheerāh'], Hirah; *nobility, noble origin,* comp. חוּר.

חִירוֹם [kheerōhm'] and חִירָם [kheerāhm'], Hiram; i. q. חוּרָם q. v. comp. the preceding, and חוּר.

חֲכִילָה [khăkheelāh'], Hachilah; *obscurity,* collated with the Arabic (S).

חֲכַלְיָה [khăkhal-yāh'], Hachaliah; *hoping* or *hope in the Lord,* contracted from חָכָה of חָכָה to wait with confidence, and לְיָהּ to or in Jah. But if compared with the preceding, it may signify, [whom] the Lord has troubled.

חַכְמוֹנִי [khakhmōhnee'], Hachmonite ; wise, from חָכַם to be wise.

חֶלְאָה [khel-āh'], Helah ; rust, compare Appellatives. Or perhaps, ornament, necklace, i. q. חֲלִי pl. חֲלָאִים.

חֶלְאָם [khēhlahm'], Helam ; in Chethib for חֵילָם q. v.

חֵלֶב [khēh'lev], Heleb; fat, fatness, comp. Appellatives.

חֶלְבָּה [khelbāh'], Helbah ; id.

חֶלְבּוֹן [khelbōhn'], Helbon ; fat.

חֵלֶד [khēh'led], Heled ; only once (1 Chr. xi. 30.) instead of חֵלֶב (2 Sam. xxiii. 29). both of which Simonis thinks to be the same in sense, by a collation with Arabic.

חֻלְדָּה [khooldāh'], Huldah; weasel, comp. Appellative חֹלֶד.

חֶלְדַּי [khelday'], Heldai ; lively, worldly, from חֶלֶד life, world (S).

חֹלוֹן [khōhlōhn'], Holon; sandy, from חוֹל sand (G.).

חָלַח [khălakh'], Halah ; perfection, i. q. כָּלַח by permutation of כ into ח.

חַלְחוּל [khalkhool'], Hallul; trembling, from חוּל ; comp. Appellative חַלְחָלָה.

חֲלִי [khălee'], Hali ; ornament, necklace, comp. Appellatives.

חֵלֶם [khēh'lem], Helem ; fat, from חָלַם to be fat.

חֵלוֹן [khēhlōhn'], Helon ; strong, from חוּל, comp. חַיִל.

חֵלֶף [kheh'leph], Heleph ; exchange, comp. Appellative חָלַף.

חֵלֶץ and חֶלֶץ [khēh'lets], Helez ; deliverance, from חָלַץ to draw out, in Piel, to deliver.

חָלָק [khāhlāhk'], Halak ; margin smooth, comp. Appellatives. This may, perhaps, be better taken as an Appellative.

חֵלֶק [kheh'lek], Helek ; portion, comp. Appellatives.

חֶלְקִי [khelkee'], Helkite ; patronymic of the preceding.

חֶלְקַי [khelkay'], Helkai ; portion of the Lord, abbreviated of the following.

חִלְקִיָּה [khilkiy-yāh'], and חִלְקִיָּהוּ [khilkiy-yāh'hoo], Hilkiah; portion of the Lord, from חֵלֶק portion and יָהּ, and יָהוּ, more fully of יְהוָֹה.

חֶלְקַת [khelkāhth'], Helkath ; portion, possession, hence i. q. Chald. חַקְלָא (by transposition) a field, possession, from חָלַק to divide.

חֶלְקַת הַצֻּרִים [khelkath hats-tsooreem'], Helkath-hazzurim ; marg. the field of strong men, but more correctly, field of swords, comp. the preceding and Appellative צוּר sharpness, edge.

חָם [khāhm'], Ham; *black*, from חָמַם collated with the Arabic and Coptic (S,).

חֶמְדָּן [khemdāhn'], Hemdan; *desirable, pleasant* from חָמַד *to desire*.

חַמּוּאֵל [khammoo-ēhl'], Hamuel; *heat* (i. e. anger) *of God*, from חָמַם *to be hot* and אֵל *God*.

חֲמוּטַל [khămootal'], Hamutal; *father-in-law of dew* i. e. *of benevolence*, from חָם and טַל, comp. Appellatives.

חָמוּל [khāhmool'], Hamul; *spared*, part. pass. of חָמַל *to pity, spare*.

חָמוּלִי [khāhmoolee'], Hamulite; patronymic of the same.

חַמּוֹן [khammōhn'], Hammon; *sunny*, from חַמָּה *sun*.

חֲמוֹר [khamōhr'], Hamor; *ass*, comp. Appellatives.

חֻמְטָה [khoomtah'], Humtah; *lizard*, comp. Appellatives חֹמֶט.

חֲמִיטַל [khămeetal'], Hamutal; i. q. קרי חֲמוּטַל, comp. אֲבִיגַיִל כתיב and אֲבִיגַיִל.

חַמְרָן [khamrāhn'], Amram, marg. Hemdan; only (1 Chr. i. 44) stands for חֶמְדָּן (Gen. xxxvi. 26).

חֲמָת [khămāhth'], Hamath; *fortification*, collated with the Arabic (S.); comp. Appellative חוֹמָה *wall*, from the obsolete חָמָה.

חַמַּת [khammath'], Hammath; *hot bath*, the name of a city in the tribe Naphtali, which is thus interpreted by Josephus (G.); its deriviation is from חָמַם *to be hot, warm*.

חַמֹּת דֹּאר [khammōhth'dohr'], Hammoth; *hot baths of Dor*, comp. the preceding and דֹּאר.

חֲמָתִי [khămāhthee'], Hemathite; gentile noun of חֲמָת.

חֵן [khēhn'], Hen; *grace, favor*, comp. Appellatives.

חֵנָדָד [khēhnāhdāhd'], Henadad; *favor of Hadad*, for חֵן הֲדַד comp. the preceding and הֲדַד (G.). But, perhaps, contracted from חֵן נָדַד *favor is departed*, comp. נָדַד and נוּד *to wander*.

חַנָּה [khannāh'], Hannah; *grace, favor* i. q. חֵן.

חֲנוֹךְ [khănōhkh'], Enoch; *initiated, dedicated*, from חָנַךְ *to initiate*.

חָנוּן [khāhnoon'], Hanun; *favored, or graciously given*, part. pass. of חָנַן *to be gracious, favorable, give graciously*, comp. חֲנַנְאֵל.

חַנִּיאֵל [khannee-ēhl'], Haniel; *grace or favor of God*, comp. חֵן and אֵל *God*.

חֲנֹכִי [khănōhkhee'], Hanochite; patronymic of חֲנוֹךְ.

חֲנַמְאֵל [khānamēhl'], Hanameel; prob. for חֲנַנְאֵל (G.). q. v.

חָנָן [khāhnāhn'], Hanan; [*whom God*] *has graciously given*, comp. חָנוּן. Gesenius supposes this to be an abbreviation of יוֹחָנָן [*whom*] *the Lord gave*.

חֲנַנְאֵל [khănan-ēhl'], Hananeel; [whom] God has graciously given, for this sense of חָנַן, Gen. xxxiii. 5.

חֲנָנִי [khănāhnee'], Hanani; He [God] has been gracious to me, or perhaps an abbreviation of the following.

חֲנַנְיָה and חֲנַנְיָהוּ [khănan-yāh', and khănnan-yāh'hoo], Hananiah; [whom] the Lord has graciously given, comp. חֲנַנְאֵל.

חָנֵס [khāhnēhs'], Hanes; of doubtful signification.

חַנָּתֹן [khannāhthōhn'], Hannathon; procured by favor, from חָנָה see, above, with the addition of the termination וֹן.

חֶסֶד [kheh'sed], Hesed; kindness, love, comp. Appellatives.

חֲסַדְיָה [khăsad-yāh'], Hasadiah; [whom] the Lord loves (G.), compare the preceding, comp. also the Hithpael of חָסַד to show one's self kind.

חֹסָה [khōhsāh'], Hosah; refuge, from חָסָה to seek shelter.

חַסְרָה [khasrāh'], Hasrah; poverty, indigence, from חָסַר to want.

חֻפָּה [khooppah'], Huppah; a covering, comp Appellatives.

חֻפִּים [khooppeem'], Huppim; coverings, from the singular חֹף a covering, and the verb חָפַף to cover, protect.

חָפְנִי [khophnee'], Hophni; perhaps, champion, fighter (G.), from חֹפֶן, as an Appellative only occurring in the Dual חָפְנַיִם the hollow hands, hence here probably the fist, personified by the termination י, lit. a fister, comp. pugnus and pugnator.

חֶפְצִי־בָהּ [khephtsee-vāh'], Hephzibah; my delight is in her, from חֵפֶץ; compare Appellatives, with suffix and the preposition בְּ with suffix.

חֵפֶר [khēh'pher], Hepher; a well, pit, from חָפַר to dig.

חֶפְרִי [khephree'], Hephrite; patronymic of the same.

חֲפָרַיִם [khăphāhrah'-yim], Haphraim two wells, Dual of חֵפֶר q. v.

חָצוֹר [khāhtsohr'], Hazor; a court, fortification comp. חָצֵר and Appellatives חָצֵר.

חָצוֹר חֲדַתָּה [khāhtsohr' khădattāh'], Hazor, Hadattah: new-castle or new Hazor, comp. the preceding; and as to the second word, it is Chaldee, i.q. Hebrew חֲדָשָׁה feminine of חָדָשׁ new. The translators of the English Version, however, have taken this to denote two different places (Josh. xv. 25).

חֲצִי הַמְּנֻחוֹת [khătsee hamměnookhohth'], half of the Manahethites, marg. half of the Menuthites, or Hatsihammenuchoth; [born] midst quiet or resting places, comp. Appellatives חֲצִי and מְנוּחָה.

חֲצִי הַמְּנַחְתִּי [khătsee hammāhnakhtee'], half of the Manahethites; patronymic of the same. According to this punctuation, the sense of the preceding may be half of the presents, or *gifts*; the second word as a Participle feminine of מִנַח, compare Appellatives מִנְחָה, and not from נוּחַ.

הָצְצוֹן תָּמָר and חֲצְצוֹן [*khăhts'tsōhn'* or *khāhtsătsōhn' tāhmāhr'*], Hazazon and Hazezon-tamar; *a cutting off of palm trees*, viz. a place abounding with palm-trees, where many were wont to be cut down for use. For the first word compare Pual of חָצַץ, and for the second, Appellatives.

חֲצַר אַדָּר [*khăzăr' addāhr'*], Hazar-addar; *village of Addar*, prob. built by Addar; the first in construction of חָצֵר *a court, village*, comp. Appellatives; see also אַדָּר.

חֲצַר גַּדָּה [*khātsar' gaddāh'*], Hazar gaddah; *village of fortune* (G,), comp. גַּד.

חֶצְרוֹ [*khetsrōh'*], Hezro; prob. an abbreviation of חֶצְרוֹן.

חֶצְרוֹן [*khetsrōhn'*], Hezron; *fortification*, comp. חָצִיר.

חֶצְרוֹנִי [*khetsrōhnee'*], Hezronite; patronymic of the same.

חֲצֵרוֹת [*khătsēhrōht'*], Hazeroth; *villages*, comp. חֲצַר אַדָּר.

חֶצְרַי [*khetsray'*], Hezrai; *villager*, comp. the above.

חֲצֵרִים [*khătsēhreem'*], Hazerim; *villages*, comp. חֲצֵרוֹת.

חֲצַרְמָוֶת [*khătsarmāh'veth*], Hazarmaveth; *court of death*, for חֲצַר comp. חֲצַר אַדָּר, & מָוֶת *death*. comp. Appellatives.

חֲצַר סוּסָה [*khătzar soosāh'*], Hazar-susah; *village of a mare, or mares, mare-village*, comp. the preceding and Appellatives.

חֲצַר סוּסִים [*khătsar' sooseem'*], Hazar-susim; *village of horses, horse-village*, comp. Appellatives.

חֲצַר עֵינוֹן [*khătsar' ngēhnōhn'*], Hazar-enon: *village of the fountain, fountain village*, compare the articles above עֵינוֹן i. q. עַיִן *fountain*.

חֲצַר עֵינָן [*khătsar' ngēhnāhn'*], Hazar-enan, id.

חֲצַר שׁוּעָל [*khătzar' shoo-ngāhl'*] Hazar-shual; *village of the fox, fox-village*, comp. Appellatives.

חָצֵר הַתִּיכוֹן [*khāhtsēhr' hatteekōhn'*], Hazar-hatticon; *middle village*, comp. Appellatives.

חֲקוּפָא [*khăkoophāh'*], Hakupha; *bent, bowed*, collated with the Arabic (G.).

חוֹרֵב sse חרב.

חַרְבוֹנָה and חַרְבוֹנָא [*kharvōhnāh'*], Harbona, Harbonah; *warlike* (S.); according to Bohlenius by Gesenius, *ass-driver*, both collated with the Persic.

חֹר הַגִּדְגָּד [*khōhr haggidgāhd'*], Hor-hagidgad; *cavern of* (i. e. *near*) *Gidgad*; *cavern of thunder* (G.)), collated with the Ethiopic; comp. חוֹר and גִּדְגָּד.

חֲרָדָה [*khărāhdāh'*], Haradah; *terror, fear*, comp. Appellatives.

חֲרֹדִי [khărōhdee'], Harodite; gentile noun of חֲרוֹד.

חַרְהֲיָה [kharhăyah'], Harhaiah; *there was a parching, drought*, from חַר of חָרַר *to be burned, dried up*, and הָיָה *he was*.

חֲרוּמַף [khăroomāph'], Harumaph; *flat-nosed*, contracted from אַף comp. Appellatives; חָרוּם participle of אַף and חָרַם.

חֲרוּפִי [khăroophee'], Haruphite; either a patronymic or gentile noun from חָרוּף *reproached* (comp. Appel.) nowhere occurring in this form.

חָרוּץ [khāhroots'], Haruz; *diligence*, compare Appellatives.

חַרְחוּר [kharkhoor'], Harhur; *inflammation, fever*, comp. Appellative חַרְחַר.

חַרְחַס [kharkhas'], Harhas; only once (2 Kin. xxii. 14) instead of which (1 Chr. xxxiv. 22) it is written חַסְרָה q. v.

חָרִיף [khāhreeph'], Hariph; *autumnal rain*; collated with the Arabic; instead of which we find (Ezr. ii. 18) יוֹרָה of the same signification (S.).

חָרִם [khahreem'], Harim; *flat-nosed*, i. q. חָרוּם (Lev. xxi. 18), for this passive form, comp. דָוִד, see also חֲרוּמַף *above*, which may be considered an expletive form of this.

חָרִם [khāhrēhm'], Harem; *devoted*, comp. חָרְמָה.

חָרְמָה [khormāh'], *a devoting, desolate place*, from חָרַם *to devote*.

חֶרְמוֹן [khermōhn'], Hermon; *high mountain*, collated with the Arabic (Clericus).

חָרָן [khāhrāhn'], Haran; *parched, day*, from חָרַר *to be burnt, dried*.

חֹרֹנִי [khōhrōhnee'], Horonite; gentile noun of חֹרֹנַיִם.

חֹרֹנַיִם [khōhrōhnah'-yim], Horonaim; *two caverns* dual of חֹרוֹן, i. q. חוֹר or defective חֹר *a cavern*.

חַרְנֶפֶר [kharneh'pher], Harnepher; *snorting of the breath*, for נְחַרְנֶפֶר, from נָחַר *to snort*, comp. Appellative נַחַר *a snorting*, and נפר according to the Syriac, *to breathe* (S.).

חֶרֶס [kheh'res], Heres; *the sun*, comp. Appellatives, once (Jud. i. 35), preceded by הַר; *mount of the sun*.

חָרֵף [khāhrēph'] Hareph; *picking*, (G.).

חֶרֶשׁ [kheh'resh], Heresh; *silence*, comp. Appellatives.

חַרְשָׁא [kharshāh'], Harshah; prob. for חֲרָשָׁה id.

חֲרָשִׁים [khărāhsheem'], Charashim, *craftsmen*; this is better taken as an Appellative altogether.

חֲרֹשֶׁת הַגּוֹיִם [khăroh'sheth haggōh-yim'], Harosheth of the Gentiles; חֲרֹשֶׁת *a working* in wood or stone, *a working place*, comp. Appellatives.

חָרֶת [kheh'reth], in pause חָרֶת, Hareth; *a cutting*, the name of a forest, from the wood which was cut there; comp. חַצְצוֹן תָּמָר, from חָרַת in the

Appellatives only in the sense of engraving, but doubtless also i. q. כָּרַת.

חֲשׂוּפָא and חֲשֻׂפָּא [khăsoophāh'], Hasupha; *nakedness*, from חָשַׂף *to make bare*.

חֲשֻׁבָה [khăshoovāh'], Hashubah; *esteemed*, participle passive of חָשַׁב *to count, esteem*.

חֲשֻׁבַּדָּנָה [khashbaddāh'nāh], Hashbadana; *linen girdle*, from חָשַׁב *a girdle*, and בַּד i. q. Appellative בַּד *linen* with ה paragogic, therefore with the accent on the penultimate.

חֶשְׁבּוֹן [kheshbōhn'], Heshbon; *a reckoning, counting*, from חָשַׁב *to reckon, count*.

חֲשַׁבְיָה [khăshav-yāh'], Hashabiah; [whom] *the Lord esteemed, loved*, comp. חֲשֻׁבָה, and יָה *Jah*.

חֲשַׁבְיָהוּ [khăshav-yāh'hoo,] Hashabiah; id.

חֲשַׁבְנָה [khăshavnāh'], Hashabnah: Gesenius supposes this to be the same with the preceding, י being changed into נ.

חֲשַׁבְנְיָה [khăshavn'yāh'], Hashabniah; id. But this appears rather to be an epenthetic נ between חשׁב and יה, as it is often the case before the suffixes; comp. יְבָרְכֶנְהוּ (Ps. lxxii. 15), from which the preceding may be contracted.

חָשׁוּב [khash-shoov'], Hashub; *esteemed*, comp. חֲשֻׁבָה.

חֻשִׁים see חוּשִׁים.

חֻשִׁים [khoosh-sheem'], Hushim; i.q. חוּשִׁים *hastening, haste*.

חָשֻׁם [khāhshoom'], *fat, rich*, from obsolete חָשַׁם *to be fat*.

חָשֻׁם see חוּשִׁם.

חֶשְׁמוֹן [kheshmōhn'], Heshmon; *fatness*, from an obsolete חָשַׁם *to be fat*.

חַשְׁמֹנָה [khashmōhnāh'], Hashmonah; id.

חֻשָׁתִי [khooshāhthee'], Hushathite; patronymic of חוּשָׁה.

חַת [khēhth'], Heth; *terror*, from חָתַת *to be broken, terrified*.

חִתִּי [khittee'], Hittite; patronymic of the same, and then a gentile noun.

חִתִּים [khitteem'], Pl. of the same.

חִתִּית [khitteeth'], singular fem. of חִתִּי.

חֶתְלֹן [khethlōhn'], Hethlon; *shelter, retreat*, from חָתַל *to wrap up, cover, hide*.

חֲתַת [khăthath'], Hathath; *terror*, compare Appellatives.

ט

טָבְאֵל [tāhv'ēhl'], Tabeel; in pause טָבְאַל [tah-v'al'], Tabeal; *goodness of God*, compound of טָב *goodness*, a Syriac form, i. q. Hebrew טוֹב, and אֵל *God*.

טֶבַח [teh'vakh], Tebah; *slaughter*, compare Appellatives.

טִבְחַת [tivkhath'], Tibhath; once (1 Chr. xviii. 8), for which, in the parallel passage (2 Sam. viii. 8), it is בֶּטַח; here probably by transposition for בְּטָחַת confidence, security, as the construct of בְּטָחָה.

טְבַלְיָהוּ [t'valyāh'hoo], Tebaliah; [whom] the Lord immersed, i. e. purified, compound from טָבַל, in a transitive sense, and יחו abbreviated for יהוה.

טַבָּעוֹת [tabbāh-ngōhth'], Tabbaoth; seal-rings, rings, compare Appellative טַבַּעַת.

טַבְרִמּוֹן [tavrimmōhn'], Tabrimon; the goodness of Rimmon, comp. טָבְאֵל. Rimmon, the name of a Syriac idol.

טַבָּת [tabbāhth'], Tabbath; famous, collated with the Chaldee (S.).

טֵבֵת [tēhvēhth'], Tebeth; the name of a Hebrew month, the signification of which is doubtful.

טוֹב [tohv'], Tob; good, compare Appellatives.

טוֹב אֲדוֹנִיָּה [tōhv ădōhniy-yāh'], Tob-adonijah; the good or kindness of the or my Lord Jah, comp. the preceding and אֲדוֹנִיָּהוּ.

טוֹבִיָּה [tōhviy-yāh'], Tobiah; the Lord (is) good, or the good or kindness of the Lord, comp. the preceding.

טוֹבִיָּהוּ [tōhviy-yāh'hoo], Tobiah; id.

טְלָאִים [t'lāh-eem'], Telaim; young lambs. From טָלִי: by some considered to be an Appellative.

טֶלֶם [tēh'lem], Telem; oppression collated with the Arabic. [Kimchi and Clericus].

טַלְמוֹן [talmōhn'], Talmon; oppressed, compare the preceding.

טָפַת [tāhphath'], Taphath; drop, construct (comp. טִבְחַת, גִּבְעַת, אַחַת) of טָפָה from the root טוּף in the Chaldee, i. q. נָטַף to distil, drop.

טַרְפְּלָיֵא [tarp'lāh-yēh'], Tarpelites; a Chaldee gentile name. Simonis compares it with Tauropylæi, i. e. the inhabitants of the passages of Taurus. The Chaldæans may have retained foreign names of this kind.

יֹאושִׁיָּהוּ [yōhshiy-yāh'hoo], once (Jer. xxvii. 1.) in Kethib for the usual יֹאשִׁיָּהוּ, which see.

יַאֲזַנְיָה [yah-ăzan-yāh'], Jaazniah; may the Lord hear [him], compound of Hiph. future of אָזַן, comp. Appellatives, and יָהּ Jah.

יַאֲזַנְיָהוּ [yah-ăzan-yāh'hoo], Jaazaniah; id.

יָאִיר [yāh-eer'], Jair; may He [God] enlighten [him], Hiph. future of אוֹר. Compare Appellatives.

יָאִירִי [yāh-eeree'], Jairite; patronymic of the same.

יֹאשִׁיָּה [yōhshiy-yāh'], only once (Zech. vi. 10,) but in all other occurrences,

יֹאשִׁיָּהוּ [yōhshiy-yāh'hoo], may the Lord heal [him], compound of the fut. of אשה collated with the Arabic to *heal*, and יָהּ or יָהוּ (G.).

יְאָתְרַי [*y'ähth'ray'*], Jeatrai; [*whom*] *the Lord shall cause to remain*. Only 1 Chr. vi. 6. supposed by Simonis to stand for יְאַתֵּר חַי, the א taking the place of י, instead of יְיַתֵּר, from the verb יתר *to remain*. For the termination י see note under אֲחֹזַי. Note, other copies read יְאָתְרָי.

יְבוּס [*y'voos'*], Jebus; *a treading under foot*. From בוּס *to tread under foot*, like יְקוּם from קוּם.

יְבוּסִי [*y'voosee'*], Jebusite; *a gentile noun of the same*.

יִבְחָר [*yivkhähr'*], Ibhar; *may the Lord choose* [him]. Fut. of בָּחַר *to choose*.

יָבִין [*yähveen'*], Jabin; *may the Lord consider* [him], comp. Hiph. fut. of בוּן.

יָבֵישׁ see יָבֵישׁ.

יָבָל [*yähvahl'*], Jabal: *stream*, compare Appellatives.

יִבְלְעָם [*yiv-l'ngähm'*], Ibleam; *he consumeth to* or *shall consume the people*. Fut. of בָּלַע *to swallow, consume*, and עָם *people*. According to Gesenius, for יִבְלֶה עָם, but the verb בָּלָה nowhere occurs in a transitive sense.

יַבְנְאֵל [*yav-n'ëhl'*], Jabneel; *may God cause* [him] *to be built up*, lit, *cause him to build*, compound of Hiph. fut. of בָּנָה *to build*, and אֵל *God*.

יַבְנֶה [*yavneh'*], Jabneh; *may He cause* [him] *to be built up*, comp. the preceding.

יִבְנְיָה [*yivn'yäh'*], Ibneiah; *may the Lord build* [him] *up*, comp. the preceding.

יִבְנִיָּה [*yivniy-yäh'*], Ibnijah; id.

יְבֻסִי see יְבוּסִי.

יַבֹּק [*yabbōhk'*], Jabbok; *a pouring out, emptying*. From בָּקַק *to pour itself out, empty itself*.

יְבֶרֶכְיָהוּ [*y'vehrekhyäh'hoo*], Jeberechiah; *may the Lord bless* [him]. Compound of Piel fut. of בָּרַךְ *to bless*, and יְהֹו *the Lord*.

יִבְשָׂם [*yivsähm'*], Ibsam; *he shall be pleasant, sweet*. Fut. of an obsolee בָּשַׂם, whence בֶּשֶׂם *sweet odour*.

יָבֵשׁ and יָבִישׁ [*yähvëhsh'*], Jabesh; *dry*, compare Appellatives.

יָבֵשׁ גִּלְעָד [*yähvëhsh gil-ngähd'*], Jabesh Gilead; *Jabesh of* or *in Gilead*, comp. the preceding and גִּלְעָד.

יִגְאָל [*yig-ähl'*], Igal, Igeal; *may He* [God] *redeem* [him]. Fut. of גָּאַל *to redeem*, comp. Appellatives.

יָגְבְּהָה [*yogb'häh'*], Jogbeah; *it shall be exalted*. ה is paragogic, the simple form of which would be יִגְבַּהּ, Hoph. fut. from גָּבַהּ *to be high*.

יִגְדַּלְיָהוּ [*yigdalyäh'hoo*], Igdaliah; *the Lord shall be exalted*, compound of the fut. of גָּדַל *to be great*, and יְהֹו *the Lord*.

יָגוּר [*yähgoor'*], Jagur; *an inn*, from גוּר *to sojourn, live as not at home*.

יָגְלִי [*yoglee'*], Jogli; *He* [God]

revealeth Himself. Hoph. fut. of גָּלָה *to uncover, open.*

יְגַר שָׂהֲדוּתָא [*y'gar sāhhădoothāh'*], Jegar-sahadutha ; *margin, the heap of witness.* Two Aramaic words.

יִדְאֲלָה [*yidălāh'*], Idalah : [which] God *exalteth* or *shall exalt.* Simonis takes it as a Syriacism for יִדְלְלָה, with ה paragogic.

יִדְבָּשׁ [*yidbāhsh'*], Idbash ; *he is sweet as honey.* Fut. of דבשׁ, compare Appellative דְּבַשׁ.

יִדּוֹ [*yiddōh'*], Iddo ; *loving, given to love.* For יְדוֹן (G.). from יָדַד *to love.*

יָדוֹן [*yāhdōhn'*], Jadon ; *He* [God] *shall judge ;* [Judex] judge (G.). Either fut. of דּוֹן *to judge,* or a noun derived from the same verb.

יַדּוּעַ [*yaddoo'-ăng*], Jaddua ; *known,* from יָדַע *to know.*

יַדַּי [*yadday'*], according to Keri, Jadau (Ex. x. 43.) in the English version it is according to Kethib ; prob. i. q. יִדּוֹ.

יְדוּתוּן and יְדִיתוּן [*y'doothoon'*], Jeduthun ; *praising.* From an obsolete noun יְדוּת *praise,* from יָדָה in Hiph. *to praise,* with the termination וּן added. (G.). This termination gives the word its personification.

יְדִידָה [*y'deedāh'*], Jedidah ; *beloved.* A passive form of יָדַד *to love,* like דָּוִד from דּוּד=דָּנַד, compare Appellative יָדִיד, of which this is the feminine form.

יְדִידְיָה [*y'dee-d'yāh'*], Jedidiah ;

beloved of the Lord, comp. the preceding.

יְדַיָה [*y'dāh-yāh'*], Jedaiah ; *praise the Lord.* From יָדָה, in Hiph. *to praise* יָהּ *the Lord.*

יְדִיאֵל [*y'dee-ngăēhl'*], Jediael ; *known of God.* From יָדַע a passive form of יָדַע, (comp. יְדִידְיָה), and אֵל God.

יְדִיתוּן Kethib for יְדוּתוּן.

יִדְלָף [*yidlāhph'*], Idlaph ; *he weepeth.* Fut. of דָּלַף *to drip, shed tears.*

יָדַע [*yāhdāhng'*], Jada ; *wise.* From יָדַע *to know.*

יְדַעְיָה [*y'dang-yāh'*], Jedaiah ; *may the Lord know* [him] i. e. *care for him,* comp. the preceding, and יָהּ *the Lord.*

יְדוּתוּן see יְדִיתוּן.

יָהּ [*yah'*], the Lord, once (Ps. lxviii. 4). Jah ; unanimously acknowledged to be an abbreviation of יהוה, whatever the true pointing of the latter ought to have been originally, comp. יְהוָה ; it is frequently found in composition with other proper names, such as אֵלִיָּה. In which case another less abbreviated form יָהוּ is often used instead, as אֵלִיָּהוּ, which additional ו confirms the above derivation of this name.

יָהֻד see יְהוּד.

יֶהְדָּי [*yehdāy'*], Jahdai ; *may the Lord direct* [him]. Fut. of הָדָה *to direct,* and י see אַחְוִי.

יְהֻדִיָּה [*y'hoodiy-yāh'*], Jehudiah ;

Jewess. The feminine of the gentile noun יְהוּדִי *Jew* used as a proper name.

יֵהוּא [*yēhhoo'*], Jehu; *He* [is] *Jehovah.* For יְהוֹ הוּא (G.). or הוּא יֶהֱוֶה the latter as the regular pointing of יְהֹוָה (S.). The inconvenience of an audible H being repeated in the pronunciation, makes such a contraction not unlikely.

יְהוֹאָחָז [*y'hōh-āhkhāhz'*], Jehoahaz ; [*whom*] *the Lord holdeth.* contracted from יְהֹוָה and אָחַז, comp. Appellatives.

יְהוֹאָשׁ [*y'hōh-āhsh'*], Jehoash ; [*whom*] *the Lord has given.* From the same, and אָשׁ preterite of an obsolete אוּשׁ *to give,* (S.). collated with the Arabic.

יְהוּד [*y'hood'*], Judah, Judea, Jewry ; the Chaldee for the Hebrew name יְהוּדָה [*Judah*], but only as referring to the country or people of that name.

יְהוּדָאִין [*y'hoodāh-een'*], Jews ; the plural of the Chaldee gentile noun of יְהוּד.

יְהוּדָה [*y'hoodāh'*]. Judah ; *praise.* From יָדָה (compare Gen. xxix. 35. and xlix. 8). According to Gesenius *praised,* verbal of Hoph. future of the same.

יְהוּדִי [*y'hoodee'*], Jew, Jehudi ; a gentile noun of the same, but used also as a proper name.

יְהוּדִית [*y'hoodeeth'*], the Jews' language, Judith ; the feminine of the gentile noun יְהוּדִי *Jewish,* in reference to the language, and used also as a proper name of a woman.

יְהֹוָה [*y'hōhvāh'*], the Lord, Jehovah, and, when pointed יֱהֹוִה, God ; *The Eternal.* Whether the pronunciation according to the present pointing be the original* or not, the consonants

---

* That the pronunciation of this name according to its consonants has been considered unlawful among the Jews from a very remote period, is not only well attested by their doctors, but also by the fact of the adoption of two sets of vowel points for the same consonants, יְהֹוָה and יֱהֹוִה, for the former of which they substituted, and still do substitute אֲדֹנָי (Lord), and for the latter אֱלֹהִים (God), so that in neither case are the consonants pronounced. The Jews maintain that the pronunciation was not known generally, but only to some, and that traditionally. But no trace of that supposed mystical pronunciation being now left, the whole fact of there *ever* having existed *another* besides the one יְהֹוָה may fairly be questioned, from the following considerations. 1. If the vowels of יְהֹוָה be those of אֲדֹנָי, we should have expected under י in the same way as we find under the same for אֱלֹהִים. But the fact may have been, that יְהֹוָה was the true pronunciation, but the Jews, led away by tradition, and perhaps based upon Ex. xx. 7, and Lev. xxiv. 31, read אֲדֹנָי instead, independent of the proper, standing vowels. But in the case of אֲדֹנָי יהוה, where the first would have been repeated twice, and for some cause or other unwilling to do so, read according to, and substituted the vowels of אֱלֹהִים, hence the form יֱהֹוִה in the one, and not יְהֹוָה in the other case. And let it also be remarked that the circumstance of the Septuagint rendering the words אדני יהוה by Κυριος Κυριος sets some bounds to the antiquity of that practice.
2. The preservation of the vowels of יְהֹוָה as found in the composition of this name with other proper names of the greatest antiquity, as יְהוֹשֻׁעַ, יְהוֹנָתָן, יְהוֹשָׁפָט &c, the vowel ְ being found again

in comparison with (Ex. iii. 14.) sufficiently attest the signification of the name. אֶהְיֶה אֲשֶׁר אֶהְיֶה *I am that I am*, i. e. I am He who am *always*, and doubtless also, with reference to His *unchangeableness*, I am *the same* that I am; of which the relative אֲשֶׁר easily admits. But, however suitably in a grammatical point of view, the Hebrew form of the future may stand here for *the present*, as expressing *continuance*, yet ought the fact of its being the future, *I shall be* that *I shall be*, not to be lost sight of. Nay, the assurance of God's existence throughout all *futurity* is the prominent point of the Spirit's expression to Israel, surrounded by Egypt's idols and idol-worship. Pre-existence may have been ascribed to them by their worshippers, the eye-witnesses of their then present existence, but questions of the character " Where are the gods of Hamath and of Arpad? &c." were doubtless nothing unusual then with regard to those perishable elements. But God in His future, uninterrupted, blessed existence, assures them of deliverance not only from their then present bondage, but *always*, in opposition to those dumb idols, as He does afterwards (Is. xl. xliii. and xliv.) when sending them a message of deliverance. The looking forward to futurity is the true exercise of faith in the children of God, even as it is now with us, to whom the things of God prepared for them that love him, which "eye hath not seen nor ear heard, neither have entered into the heart of man" are revealed by His Spirit. As we have learned to know Him as the Alpha, we are now, or at least ought to be, looking forward for the future vindication of His power and glory, when He shall be all in all, as the Omega.

in the abbreviated form יְהֹ and its compounds, as אֲבִיָּה, אֲדֹנִיָּה &c., by permutation of ו into י. In these cases, we should have expected the true vowels again, if there had been any other; the full word יהוה not being found in either. For the Jews assert that the teaching of the pronunciation of this name was by pointing out each letter separately, so as not to pronounce the whole of the name at once, which need not be feared in compounds. And this must prove for the present pronunciation of יְהֹוָה, unless we extravagantly suppose, that the punctuators did, with these compound names, the same as they did with this name itself, establish the tradition of the unlawfulness of the pronunciation of this name, as a truth vouched for by its so very remote antiquity even up to Moses, and that we have not the right pronunciation even of these proper names.

The fact that בְּ and לְ have before this name *Pattah*, as if they were prefixed to אֲדֹנָי (בַּיהוָֹה and לַיהוָֹה), can prove nothing more but the punctuators' consistency with the tradition they had received and believed.

הוה, the more antique, and indeed acknowledged as the primitive form of הָיָה *to be*, stands in this name in the third person future. Thus, God speaking of His blessed Self, speaks and reveals Himself as the *I shall be* "*I am (I shall be) has sent me unto you*". The believers in Him with an Amen upon their lips call Him יהוה *He shall be*.

יְהֹוָה יִרְאֶה [*y'hōhvāh' yir-ēh'*], Jehovah-jireh; marg. *the Lord will see* or *provide*. From the same, and fut. of רָאָה, compare Appellatives.

יְהֹוָה נִסִּי [*y'hōhvāh nissee'*], Jehovah-nissi; marg. *the Lord my banner*. From the same, and נס *a banner*, see Appellatives.

יְהֹוָה שָׁלוֹם [y'hōh-vāh shāhlōhm'], Jehovah-shalom, marg. *the Lord* [send] *peace;* lit. *the Lord* (is) *peace.* From the same, and שָׁלוֹם *peace.*

יְהוֹזָבָד [y'hōhzāhvāhd'], Jehozabad; [whom] *the Lord has bestowed,* compound of יְהֹוָה and זָבַד *to give as a present,* comp. Appellatives.

יְהוֹחָנָן [y'hōhkhāhnāhn'], Johanan; [whom] *the Lord has graciously given.* From the same and חָנַן *to be gracious, give graciously.*

יְהוֹיָדָע [y'hōh-yāhdāhng'], Jehoiada; [whom] *the Lord hath known.* From the same and יָדַע *to know.*

יְהוֹיָכִין [y'hōh-yāhkheen'], Jehoiachin; *may the Lord establish* [him]. From the same and יָכִין Hiph. fut. of כּוּן, comp. Appellatives.

יְהוֹיָקִים [y'hōh-yāhkeem'], Jehoiakim; *may the Lord establish* [him]. From the same and the Hiph. fut. of קוּם, comp. Appellatives.

יְהוֹיָרִיב [y'hōh-yāhreev'], Jehoiarib; *the Lord plead for* [him]. From the same, and fut. of רִיב.

יְהוּכַל [y'hookhal'], Jehuchal; *may he prevail.* Hoph. fut. of יָכֹל.

יְהוֹנָדָב [y'hōhnāhdāhv'], Jehonadab; [whom] *the Lord has freely given.* From יְהֹוָה and נָדַב of which comp. Hiph. in the Appellatives.

יְהוֹנָתָן [y'hōhnāhthāhn'], Jehonathan [whom] *the Lord has given.* From the same, and נָתַן *to give.*

יְהוֹסֵף [y'hōhsēhph'], Joseph; *He* [God] *shall add,* comp. Gen. xxx. 24. An uncontracted Hiph. form of יָסַף *to add.*

יְהוֹעַדָּה [y'hōh-ngaddāh'], Jehoadah; [whom] *the Lord has adorned.* From יְהֹוָה, and Piel of עָדָה *to adorn.*

יְהוֹעַדִּין [y'hōh-ngaddeen'], Jehoaddan; in Kethib prob. the same as the following.

יְהוֹעַדָּן [y'hōh-ngaddāhn'], Jehoadan; *the Lord's delight.* From the same, and עָדָן, comp. the verb עָדַן, and the noun עֵדֶן.

יְהוֹצָדָק [y'hōhtsāhdāhk'], Jehozadak; *the Lord is righteous.* From the same, and צָדַק *to be just, righteous.*

יְהוֹרָם [y'hōhrāhm'], Jehoram; *the Lord is exalted.* From the same, and רָם preterite of רוּם *to be high.*

יְהוֹשֶׁבַע [y'hōhsheh'vang], Jehosheba; *the Lord's oath;* or *the Lord* (is his) *oath,* i. e. he swears by, worships the Lord, comp. Is. xlviii. 1. From the same, and שֶׁבַע, *oath,* occurring only in this sense in compound proper names, comp. בְּאֵר שֶׁבַע with Gen. xxi. 31.

יְהוֹשַׁבְעַת [y'hōhshav-ngath'], Jehoshabeath; found 2 Chr. xxii. 11. for the preceding.

יְהוֹשׁוּעַ and יְהוֹשֻׁעַ [y'hōhshoo'ăng], Jehoshua, Joshua; *the Lord's salvation,* contracted of the same, and יֶשַׁע *help.*

יְהוֹשָׁפָט [y'hōhshāhphāht'], Jehoshaphat; [whom] *the Lord judges.* From the same, and שָׁפַט *to judge.*

יְהַלֶּלְאֵל [y'hallel-ēhl'], Jehaleleel; *may he praise God.* From יְהַלֵּל Piel fut. of הָלַל only in Piel, *to praise,* and אֵל *God.*

יַהַץ [yah'haz], Jahaz; *a place trodden down,* prob. a threshing-floor (G.), collated with the Arabic יהץ *to tread under foot.*

יַהְצָה [yahtsāh'], Jahazah; id.

יוֹאָב [yōh-āhv'], Joab; [whose] *father* (is) *the Lord.* Contracted for יְהוֹאָב, comp. the preceding compounds of יהוה, as יְהוֹאָחָז, יְהוֹאָשׁ &c.

יוֹאָח [yōh-āhkh'], Joah; [whose] *brother* [i. e. *helper*] *is the Lord.* Compound of יְהוָֹה and אָח *brother.*

יוֹאָחָז [yōh-āhkhāhz'], Joahaz, Jehoahaz; contracted from יְהוֹאָחָז q.v.

יוֹאֵל [yōh-ēhl'], Joel; *the Lord* (is his) *God.* Contracted for יְהוֹאֵל, יְהוָֹה *the Lord,* and אֵל *God.*

יוֹאָשׁ [yōhāhsh'], Joash; contracted from יְהוֹאָשׁ q. v.

יוֹב [yōhv'], Job; *desire.* For יָאוֹב from יָאַב *to desire,* comp. Appellatives (S); or *cry,* from יָבַב compare the following. But this name only occurs (Gen. xlvi. 13.) for יָשׁוּב (Num. xxvi. 24).

יוֹבָב [yōhvāhv'], Jobab; *desert, wilderness,* properly *a howling,* a place where wild beasts howl, collated with the Arabic (G.).

יוּבָל [yoovāhl'], Jubal; *river,* compare Appellative יוּבָל.

יוֹזָבָד [yōhzāhvāhd'], Jozabad; contracted from יְהוֹזָבָד q. v.

יוֹזָכָר [yōhzāhkhāhr'], Jozachar; [whom] *the Lord remembers.* Contracted for יְהוֹזָכָר, compare the preceding, from יְהוָֹה *the Lord,* and זָכַר *he remembered.*

יוֹחָא [yōhkhāh'], Joha; *haste.* For יוֹחָה from the Chaldee יחה in Aph. *to make haste* (S.).

יוֹחָנָן [yōhkhāhnāhn'], Johanan; contracted from יְהוֹחָנָן q. v.

יוּטָה [yootāh'], Juttah; i. q. יֻטָּה.

יוֹיָדָע [yōh-yāhdāhng'], Joiada, Jehoiada; contracted from יְהוֹיָדָע q. v.

יוֹיָכִין [yōh-yāhkheen'], Jehoiachin; contracted from יְהוֹיָכִין q. v.

יוֹיָקִים [yōh-yāhkheem'], Joiakim, Jehoiakim; contracted from יְהוֹיָקִים q. v.

יוֹיָרִיב [yōh-yāhreev'], Joiarib; contracted from יְהוֹיָרִיב q. v.

יוֹכֶבֶד [yōhkheh'ved], Jochebed; [whose] *glory* [is] *the Lord.* Contracted from יְהוֹכֶבֶד, יְהוָֹה *Lord,* and כָּבֵד *glory,* comp. Appellative כָּבֵד.

יוּכַל [yookhal'], Juchal; contracted from יְהוּכַל q. v.

יָוָן [yāhvāhn'], Javan, Greece, Grecia; *soft* (S.),

יוֹנָדָב [yōhnāhdāhv'], Jonadab; contracted from יְהוֹנָדָב q. v.

יוֹנָה [yōhnāh'], Jonah; dove. Compare Appellatives.

יְוָנִים [y'vāhneem'], Grecians; patronymic of יָוָן.

יוֹנָתָן [yōhnāhthāhn'], Jonathan; contracted from יְהוֹנָתָן, q. v.

יוֹסֵף [yōhsēhph'], Joseph; contracted from יְהוֹסֵף, q. v.

יוֹסִפְיָה [yōhsiph-yāh'], Josipiah; [whom] the Lord shall increase, enlarge. From Hiph. fut. of יָסַף, to add, increase, and יָהּ Jah,

יוֹעֵאלָה [yōh-ngēhlāh'], Joelah; perhaps may He help. For יוֹעֵלָה (G.); or perhaps a contraction for יוֹעֵל may God help: from the Hiph. fut. of יָעַל and אֵל.

יוֹעֵד [yōh-ngēhd'], Joed; the Lord [is] witness, contracted from יְהוֹעֵד, comp. the preceding compounds with יְהוֹ and יוֹ from יְהֹוָה the Lord, עֵד witness, comp. Appellatives.

יוֹעֶזֶר [yōh-ngeh'zer], Joezer; the Lord [is his] help; contracted from יְהוֹעֶזֶר comp. the preceding and עֵזֶר help, among the Appellatives.

יוֹעָשׁ [yōh-ngāhsh'], Joash; the Lord is gathering together. For יְהוֹעָשׁ, from יְהֹוָה the Lord and עָשׁ from עוּשׁ; in Joel iv. 11. in an intransitive, here perhaps in a transitive sense.

יוֹצָדָק [yōhtsāhdāhk'], Jozadak; contracted from יְהוֹצָדָק q. v.

יוֹקִים [yōkeem'], Jokim; contracted from יוֹיָקִים q. v.

יוֹרָה [yōhrāh'], Jorah; early rain, i. q. יוֹרֶה Appellative.

יוֹרַי [yōhrah'y], Jorai; may the Lord instruct [him]; contracted from יוֹרֶה Hiph. fut. of יָרָה; see Appellatives, and יְ _ the Lord; comp. אֲחוַי.

יוֹרָם [yōhrāhm'], Joram; contracted from יְהוֹרָם q. v.

יוּשַׁב חֶסֶד [yooshāhv'kheh'sed], Jushab-hesed; grace is restored. יוּשַׁב Hoph. fut. of שׁוּב to return, חֶסֶד kindness, grace.

יוֹשִׁבְיָה [yōhshiv-yāh'], Josibiah; may the Lord cause [him] to dwell, i.e. safely, quietly. From יוֹשִׁיב Hiph. fut. of יָשַׁב to dwell, and יָהּ the Lord.

יוֹשָׁה [yōhshāh'], Joshah; perhaps existence. From the obsolete root יָשָׁה; comp. the following article.

יוֹשַׁוְיָה [yōhshav-yāh'], Joshaviah; [whom] the Lord raises (G.). perhaps as Hiph. form of יָשָׁה to stand, stand upright, exist, with יָהּ the Lord.

יוֹשָׁפָט [yōhshāphāht'], Joshaphat; contracted from יְהוֹשָׁפָט q. v.

יוֹתָם [yōhthāhm'], Jotham; the Lord [is] perfect. For יְהוֹתָם, from יְהֹוָה and תָּם perfect, compare Appellatives.

יְזוּאֵל [y'zoo-ēhl'], Kethib, for

יְזִיאֵל [y'zee-ēhl'], Keri, Jeziel; assembly of God. יְזִי from יָזָה collated with the Arabic to come together (G.), and אֵל God.

יִזִּיָּה [yizziy-yāh'], Jeziah; may

I

the Lord besprinkle, i. e. *purify* [him]. Fut. of בָּזָה *to sprinkle*, and יָהּ *the Lord*.

יָזִיז [*yāhzeez'*], Jaziz; *he shall shine*. Fut. of זוז comp. יָזָא!.

יִזְלִיאָה [*yizlee-āh'*], Jezliah; *may he draw* [him] *out*, i. e. *save*. From an obsolete זָלָא perhaps i. q. דָּלָה (G.), and perhaps by transposition for יִזְלָאיָה.

יִזַנְיָה [*y'zan-yāh'*], Jezaniah; contracted from יַאֲזַנְיָה.

יִזַנְיָהוּ [*y'zan-yāh'hoo*], id.

יִזְרָח [*yizrāhkh'*], the Israhite; with the article ה, הַיִּזְרָח once (1 Chron. xxvii. 8) for the patronymic אֶזְרָחִי.

יִזְרַחְיָה [*yizrakh-yāh'*], Jezrahiah; *the Lord shall rise*, i. e. *shine forth* (as the sun). Fut. of זָרַח *to rise* (as the sun) and יָהּ *the Lord*.

יִזְרְעֶאל [*yizr'ngēhl'*], Jezreel; [which] *God shall sow* or *plant*. Fut. of זָרַע *to sow, plant*, and אֶל *God*.

יִזְרְעֵאלִי [*yizr'ngēhlee'*], Jezreelite; gentile noun of the same.

יִזְרְעֵאלִית [*yizr'ngēhleeth'*], Jezreelitess; feminine of the same.

יַחְדּוֹ [*yakhdōh'*], Jahdo; *united*, for יַחְדּוֹן.

יַחְדִּיאֵל [*yakhdee-ēhl'*], Jahdiel; *may God make* [him] *to rejoice*. Fut. of חָדָה *to rejoice*, and אֵל *God*.

יֶחְדְּיָהוּ [*yekh-d'yāh'hoo*], Jehdeiah; *may the Lord make* [him] *to rejoice*; comp. the preceding.

יְחַוְאֵל [*y'khav-ēhl'*], Kethib for יְחִיאֵל; *may God preserve* [him] *alive*. For יְחַוֶּה from חָוָה (G.), i. q. חָיָה *to live*, in Piel *to preserve alive*.

יַחֲזִיאֵל [*yakhzee-ēhl'*], Jahziel; *he shall behold God*. Fut. of חָזָה *to see* אֵל *God*.

יַחְזְיָה [*yakhz-'yāh'*], Jahaziah; *he shall behold the Lord*; comp. the preceding.

יְחֶזְקֵאל [*y'khezk'ēhl'*], Ezekiel; *may God strengthen* [him]. This stands, according to Gesenius, for יְחֶזְקָאל like יְחִזְקָאל like אָכְלָה Ex. xxxiii. for אֹכְלָה Piel fut. of חָזָה *to be strong*, and אֵל *God*.

יְחִזְקִיָּה [*y'khizkiy-āh'*], Hezekiah; *may the Lord strengthen him*; comp. the preceding.

יְחִזְקִיָּהוּ [*y'khezkiy-āh'hoo*], id.

יַחְזְרָה [*yakh-zēhrāh'*], Jahzehrah; *may he bring back*. Hiph. of חזר, according to the Chaldee *to go back*.

יְחִיאֵל [*y'khee-ēhl'*], Jehiel; *may God preserve* [him] *alive*. For אֵל יְחַיֶּה, Piel of חָיָה *to live*, and אֵל *God*.

יְחִיאֵלִי [*y'khee-ēhlee'*], Jehieli, better Jehielite; patronymic of the preceding.

יְחִיָּה [*y'khiy-yāh'*], Jehiah; *may the Lord preserve* [him] *alive*; comp. יְחִיאֵל.

יַחְלְאֵל [*yakhl'ēhl'*], Jahleel; *expectation of God*, i. e. [a son] *expected of God* (S.). From יָחַל in Piel *to wait, hope*. According to Gesenius

יַחֲלָה [whom] *God has made sick*. From Hiph. of חָלָה *to be sick*, and אֵל *God*.

יַחְלְאֵלִי [yakhl'ēhlee'], Jahleelite; patronymic of the same.

יַחְמַי [yakhmah'y], Jahmai; *may the Lord keep* or *preserve* [him]. Fut. of an obsolete חמה whence חוֹמָה *a wall* is derived, and יְ *the Lord*; comp. אֲחָזִי.

יַחְצְאֵל [yakhts'ēhl'], Jahzeel; [whom] *God does bestow*, i. e. as a portion bestowed by God. Hiph. fut. of חָצָה *to divide* and אֵל *God*.

יַחְצְאֵלִי [yakhts'ēhlee'], Jahzeelite; patronymic of the same.

יַחְצִיאֵל [yakhtsee-ēhl'], Jahziel; i. q. יַחְצְאֵל.

יַחַת [yah'khath], Jahath; *He shall take away*. Apocopated form of Hiph. fut. יַחְתֶּה from חָתָה *to take away*. According to Gesenius *unition;* a contraction for יַחְדַת.

יָטְבָה [yotvāh'], Jotbah; *goodness*. From יָטַב *to be good*.

יָטְבָתָה [yotvāhtāh'], Jotbathah; id. with paragogic ה.

יֻטָּה [yoottāh'], Juttah; *extended* Verbal of Hoph. fut. of נָטָה (G.).

יְטוּר [y'toor'], Jetur; *enclosure, village of Nomades*, i. q. טִירָה, from an obsolete טוּר *to surround*, according to the form יְקוּם from קוּם (G.).

יְכוֹנְיָה [y'khoonyāh'], Kethib for יְכָנְיָה.

יְכִילְיָה [y'kheel'yāh'], Kethib for יְכָלְיָה.

יָכִין [yahkheen'], Jachin; *may He establish* [him]. Hiph. fut. of כּוּן compare Appellatives.

יָכִינִי [yāhkheenee'], Jachnite; patronymic of the same.

יְכָלְיָה [y'khol-yāh'], Kethib for יְכָלְיָהוּ [y'khol-yāh'hoo], Jecholiah; [for whom] *the Lord hath shewn himself mighty*. From יָכֹל *to be able, to prevail,* and יָהוּ *the Lord.*

יְכָנְיָה [y'khon-yāh'], Jeconiah; *may the Lord establish* [him]. For יָכֹן יָהּ fut. of כּוּן here in a transitive sense.

יְכָנְיָהוּ [y'khon-yāh'hoo], Kethib id.

יָלוֹן [yāhlōhn'], Jalon; *may he remain.* Fut. of לוּן *to pass the night,* also *to abide, remain.*

יְמוּאֵל [y'moo-ēhl'], Jemuel; *may God circumcise* [him]. For יָמוּל אֵל, future from מוּל, instead of which Num. xxvi. 12, and 1 Chr. xxiv. 4; we find נְמוּאֵל for אֵל נָמוּל *circumcised of God,* from נָמַל *to circumcise* (S.); *day of God* i. q. יוֹם, יְמוּ i. q. שֵׁם, שְׁמוּ מֵתוּ i. q. מֵת (G.).

יְמִימָה [y'meemāh'], Jemimah; *dove;* collated with the Arabic. Kromayer by Simonis.

יָמִין [yāhmeen'], Jamin; *the right* or *right hand*, compare Appellatives.

יְמִינִי [yāhmeenee'], Jaminite; patronymic of the same.

יְמִינִי [y'meenee'], Jemini; found elliptically for the patronymic בֶּן־יְמִינִי.

יִמְלָא [yimlāh'], Imla; *He shall fill* or *fulfil*. Fut. of מָלָא compare Appellatives.

יִמְלָה [yimlāh'], Imlah; id.

יַמְלֵךְ [yamlēhkh'], Jamlech; *may He make* [him] *to reign*. Hiph. fut. of מָלַךְ, *to reign*.

יִמְנָה [yimnāh'], Imnah; *felicity*, collated with the Arabic (S.).

יִמְנָע [yimnāhng'], Imna; *may He spare* [him]. Fut. of מָנַע *to hold back, withhold*,

יִמְרָה [yimrāh'], Imrah; *rebellion* (G.). From מָרָה *to be perverse, rebellious*.

יָנוֹחַ [yāhnōh'ăkh], Janoah; *rest, quiet*. From נוּחַ comp. Appellatives.

יָנוּם [yāhnoom'], Keri; יָנִים [yāh-neem'], Kethib; Janum; *slumber*. From נוּם *to sleep, slumber*.

יִסְכָּה [yiskāh'], Iscah; *covering*. It has the form of יָסַךְ, but the signification of נָסַךְ or סָכָה *to cover* (S.).

יִסְמַכְיָהוּ [yismakh-yāh'hoo], Ismachiah; *the Lord support* [him]. From סָמַךְ comp. Appellatives, and יָהוּ *the Lord*.

יַעְבֵּץ [yangbēhts'], Jabez; *who causeth pain*. By transposition for יַעֲצֵב Hiph. fut. of עָצַב, comp. 1 Chr. iv. 9, 10.

יֶעְדּוֹ [yengdōh'], Keri; יֶעְדִּי [yeng-dah'y], Kethib, Iddo; once (2 Chr. ix. 29) for עִדּוֹ probably of the same signification, *seasonable;* comp. the verb יָעַד.

יְעוּאֵל [y'ngoo-ēhl'], Jeuel; *treasure of God*. From יָעָה collated with the Arabic *to gather, preserve*, (G.), and אֵל *God*.

יְעוּץ [y'ngoots'], Jeuz; *counsel*. From עוּץ *to advise*, like יְקוּם from קוּם.

יָעוּר [yāh-ngoor'], Kethib for יָעִיר.

יְעוּשׁ [y'ngoosh'], Jeush; *assembly*. From עוּשׁ *to come together;* comp. יְעוּץ.

יַעֲזִיאֵל [yah-ngăzee-ēhl'], Jaaziel; *may God console* [him]. Hiph. fut. of עָזָה, collated by Simonis with the Arabic עזי *to be comforted*, and אֵל *God*.

יַעֲזִיָה [yah-ngăziy-yāh'], Jaaziah; *may the Lord console* [him]; compare the preceding.

יַעֲזֵיר [yah-ngăzēhr'], יַעְזֵר [yangzēhr'], Jazar; *may He help* [him]. Hiph. fut. of עָזַר compare Appellatives.

יְעִיאֵל [y'ngee-ēhl'], Jeiel; i. q. יְעוּאֵל.

יָעִיר [yāh-ngeer'], Jair; *may He stir* [him] *up*. Hiph. fut. of עוּר *to be awake*.

יְעִישׁ [y'ngeesh'], Kethib for יְעוּשׁ.

יַעְכָּן [yang-kāhn'], Jachan; *afflicted*. From an obsolete עָכַן prob. i. q. עָכַר (G.).

יָעֵל [yāh-ngēhl'], Jael; *wild he-goat*, comp. Appellatives.

יַעֲלָא [yah-ngălāh'], Jaalah, i. q. יַעֲלָה.

יַעֲלָה [yah-ngălāh'], Jaalah; *wild she-goat*, feminine of יָעֵל q. v.

יַעְלָם [yang-lāhm'], Jaalam; *may He hide*, i. e. protect him. Hiph. fut. of עָלַם, comp. Appellatives.

יַעַן see יָעַן דָּן

יַעֲנַי [yangnah'y], Jaanai; *may the Lord answer* [him]. Fut. of עָנָה *to answer*, יְ _, comp. אֲחַי.

יַעֲקֹב, a few times also in Kethib יַעֲקוֹב [yah-ngăkōhv'], Jacob; *laying hold by the heel, supplanter*. From עָקֵב *a heel*, compare Gen. xxv. 26.

יַעֲקֹבָה [yah-ngăkōh'vāh], Jaakobah; id.

יַעְקָן [yah-ngăkāhn'], Jakan; *he shall adorn*. Fut. of עָקַן i. q. עָנַק *to surround like a necklace* (S.). Gesenius compares עָקַן with the Aramaic עקם *to wreathe, twist*.

יַעְרָה [yang-rāh'], Jarah; only once (1 Chron. ix. 42.) for יְהוֹעַדָּה.

יַעְרֵי אֹרְגִים [yah-ngărēh' ōhr'geem'], Jaare-oregim; only once 2 Sam. xxi. 19, for יָעִיר 1 Chron. xx. 5. Doubtless *the woods of the weavers*, but not suitable when compared with the latter passage.

יַעֲרֶשְׁיָה [yah-ngăresh-yāh'], Jaresiah; [whom] *the Lord nourishes*.

From עָרַשׂ after the Syriac *to fatten* (G.) and יָה *the Lord*.

יַעֲשַׂי [yah-ngăsāh'y], Jaasau (according to Kethib יעשו); contracted from יַעֲשָׂיָה (G.), *the Lord does* [it]. Fut. of עָשָׂה *to do*, and יָה *the Lord*.

יַעֲשִׂיאֵל [yah-ngăsee-ēhl'], Jasiel; *God does it*, comp. the preceding.

יִפְדְיָה [yiphd'yāh']. Iphedeiah; *the Lord redeem* [him]. Fut. of פָּדָה *to redeem*, and יָה *the Lord*.

יָפוֹ and יָפוֹא [yāhphōh'], Joppa; *beauty*. From יָפָה *to be beautiful*.

יָפִיעַ [yāhphee'ăng], Japhia; *shining*. From יָפַע; comp. Appellatives.

יַפְלֵט [yaphlēht'], Japhlet; *may He deliver* [him]. Hiph. fut. of פָּלַט *to escape*.

יַפְלֵטִי [yaphlēhtee'], Japhleti, better Japhletite; patronymic of the same.

יְפֻנֶּה [y'phoonneh'], Jephunneh; *may he be regarded with favor*. Pual fut. of פָּנָה *to turn, turn one's eyes, look graciously*.

יֶפֶת [yeh'pheth], Japheth; *enlargement*, from פָּתָה *to be open, wide*, in Hiph. *to enlarge*, compare Gen. ix. 27.

יִפְתָּח [yiphtāhkh'], Jephthah; *may He free* [him]. Fut. of פָּתַח *to open, set free*.

יִפְתַּח־אֵל [yiphtākh-ēhl'], Jiphthahel; [which] *the Lord openeth*, comp. the preceding.

יִצְהָר [yits-hähr'], Izhar; *oil*, comp. Appellatives.

יִצְהָרִי [yits-hähree'], Izeharite; patronymic of the same.

יִצְחָק [yitskhähk'], Isaac; *he laugheth*. Fut. of צָחַק *to laugh*, comp. Gen. xvii. 17, &c.

יֵצֶר [yēh'tser], Jezer; *form*, comp. Appellatives.

יִצְרִי [yitsree'], Jezerite; patronymic of the same.

יְקַבְצְאֵל [y'kavts'ēhl'], Jekabzeel; [which] *God shall gather*. Piel fut. of קָבַץ *to gather together*, and אֵל *God*.

יָקְדְעָם [yok-d'ngähm'], Jokdeam; *burning of the people*. יָקְדָה or יָקַד *a burning*, from יָקַד *to kindle, burn*, עָם *people*.

יָקֶה [yähkeh'], Jakeh; *pious*. From יקה according to the Arabic *to venerate, fear God, be pious* (G.).

יְקוּתִיאֵל [y'koothee-ēhl'], Jekuthiel; *godly piety*, lit. *piety of God*. Compound of יְקוּת *piety*, comp. the preceding, joined to אֵל [God] by י conjunctive.

יָקְטָן [yoktähn'], Joktan; *diminished*. Verbal of the Hoph. fut. of קָטַן *to be small*.

יָקִים [yähkeem'], Jakim; *may He raise* [him]. Hiph. fut. of קוּם *to arise*.

יְקַמְיָה [y'kam-yäh'], Jekamiah; [whom] *the Lord gathereth*. For יָקִימָה יָהּ, Piel fut. of קָמָה according to the Arabic *to gather* (G.).

יְקַמְעָם [y'kam-ngähm'], Jekameam; [who] *gathereth the people*. For קָמָה עָם (G.) Piel fut. of קָמָה, comp. the preceding.

יָקְמְעָם [yokm'ngähm'], Jokmeam; *gathered of the people*. Of Hoph. fut. of קָמָה, comp. the preceding, עָם *people*.

יָקְנְעָם [yokn'ngähm'], Jokneam; *possessed of the people*. For יָקְנָה עָם, Hoph. fut. of קָנָה *to possess*, and עָם *people*.

יָקְשָׁן [yokshähn'], Jokshan; *fowler*. From יָקַשׁ *to lay snares*.

יָקְתְאֵל [yokth'ēhl'], Joktheel; *subdued by God*. For יָקְתָה אֵל, Hoph. of קָתָה according to the Arabic *to serve as a slave* (G.).

יִרְאוֹן [yir-ōhn'], Iron; *fearing* [God]. From יָרֵא *to fear, reverence*.

יִרְאִיָּה [yir-iy-yäh], Irijah; *the Lord look upon* [him]. Fut. of רָאָה *to see, look upon*, and יָהּ *the Lord*.

יָרֵב [yährēhv'], Jareb; only Hos. v. 13 and x. 6, perhaps more correctly rendered as an Appellative, as it is in the margin, [the king that] *should plead*. Fut. of רִיב.

יְרֻבַּעַל [y'roobbah'-ngal], Jerubbaal; marg. (to Judg. vi. 32) *Let Baal plead*. For יָרֵב בַּעַל, comp. Appellatives for רִיב and בַּעַל.

יָרָבְעָם [yährov-ngähm'], Jeroboam; [whose] *people is numerous*. Fut. apoc. of רָבַב *to be numerous, many*, and עָם *people*.

יְרֻבֶּשֶׁת [y'roobbeh'sheth], Jerubbesheth ; *let shame* (i. e. the shameful idol) *plead.* Once (2 Sam. xi. 21) for יְרֻבַּעַל, q. v. בֶּשֶׁת *shame*, i. q. בֹּשֶׁת, comp. Appellatives.

יֶרֶד [*yeh'red*], Jared, Jered ; *descent.* From יָרַד *to descend.*

יַרְדֵּן [*yardēhn'*], Jordan ; *flowing down.* From יָרַד *to descend.* According to Simonis, *continual noise, murmuring.* From רָדַן *to make a bustling noise.*

יְרוּאֵל [*y'roo-ēhl'*], Jeruel ; *founded by God.* Part. pass. יָרָה *to cast, lay foundation,* and אֵל *God.*

יָרוֹחַ [*yāhrōh'ăkh*], Jeroah ; *moon;* i. q. Appellative יָרֵחַ.

יְרוּשָׁה, יְרוּשָׁא [*y'rooshāh'*], Jerusha, Jerushah ; *possessed.* From participle pass. fem. יָרַשׁ *to possess.*

יְרוּשָׁלַיִם [*y'rooshāhlah'-yim*] ; only 2 Chron. xxxii. 9, Est. ii. 6, and according to some copies also 1 Chron. iii. 5, in all other places יְרוּשָׁלֵם (in pause ־לֵם), Jerusalem ; *possession of quietness*, i. e. *a quiet possession.* For יְרוּשׁ שָׁלַיִם from יָרַשׁ *to possess,* and dual of שַׁל *quietness,* שָׁלָה. But the correctness of this dual punctuation may fairly be questioned, since the dual י only occurs in the above-mentioned three passages out of 643 times of this word's occurrence. It is most likely a later adopted Chaldee form (compare Hebrew שֹׁמְרוֹן and Chaldee שָׁמְרַיִן) according to which it was pointed. In the Chaldee part of the Scriptures it is יְרוּשְׁלֶם and יְרוּשְׁלָם. All this would speak for the opinion that the ם is radical, and with the vowels of שָׁלֵם (comp. Gen. xiv. 18,

and Ps. lxxvi. 3) signifies *peace.* Hence according to Saadia, *house of peace,* יְרוּ collated with the Arabic *habitation, house,* in the Hebrew literally *founded,* as a participle of יָרָה.

יְרוּשָׁלֵם & יְרוּשְׁלֶם [*y'rooshlēhm'* & *y'rooshlem'*], Chald. Jerusalem ; id.

יֶרַח [*yeh'rakh'*], in pause יָרַח, Jerah ; *month,* comp. Appellatives.

יְרֵחוֹ [*y'rēhkhōh'*], Jericho; *sweet odour.* From רֵיחַ for יְרֵחוֹן.

יְרֹחָם [*y'rōhkhāhm'*], Jeroham ; *may he be loved.* Pual fut. of רָחַם *to love.*

יְרַחְמְאֵל [*y'rakhm'ēhl'*], Jerahmeel; *may God have compassion upon* [him]. Compound of Piel fut. of רָחַם *to pity, love,* and אֵל *God.*

יְרַחְמְאֵלִי [*y'rakhm'ēhlee'*], Jerahmeelite ; patronymic of the same.

יַרְחָע [*yarkhāhng'*], Jarha ; of uncertain signification, probably of Egyptian derivation, since it is the name of an Egyptian servant, 1 Chr. ii. 34, 35.

יְרִיאֵל [*y'ree-ēhl'*], Jeriel ; *established of God,* for יְרִי—יָרִי אֵל, a passive form for יָרָה, comp. יְרוּאֵל, see also יִרְמְיָה.

יָרִיב [*yāhreev'*], Jarib ; *adversary.* From רִיב *to contend,* compare Ps. xxxv. 1.

יְרִיבַי [*y'reevah'y*], Jeribai ; id. with the adjective termination ־ַי (G.).

יְרִיָּה [*y'riy-yāh'*]. Jerijah ; *estab-*

lished of the Lord, for יָהּ יְרִי, comp. יְרוּאֵל and יְרִיאֵל.

יְרִיָּהוּ [y'riy-yāh'hoo], Jeriah; id.

יְרִיחוֹ (only once 1 Kin. xvi. 34.) and יְרֵיחוֹ [y'reekhōh'], Jericho; i.q. יְרִחוֹ.

יְרִימוֹת [y'reemōhth'], Jerimoth; elevations, high places, comp. יְרֵמוֹת.

יְרִימוֹת [y'rehmōhth'], Jerimoth; id.

יְרִיעוֹת [y'ree-ngōhth'], Jerioth; curtains. Pl. of יְרִיעָה, comp. Appellatives.

יַרְמוּת [yarmooth'], Jarmuth; elevation, high place. From יָרַם i.q. רוּם and אָרַם to be high (G.).

יְרֵמוֹת [y'rēmōhth'], Jeremoth; elevations, high places, compare the preceding.

יִרְמַי [y'rēhmah'y], Jeremai; inhabiting high places (G.). comp. the preceding, יִ an adjective form.

יִרְמְיָה [yirm'yāh'], Jeremiah; may the Lord establish [him]. Future of רמה i.q. Chaldee רְמָא or רְמָה to cast, set, place, and יָהּ the Lord.

יִרְמְיָהוּ [yirm'yāh'hoo], Jeremiah; id.

יִרְפְּאֵל [yirp'ehl'], Irpiel; may God heal [him]. Fut. of רָפָא to heal, and אֵל God.

יָרְקְעָם [york'ngāhm'], Jorkoam; may the people spread themselves. Hoph. fut. of רָקַע to spread out, and עָם people.

יִשְׂחָק [yiskhāhk'], Isaac; (i.q. יִצְחָק) from צָחַק to laugh.

יְשִׂימִאֵל [y'seemee-ēhl'], Jesimiel; may God establish [him]. Hiph. fut. of שׂוּם to set, place, establish, and אֵל God.

יִשְׂרָאֵל [yisrāh-ēhl'], Israel; he shall be a prince with God, Fut. of שָׂרָה to be a prince, shew one's self a prince. Others, to contend, struggle, hence this name, a wrestler with God comp. Gen. (xxxii. 24.) אֵל God.

יִשְׂרְאֵלִי [yisr'ēhlee'], Israelite; a man of Israel; gentile noun of the same.

יִשְׂרְאֵלִית [yisr'ēhleeth'], Israelitish [woman], fem. of the same.

יִשָּׂשכָר [yissāhkhāhr'], Issachar; He [i.e. God] brings reward. Without regard to the points, יִשָׂשכָר for יִשָּׂא he beareth, fut. of נָשָׂא and שָׂכָר reward, compare Gen. xxx. 18. But according to the pointing, יִשְׂכָר he is hired, i. e. gotten by hire (as Niph. fut. of שָׂכַר), compare ver. 16.

יֶשְׁבְאָב [yehshev-āhv'], Jeshebeab; seat of the father. From יָשַׁב to sit, dwell, and אָב father.

יֹשֵׁב בַּשֶּׁבֶת [yōhshēv' bashsheh'veth] sat in the seat. This is according to some taken as a a proper name, with the signification dwelling quietly, lit. dwelling in [his own] seat.

יִשְׁבּוֹ בְּנֹב Kethib [yishbōh b'nōhv'] Ishbi-benob; whose seat is Nob. From יֶשֶׁב seat, with suffix, and נֹב with prefix.

יִשְׁבַּח [yishbakh'], Ishbah; may he

ישב (65) ישן

praise [God]. Fut. of שָׁבַח (in Piel) *to praise.*

יָשֻׁבִי [*yāhshoovee'*], Jashubite; patronymic of יָשׁוּב.

יִשְׁבִּי בְּנֹב [*yishbee b'nōhv'*], Keri, Ishbi benob; *my seat is in Nob*, comp. יָשְׁבוּ בְּנֹב.

יָשֻׁבִי לֶחֶם [*yāhshoovee' leh'khem*], Jashubilehem; *may bread return* (perhaps *to me*). Fut. of שׁוּב *to return*, perhaps for לִי, and לֶחֶם *bread*.

יָשָׁבְעָם [*yāhshov-ngāhm'*], Jashobeam; *the people shall return.* Fut. apocopated of שׁוּב *to return*, and עָם *people.*

יִשְׁבָּק [*yishbāhk'*], Ishbak; *he shall leave.* Fut. of שָׁבַק in the Chaldee, *to leave.*

יָשְׁבְּקָשָׁה [*yoshb'kāh'shāh*], Joshbekashah; *seek a dwelling.* For יָשׁב, יָשֵׁב בְּקָשָׁה *a dwelling*, בְּקָשָׁה, imperative of בָּקַשׁ *to seek*, with ה paragogic.

יָשׁוּב [*yāhshoov'*], Jashub; *he shall return.* Fut. of שׁוּב *to return.*

יִשְׁוָה [*yishvāh'*], Ishvah; *likeness, similarity.* From שָׁוָה *to be like, similar.*

יְשׁוֹחָיָה [*y'shōhkhāh-yāh'*], Jeshohaiah; *the Lord boweth down, humbles.* For יָשׁוּחַ *to bow*, fut. of שׁוּחַ *to bow down*, (trans.), and יָה *the Lord.*

יִשְׁוִי [*yishvee'*], Ishui; *like, similar.* From שָׁוָה *to be like, similar.* Also as a patronymic, English version, *Jesuite.*

יֵשׁוּעַ [*yēhshoo'ăng*], Jeshua; a contracted form for יְהוֹשֻׁעַ, q. v.

יִשַׁי [*yeeshah'y*], Jesse; of doubtful signification. According to some, *rich*, from the obsolete יָשָׁה.

יָשִׁיב [*yāhsheev'*], Jashub; *he shall bring back*, once (1 Chron. vii.1), in Kethib for יָשׁוּב, q. v.

יִשִׁיָּה [*yishshiy-yāh'*], Ishiah (1 Chron. vii. 3), Jesiah (xxiii. 20) Isshiah (xxiv. 21), Ishijah (Ez. x. 31); [whom] *the Lord lendeth.* Fut. of נָשָׁה *to lend*, יָה *the Lord.*

יִשִׁיָּהוּ [*yishshiy-yāh'hoo*], Jesiah; id.

יְשִׁישַׁי [*y'sheeshah'y*], Jeshishai; [born] *of an old man* (G.). From יָשִׁישׁ *an old man.*

יִשְׁמָא [*yishmāh'*], Ishma; *desolation.* From שָׁמֵם *to be desolate.*

יִשְׁמָעֵאל [*yishmāhngēhl'*], Ishmael; *God heareth.* Fut. of שָׁמַע *to hear* and אֵל *God.* Compare Gen. xvi. 11.

יִשְׁמְעֵאלִי [*yishm'ngēhlee'*], Ishmaelite; patronymic of the same.

יִשְׁמַעְיָה [*yishmang-yāh'*], Ishmaiah; [whom] *the Lord heareth*, or *shall, may hear*, compare יִשְׁמָעֵאל.

יִשְׁמַעְיָהוּ [*yishmang-yāh'hoo*], Ishmaiah; id.

יִשְׁמְרַי [*yishm'rah'y*], Ishmerai; *the Lord keep* [him]. Fut. of שָׁמַר, and י the Lord, compare אֲחוַי.

יָשֵׁן [*yāhshēhn'*], Jashen; *sleeping, asleep*, compare Appellatives.

K

יְשָׁנָה [y'shāhnāh'], Jeshanah ; *old*. The fem. of יָשָׁן *old*, compare Appellatives.

יִשְׁעִי [yish-ngee'], Ishi ; *salutary*. From יֶשַׁע *help, salvation* (G).

יְשַׁעְיָה [y'shang-yāh'], Jeshaiah, Jesaiah ; *salvation of the Lord*. From יֶשַׁע *salvation* and יָהּ *the Lord*.

יְשַׁעְיָהוּ [y'shang-yāh'hoo], Isaiah ; *id*.

יִשְׁפָּה [yishpāh'], Ispah ; *eminence*. From an obsolete שפה *to stand out, be higher*.

יִשְׁפָּן [yishpāhn'], Ishpan ; *eminent*, compare the preceding.

יֵשֶׁר [yeh'sher], Jesher ; *uprightness*. Compare Appellative יָשָׁר.

יְשַׂרְאֵלָה [y'sharēh'lāh], Jesharelah ; *upright towards* or *with God*. From יָשָׁר *straight, upright,* and אֵל *God* with local ה.

יְשֻׁרוּן [y'shooroon'], *upright, righteous*. Part. pass. of יָשָׁר *straight, right*. The termination, וּן is, according to some, intensive, hence *very* or *most righteous*, according to others diminutive, *the little righteous* [people], speaking of Israel. If this be the true meaning, the word *righteous* here, ought, perhaps, be taken in the sense of *justified*.

יַתִּיר [yatteer'], Jattir ; *eminent*. From יָתִר, compare the Chaldee יַתִּיר *very great, eminent*.

יִתְלָה [yithlāh'], Jethlah ; *may He exalt* [him]. From תָּלָה according to the Chaldee *to lift up, exalt*.

יִתְמָה [yithmāh], Ithmah ; *the being without a father, orphanhood* (orbitas). From יָתוֹם *fatherless, an orphan*.

יַתְנִיאֵל [yathnee-ēhl'], Jathniel ; [whom] *God gives as a present*. Hiph. fut. of נָתַן *to give presents,* and אֵל *God*.

יִתְנָן [yithnāhn'], Ithnan ; *given* (G.), compare the preceding.

יֶתֶר [yeh'ther], Jether ; *excellence* or *excellent*, compare Appellatives.

יַתִּיר see יָתִר.

יִתְרָא [yithrāh'], Ithra ; *excellence*. For יִתְרָה, as an Appellative, *abundance*.

יִתְרוֹ [yithrōh'], Jethro ; *excellent*. For יִתְרוֹן with the above signification, since it stands for יֶתֶר, compare יִתְרָן.

יִתְרִי [yithree'], Ithrite ; patronymic of יֶתֶר.

יִתְרָן [yithrāhn'], Ithran; *excellent*. Probably i. q. יִתְרוֹן compare יִתְרוֹ.

יִתְרְעָם [yithr'-ngāhm'], Ithream ; *abundance of people*. From יֶתֶר *abundance*, compare Appellatives, and עָם *people*.

יְתֵת [y'thēhth'], Jetheth ; *pin, tent-pin*. For יְתֵדֶת (S.), from יָתֵד, compare Appellatives.

כ

כָּבוּל [kāhvool'], Cabul ; *received as a pledge* [of friendship]. From

כבל, collated with the Arabic, i. q. חבל to bind (S.), whence חֶבֶל a cord, and חֹבֵל a pledge. But Gesenius supposes it to be the same with גְבוּל limit, border.

כַּבּוֹן [kabbōhn'], Cabbon; band. From כבן collated with the Talmudic to bind (S.). But Gesenius in Thes. compares it with the Syriac כבונא a cake, under the root כָּבַב.

כְּבָר [k'vāhr'], Chebar; greatness or might. Compare the verb כָּבַר and adjective כַּבִּיר.

כְּדָרְלָעֹמֶר [k'dorlāh-ngōh'mer], Chedorlaomer; handful of sheaves. From כדר collated with the Arabic a handful, and עמר a sheaf (S.).

כּוּב [koov'], Chub; thorn (paliurus), collated with the Syriac (Hiller).

כּוּן [koon'], Chun; stability. From כון compare Appellatives.

כּוֹנַנְיָהוּ [kōhnan-yah'hoo], Cononiah; [whom] the Lord has established. According to Kethib, from Piel of כָּנַן, see כְּנַנְיָהוּ.

כּוֹר עָשָׁן [kōhr ngāhshāhn'], Chorashan; smoking furnace. כּוֹר i. q. כּוּר a furnace, compare Appellatives.

כּוֹרֶשׁ and only twice, כֹּרֶשׁ [kōh'resh], Cyrus; supposed to signify the sun, in the Persic (G.).

כּוּשׁ [koosh'], Cush, Ethiopia; terror. Collated with the Arabic and Chaldee (S.). According to some, multitude, assembly.

כּוּשִׁי [kooshee'], Ethiopian, Cushi; gentile noun of the same, and also as a proper name, probably of the same signification with the preceding.

כּוּשִׁית [koosheeth'], Ethiopian woman; feminine of the preceding gentile noun.

כּוּשָׁן [kooshāhn'], Cushan; i. q. כּוּשׁ.

כּוּשַׁן רִשְׁעָתַיִם [kooshan rish-ngāh-thah'-yim], Chushan-rishathaim; perhaps Chushan of [the city] Rishathaim, רִשְׁעָתַיִם double wickedness, i. e. great wickedness, as a dual of רִשְׁעָה.

כּוּת [kooth], Cuth; probably i. q. כּוּשׁ.

כּוּתָה [koothāh'], Cuthah; id.

כְּזִבָא [kōhzēhvāh'], Choziba; lying, false. Participle of כָּזַב to lie.

כָּזְבִּי [kozbee'], Cozbi; lying, false. Compare the preceding.

כְּזִיב [k'zeev], Chezib; a lie. Compare the preceding.

כִּידוֹן [keedōhn'], Chidon; dart, or perhaps, destruction. Compare Appellatives.

כִּיּוּן [kiy-yoon], Chiun; statue. From כּוּן to stand erect. For this form may, perhaps, be compared כִּיּוֹר from כּוּר, as also קוּם, Piel. קִיֵּם, compare Rabbinic קִיּוּם standing, existence.

כִּלְאָב [kil-āhv'], Chileab; like unto the father. For כְּלְאָב, to prevent the collision of double sh'va; at the beginning the two consonants form one syllable, compare כְּקְטֹל.

כָּלֵב [kāhlēhv'], Caleb; *rabid.* Collated with the Arabic (G.). According to others, *barker,* compare Gesenius on the obsolete כָּלַב.

כָּלֵב אֶפְרָתָה [kāhlēhv - ephrāh'thāh], Caleb-ephratah; perhaps, *Caleb on the way to Ephrath,* literally *towards Ephrath.* For the signification see the preceding, and אֶפְרָת.

כָּלִבִּי [kāhlibbee'], of the house of Caleb; patronymic of כָּלֵב. Thus it is according to Keri in its only occurrence 1 Sam. xxv. 3, but if the Kethib be correct, it may be taken as an Appellative, (וְהוּא) *and he was* כְּלִבּוֹ *according to his own heart,* i. e. his (Nabal's) actions were regulated by the impulse of his wicked heart, and not by the law of God.

כְּלוּב [k'loov'], Chelub; *cage* or *basket.* Compare Appellatives.

כְּלוּבַי [k'loovāh'y], Chelubai; once (1 Chr. ii. 9), for כָּלֵב, probably of the same signification.

כְּלוּהוּ [k'looh'hoo], Keri, כְּלוּחַי [k'loohah'y] Kethib, Chelluh; in neither case is the signification evident.

כֶּלַח [keh'lakh], only found in pause כָּלַח [kāh'lakh], Calah; *perfection* or *old age.* Compare Apellatives.

כָּל־חֹזֶה [kol khōhzeh']; Col-hozeh; *all-seeing,* כָּל *all,* חֹזֶה participle of חָזָה *to see.*

כִּלְיוֹן [kilyōhn'], Chilion; *a pining.* Compare Appellatives.

כַּלְכֹּל [kalkōhl'], Calcol; *sustenance,* from כּוּל, in Piel כִּלְכֵּל *to sustain.*

כְּלָל [k'lāhl'], Chelal; *completeness.* From כָּלַל *to be complete.*

כִּלְמַד [kilmad'], Chilmad; of doubtful signification.

כַּלְנֵה, כַּלְנֶה [kalnēh'], Calneh; and כַּלְנוֹ [kalnōh], Calno; id.

כִּמְהָם [kimhāhm'], Chimham; *longing.* From כָּמַהּ comp. Ps. lxiii. 2.

כִּמְהָן [kimhāhn'], Chimhan; id.

כְּמוֹשׁ [k'mōhsh], Chemosh; probably *subduer, vanquisher.* From כָּמַשׁ i. q. כָּבַשׁ *to subdue* (G.).

כְּמִישׁ [k'meesh], once (Jer. xlviii. 7), in Kethib for the preceding.

כַּנֵּה [kannēh'], Canneh; supposed to be a contraction of כַּלְנֶה.

כָּנְיָהוּ [kon-yāh'hoo], Coniah; abbreviated from יְכָנְיָהוּ, by dropping the י, see יְכָנְיָה.

כְּנָנִי [k'nāh'nee], Chenani; *He* (God) *has established me.* For כְּנָנְנִי to prevent the concurrence of three Nuns, from כָּנַן (only according to the derivatives) *to establish,* compare חֲנָנִי from חָנַן. Or this may merely be an abbreviation of the following.

כְּנַנְיָה [k'nan-yāh'], Chenaniah; [whom] *the Lord has established.* From כָּנַן *to establish* (compare כְּנָנִי), and יָהּ *the Lord.*

כְּנַנְיָהוּ [k'nan-yāh'hoo], Chenaniah; id.

כְּנַנְיָהוּ [kāhnan-yāh'hoo], only in Keri, Cononiah, (the English version here reading with Kethib, see כּוֹנַנְיָהוּ), id.

כְּנַעַן [k'nah'-ngan], Canaan; humiliation. From כָּנַע to be low.

כְּנַעֲנָה [k'nāh-ngănah'], Chenaanah; id.

כְּנַעֲנִי [k'nāh-ngănee'], Canaanite; gentile noun of כְּנַעַן.

כְּנַעֲנִית [k'nāh-ngăneeth'], Canaanitess, Canaanitish woman; feminine of the preceding.

כִּנְּרוֹת [kinn'rōhth'], Chinneroth; plural of the following.

כִּנֶּרֶת [kinneh'reth], Chinnereth; harp, i. q. Appellative כִּנּוֹר.

כַּשְׂדִּי for כַּשְׂדִּי q. v.

כְּסִיל [k'seel'], Chesil; perhaps i.q. Appellative כֶּסֶל confidence, hope.

כִּסְלֵו [kislēv'], Chislev; torpor Collated with the Arabic (S.).

כִּסְלוֹן [kislōhn'], Chislon; confidence, hope, compare Appellative כֶּסֶל.

כְּסָלוֹן [k'sāhlōhn'], Chesalon; id.

כְּסֻלּוֹת [k'soollōhth'], Chesulloth; hopes, compare the preceding.

כַּסְלֻחִים [kaslookheem'], Casluhim; of obscure signification.

כִּסְלֹת־תָּבוֹר [kislōhth tāhvōr'], Kisloth-Tabor; confidence of Tabor; compare כִּסְלוֹן, see also תָּבוֹר.

כַּסְפִיָא [kāhsiph-yāh'], Casiphia; the signification of this word is not evident.

כְּפִירָה [k'pheerāh'], Chephirah; probably i. q. כָּפָר village.

כְּפַר הָעַמּוֹנִי [k'phar hāh-ngammōhnee'], Kethib Chephar-haammonia; village of the Ammonites. From כְּפָר a village, compare Appellative כָּפָר and also עַמּוֹנִי. The reading according to Keri is הָעַמּוֹנָה [hah-ngammohnah], probably population. The English version reads with the vowels of Keri and the letters of Kethib.

כַּפְתּוֹר [kaphtōhr'], Caphtor; knob or pomegranate. Compare Appellative.

כַּפְתֹּרִים [kaphtōhreem'], Caphtorims; gentile noun of the same.

כְּרוּב [k'roov'], Cherub; cherub, compare Appellatives.

כְּרִית [k'reeth], Cherith; a cutting, separation. From כָּרַת to cut.

כַּרְכְּמִישׁ [kark'meesh'], Carchemish; fortress of retreat or refuge. From כָּרַךְ in the Chaldee fortress, and מִישׁ retreat, from מוּשׁ to depart, retreat. But according to some מִישׁ is taken as the name of a man, compare מֵישָׁא.

כַּרְכַּס [karkas'], Carcas; eagle. According to the Persic (S.).

כַּרְמִי [karmee'], Carmi; vinedresser. From כֶּרֶם vine-yard, compare Appellatives.

כַּרְמֶל [karmel'], Carmel; fruitful place, vine-yard, or field, compare Appellatives.

כַּרְמְלִי [karm'lee'], Carmelite; gentile noun of the same.

כַּרְמְלִית [karm'leeth'], Carmelitess; feminine of the preceding.

כְּרָן [k'rāhn'], Cheran; harp. Collated with the Arabic (G.).

כֹּרֶשׁ occurs only in this form twice, Est. i. 1, 2, otherwise כּוֹרֶשׁ which see.

כַּרְשְׁנָא [karsh' nāh'], Carshenah; collated with the Persic, some suppose it to mean *shining, illustrious,* compare כּוֹרֶשׁ, others, *pillaging of war,* i. e. *spoiler.*

כְּרֵתִי [k'rēhthee'], Cherethites; gentile noun, perhaps from some place כָּרֵת or כָּרַת (*a cutting off,* from כָּרַת *to cut off*).

כֶּשֶׂד [keh'sed], Chesed; *increase.* Collated with the Arabic (S.).

כַּשְׂדַי [kasdee'], and Chaldee [kasdah'y], Chaldean; gentile name of the preceding.

כִּתִּים [kitteem'], and כִּתִּיִּים [kittiy-yeem'], Kittim, Chittim; perhaps, better *Chittites,* as in the Latin *Chittæi;* a gentile noun of some unknown name; כָּת, a beating or breaking in pieces, from כָּתַת to beat, break in pieces.

כְּתְלִישׁ [kithleesh'], Kithlish; *wall of man.* Contracted from כֹּתֶל in Chaldee, and כֹּתֶל *wall,* and אִישׁ *man* (G.).

ל

לֹא דְבַר [lōhd'văhr'], Lo-debar; *no-pasture,* לֹא *not,* דְּבַר *pasture,* i. q. Appellative דֶּבֶר, compare מִדְבָּר *a desert,* properly, a large place whither cattle is driven for pasture.

לֵאָה [lēh-āh'], Leah; *wearied.* From לָאָה *to be wearied.*

לָאֵל [lāh-ēhl'], Lael; *of God.* אֵל *God,* with prefix לְ.

לְאֻמִּים [l'oommeem'], Leummim; *people, nations.* Plural of לְאֹם compare Appellatives.

לֹא עַמִּי [lōh-ngammee'], not my people Hos. i. 9, &c.; compare Appellatives.

לֹא רֻחָמָה [lōh-rookhāh'māh], Loruhamah; marg. *not having obtained mercy.* רֻחָמָה Pual pret. of רָחַם.

לְבָאוֹת [l'vāh-ōhth'], Lebaoth; *lions.* compare Appellatives.

לְבוֹנָה [l'vōhnāh'], Lebonah; *frankincense.* Compare Appellatives.

לֻבִּים [loobbeem'], Libyans; once (Dan. xi. 43), for לוּבִים, q. v.

לָבָן [lāhvāhn'], Laban; *white.* Compare Appellatives.

לְבָנָה and לְבָנָא [l'vāhnāh], Lebanan, Lebanah; *moon.* Compare Appellatives.

לִבְנָה [livnāh'], Libnah; *whiteness.* Compare Appellatives.

לְבָנוֹן [l'vāhnōhn'], Lebanon; *the*

white one, i. e. white mountain, snow mountain. From לָבָן white.

לִבְנִי [livnee'], Libni, Libnite; white, compare the preceding.

לֹד [lōhd], Lod; birth, nativity, for יָלֹד from יָלַד to bear, bring forth. According to Gesenius, strife, quarrel, from an Arabic root לָדַד to strive.

לְהָבִים [l'hāhveem'], Lehabim; gentile noun, in the plural Lehabites, of the singular לַהְבִי from לַהַב burning flame. Supposed to be the same with לוּבִים.

לַהַד [lah'had], Lahad; oppression. Collated with the Arabic (G.).

לוּבִים [looveem'], Lubim, Lubims; a gentile noun, in the plural Lubites (Libyans), of the singular לוּבִי, from לוּב thirst, drought, collated with the Arabic verb to thirst (S.).

לוּד [lood], Lud, Lydia; born, for יָלוּד, from יָלַד to bear, bring forth.

לוֹ דְבָר [lōh-d'vāhr'], Lo-debar; stands 2 Sam. ix. 4, 5, for לֹא דְבָר 2 Sam. xvii. 27.

לוּדִים [loohdeem'], Ludim; gentile noun of לוּד.

לוּז [looz,] Luz; almond-tree, compare Appellatives.

לוּחֹת [lookhooth'] Kethib, and לוּחִית [lookheeth'], Luhith; boarded, floored, from לוּחַ tablet, table.

לוֹחֵשׁ [lohkhēhsh'], Halohesh; only occurring with article ה the enchanter. Participle of לָחַשׁ, compare Appellatives.

לוֹט [lōht'], Lot; covering, protection, from לוּט to wrap, cover.

לוֹטָן [lōhtāhn'], Lotan; id.

לֵוִי [lēhvee'], Levi, Levite; joining, adhesion, from לָוָה to join oneself to, adhere to, compare Gen. xxix. 34, where the margin reads joined. In the singular and plural used as a patronymic.

לְוִיָּא [lēhvāh-yēh'], Levites; the Chaldee plural of the preceding.

לוּשׁ [loosh], Laish; once (2 Sam. iii. 15), for לַיִשׁ, q. v.

לְחִי [l'khee'], occurs only in pause לֶחִי [leh'khee], Lehi; jaw-bone. Compare Appellatives, and Jud. xv. 17.

לַחְמִי [lakhmee'], Lahmi; fighter, from לָחַם to fight, war.

לַחְמָס [lakhmāhs'], Lahmam (according to the reading of some MSS.); of violence, i. e. place of violence. חָמָס i. q. Appellative חָמָס, with prefix לְ.

לְטוּשִׁים [l'toosheem'], Letushim, a gentile noun in the plural, of the singular לְטוּשִׁי, as a participle passive of לָטַשׁ to sharpen, hence sharpened.

לַיִשׁ [lah'-yish], Laish; lion, compare Appellatives.

לֵכָה [lēhkhāh'], Lecah; a going, journey, for יְלֵכָה from יָלַךְ to go, compare דֵּעָה from יָדַע, צֵאָה from יָצָא

לָכִישׁ [lāhkeesh'], Lachish; *the obstinate*, i. e. impregnable, collated with the Arabic (G.).

לְמוֹאֵל [l'mōh-ēhl'], Lemuel; *of God*, i. q. לְמוֹ, לְאֵל, being a poetic form for לְ.

לְמוּאֵל [l'moo-ēhl'], Lemuel; id.

לֶמֶךְ [leh'mekh], Lemech, (in pause) Lamech; *strong*, collated with the Arabic (S.).

לַעְדָה [lang-dāh'], Laadah; *for an ornament*, for עֲדָה, לְעָדָה i. q. Appellative עֲדִי. But according to Gesenius, collated with the Arabic *order*.

לַעְדָּן [lang-dāhn'], Laadan; perhaps, id. According to Gesenius, *put in order*, compare the preceding.

לַפִּידוֹת [lappeedōhth'], Lapidoth; *torches*, i. q. Appellative לַפִּיד.

לַקּוּם [lakkoom'], Lakum; *obstruction of the way*, collated with the Arabic (S.).

לִקְחִי [lik-khee'], Likhi; *attractive*. From לָקַח *to take*.

לֶשֶׁם [leh'shem], Leshem; *Ligure*, the name of a gem, or according to Castell, *Jacinth*. Compare Appellatives.

לֶשַׁע [leh'shang], only in pause לָשַׁע [lah'shang], Lasha; *a chasm in the earth*. Compare Gesenius under the obsolete root לָשַׁע.

מ

מֵאָה [mēh-āh'], Meah; *hundred*. Compare Appellatives.

מִבְחָר [mivkhāhr'], Mibhar; *the choicest*. Compare Appellatives.

מְבֻנַּי [m'voonnahy'], Mebunai; *built up*, i. e. made prosperous, and perhaps, *of the Lord*, if י expresses *Lord*; compare אֲחֻזַּי. Pual participle of בָּנָה *to build*.

מִבְצָר [mivtsāhr'], Mibzar; *fortress*. Compare Appellatives, and Jer. vi. 27.

מִבְשָׂם [mivsāhm'], Mibsam; *sweet odour*. From בֶּשֶׂם *fragrance, spicery*.

מַגְבִּישׁ [magbeesh'], Magbish; *gathering*. Hiph. participle of גבשׁ in the Chaldee *to gather*.

מְגִדּוֹ [m'giddōh'], Megiddo; [place] *of troops*. From גָּדַד, compare Appellative גְּדוּד *a troop*.

מִגְדָּל, מִגְדּוֹל [migdōhl'], Migdol; *tower*, i. q. Appellative מִגְדָּל.

מְגִדּוֹן [m'giddōn'], Megiddon; i. q. מְגִדּוֹ.

מַגְדִּיאֵל [magdee-ēhl'], Magdiel; *precious of God*. Compound of מֶגֶד *something precious, excellent*, and אֵל *God*, compare Appellatives.

מִגְדַּל־אֵל [migdal-ēhl'], Migdal-el; *tower of God*, compare Appellatives.

מִגְדַּל־גָּד [migdal-gahd'], Migdal-gad; *tower of Gad*, compare Appellatives, and גָּד proper name.

מִגְדַּל־עֵדֶר [migdal-ngēh'der], tower of Edar; *tower of the flock.* Compare Appellatives.

מָגוֹג [māhgōhg'], Magog; *extension, or, augmentation* (S.). Compare גּוֹג.

מָגוֹר מִסָּבִיב [māhgōhr missāhveev'], Magor-missabib; marg. (Jer. xx. 3) *fear round about.* Compare Appellatives.

מַגְפִּיעָשׁ [magpee-ngāhsh'], Magpiash; *great gathering, or, assembly.* Simonis supposes this word to be a contraction of מַגְפִּישׁ i.q. מַגְפִּישׁ above, *a gathering,* and עָשׁ id. from עוּשׁ *to come together;* but Gesenius, *moth-killer,* as it were מַגִּפִיעָשׁ, from מַגֵּף Hiph. Part. of נָגַף *to smite,* and עָשׁ *a moth.* Compare Appellatives.

מִגְרוֹן [mig-rōhn'], Migron; *precipice.* From מָגַר *to cast,* Chaldee מְגַר *to cast down.*

מָדָאָה [māhdāh-āh'], Median; Chaldee gentile noun in the emphatic state; in Keri, of מָדַי.

מָדוֹן [māhdōhn'], Madon; *contention,* from דּוּן *to contend.* Compare Appellatives.

מָדַי [māhdăy'], Madai, Media, Medes; supposed to mean *middle, midst.*

מָדִי [māhdee'], Mede; gentile noun of the same.

מִדְיָן [mid-yāhn'], Midian, Midianite; *strife, contention.* Comp. Appellatives.

מִדִּין [middeen'], Middin; *measures.* From the sing. מַד, root מָדַד *to measure.*

מִדְיָנִי [mid-yāhnee'], Midianite; gentile noun of מִדְיָן.

מִדְיָנִית [mid-yāhneeth'], Midianitish woman; fem. of the preceding.

מַדְמֵן [madmēhn'], Madmen; *dunghill,* i. q. מַדְמֵנָה.

מַדְמֵנָה [madmēhnāh'], Madmenah; *dung-hill.* Compare Appellatives.

מַדְמַנָּה [madmannāh'], Madmannah; id.

מְדָן [m'dāhn'], Medan; *contention.* Compare Appellatives.

מְדָנִי [m'dāhnee'], Midianite; i. q. מִדְיָנִי.

מְדָתָא [m'dāhth'āh], Hammedatha; it occurs only in the form הַמְּדָתָא, the ה being considered radical (not the article) *twin-brother* (geminus), collated with the Persic (S).

מְהוּמָן [m'hoomāhn'], Mehuman; *faithful.* A Chaldee form, from the root אָמַן; compare מְהֵימַן (Dan. vi. 5) *faithful,* as a Part. Aph.

מְהֵיטַבְאֵל [m'hēhtav-ēhl'], Mehetabel, Mehetabeel; *God is the benefactor.* From מְהֵיטַב Hiph. Part. according to the Chaldee form of יָטַב *to be good;* in Hiph. *to do good,* and אֵל God.

מַהֲלַלְאֵל [mah-hălal-ēhl'], Mahalaleel; *praise of God.* Compound of מַהֲלַל *praise,* from הָלַל, and אֵל God. Compare Appellatives.

מַהֲרַי [mah-hărah'y], Maharai; *swift.* From מָהַר *to hasten.*

L

מַהֵר שָׁלָל חָשׁ בַּז [mah-hēhr' shāh-lāhl' khāhsh bāhz'], Maher-shalal-hash-baz (marg. *in making speed to the spoil, he hasteneth the prey*).

מוֹאָב [mōh-āhv'], Moab; *the coming in* (lying with) *of the father*. Contracted from מוֹבָא אָב, the former as derived from בּוֹא *to come in*.

מוֹאָבִי [mōh-āhvee'], Moabite; gentile noun of the same.

מוֹאָבִיָּה [mōh-ăviy-yāh'], Moabitess; feminine of the preceding.

מוֹאָבִית [mōh-āhveeth'], Moabitess; id.

מוֹלָדָה [mōhlāhdāh'], Moladah; *birth, origin*. From יָלַד *to bear*, bring forth.

מוֹלִיד [mōhleed'], Molid; *begetter, sire* (genitor). From Hiph. participial form of יָלַד *to bear, bring forth*.

מוֹמְכָן [mōhm'khāhn'], Kethib for מְמוּכָן.

מוֹסֵרָה [mōhsēhrāh'], Mosera; *band*. From אָסַר *to bind*. In the plural מֹסֵרוֹת [mōhsēhrōhth], Moseroth; *bands*.

מוֹעַדְיָה [mōh-ngad-yāh'], Moadiah; *coming together*, or, *assembly of the Lord*. Compound of מוֹעֵד *assembly*, and יָהּ; compare Appellatives. But from the comparison of Neh. xii. 5 with v. 17, it stands for מַעֲדְיָה [*ornament of the Lord*], מֹעֵד i. q. מַעַד both from עָדָה [*to adorn*], compare מֹעַל (Neh. viii. 6) from עָלָה; except we point מֹעֲדְיָה in Neh. xii. 5, which also the margin proposes there.

מוּפַעַת [moophall'-ngath], in Kethib for מֵיפַעַת.

מוֹצָא [mōhtsāh'], Moza; *fountain*. From יָצָא *to come forth*. Compare Appellatives.

מוֹרֶה [mōhreh'], Moreh; *archer*. Hiphil form of יָרָה *to throw, shoot*.

מוֹרִיָּה see מֹרִיָּה.

מוֹרֶשֶׁת גַּת [mōhreh'sheth gath], Moresheth-gath; *possession of Gath*. מוֹרֶשֶׁת from יָרַשׁ *to take possession of*, and compare Appellative גַּת.

מוֹרַשְׁתִּי [mōhrashtee'], Morasthite; gentile noun of the preceding.

מוּשִׁי [mooshee'], Mushi, Mushite; *yielding*. From מוּשׁ *to give way, yield*. As a p. n. and patronymic of the same. It is once (1 Chr. vi. 4) found מֻשִּׁי [mushshee'].

מִזָּה [mizzāh'], Mizzah; *fear*. From מזז in the Chaldee, i. q. מָסַס *to melt, be faint-hearted, fear*.

מְחוּיָאֵל [m'khoo-yāh-ēhl'], Mehujael; *smitten of God*. מְחוּי as Participle passive in the construct state of מָחָה i. q. מָחָא *to strike, smite*, and אֵל *God*. Compare מְחִיָּאֵל.

מַחֲוִים [mahkhăveem'], Mahavite; a gentile noun, only occurring 1 Chr. xi. 4. According to Simonis from מַחֲוֶה *place of assembly*, from the Arabic حوي *to gather together;* from which also حوة *a village*, is derived. But the plural form in this passage cannot easily be accounted for.

מָחוֹל [māhkhōhl'], Mahol; *dancing*.

From חוּל to dance. Compare Appellatives.

מַחֲזִיאוֹת [makhzee-ōhth'], Mahazioth ; vision. From חָזָה to see.

מְחִידָה [m'kheedāh'], Mehida; junction. From חוּד collated with the Syriac to join (S.).

מְחִיָּיאֵל [m'khiy-yāh-ēhl'], Mehujael ; smitten of God, i. q. מְחוּיָאֵל for which it stands, the form מְחִי being a Chaldee Part. pass. form.

מְחִיר [m'kheer'], Mehir ; price. Compare Appellatives.

מַחְלָה [makh-lāh'], Mahlah ; sickness, i. q. Appellatives מַחֲלָה.

מַחְלוֹן [makh-lōhn'], Mahlon; sick. From חָלָה to be in pain, be sick.

מַחְלִי [makhlee'], Mahali, Mahli, Mahlites ; id.

מַחֲלַת [mah-khǎlath'], Mahalath ; lute, guitar. Thus Gesenius renders this word, Ps. liii. 1 and lxxxviii. 1, by a collation with the Æthiopic.

מְחֹלָתִי [m'khōhlāhthee'], Meholathite; gentile noun of אָבֵל מְחֹלָה q.v.

מַחֲנֵה־דָן [mahkhǎnēh' dāhn'], Mahaneh-dan ; camp of Dan. Compare Appellatives and p. n. דָן.

מַחֲנַיִם [mahkhǎnah'-yim], Mahanaim ; marg. two hosts (Gen. xxxii. 2), better two camps. Dual of מַחֲנֶה a camp.

מַחְסֵיָה [makhsēh-yāh'], Maaseiah; [whose] refuge is the Lord. מַחְסֶה refuge, from חָסָה to take refuge, shelter, and יָה the Lord.

מַחַת [mah'khath], Mahath ; taking, grasping. Apoc. from מַחְתָּה Hiph. part. of חָתָה to take, seize.

מַטְרֵד [mat-rēhd'], Matred; propeller, driver. Hiph. Part. of טָרַד i. q. Chaldee טְרַד to thrust, drive.

מַטְרִי [mat-ree'], Matri ; perhaps better Matrite, as a patronymic of an unknown person מָטְר ; probably i. q. מָטָר rain.

מֵידְבָא [mēh-d'vāh'], Medeba; water of quiet. From מֵי construct state of מַיִם water, and דְבָא collated with the Arabic to rest, be quiet (S.).

מֵידָד [mēhdāhd'], Medad ; love. From יָדַד i. q. דוּד to love.

מֵי זָהָב [mēh' zāh-hāhv'], Mezahab; water of gold, or, gold water. מֵי const. מַיִם and זָהָב gold. Compare Appellatives.

מֵי הַיַרְקוֹן [mēh' hay-yarkōhn'], Mejarkon ; water of greenness, or, green-water. מֵי, compare the preceding, and יַרְקוֹן i. q. Appellative יָרָקוֹן, but which latter more refers to the green-yellowish colour, compare Appellatives.

מִיכָא [meekhāh'], Micha; for מִיכָה (compare 2 Sa. ix. 12, with 1 Chr. viii. 34), and as a contraction from מִיכָיָה (compare Neh. xi. 17, 22, with xii. 35) who (is) like the Lord.

מִיכָאֵל [meekhāh-ēhl'], Michael ; who (is) like unto God? Compound of מִי who, כְּאֵל as God, compare מִיכָיָה.

מִיכָה [meekhāh'], Micah; who (is) like unto the Lord? Contraction from מִיכָיָה (compare 2 Chron. xxxiv. 20 with 2 Kings xxii. 12), which see; compare also מִיכָא.

מִיכָיָה [meekhāh-yāh'], Michaiah; who (is) like unto the Lord? From מִי who, and כְּיָה as the Lord; for which form compare מִיכָאֵל, which favours this signification, so that all the preceding forms may rightly be considered contractions from this, as the references under each prove them to have been used indiscriminately; and see also מִיכָא.

מִיכָיְהוּ [meekhāh-y'hoo'], Micaiah, Micah; id., but more fully of יהוה.

מִיכַל [meekhal'], Michal; brook, i. q. Appellative מִיכָל.

מִיָּמִין [miy-yāhmeen'], Mijamin, Miamin; at the right, i. e. the most cherished. Compare Appellative יָמִין the right.

מֵי מְרִיבָה [mēh' m'reevāh'], water of Meribah; waters of contention or strife. Perhaps the whole may be best taken as a proper name, Me-meribah. מֵי const. state of מַיִם water, מְרִיבָה contention, from רוּב, or רִיב to contend (so also the plural מֵי מְרִיבוֹת).

מֵי נֶפְתּוֹחַ [mēh' nephtōh'ăkh], the waters of Nephtoah; waters of opening, i. e. waters flowing freely. Perhaps the whole may be better taken as a proper name, Me-nephtoah. מֵי compare the preceding, and נֶפְתּוֹחַ from פָּתַח to open.

מֵיפַעַת [mēhphah'ngath], Mephaath; splendour, beauty, from יָפַע to shine.

מֵישָׁא [mēhshāh'], Mesha; retreat. From Hiph. of מוּשׁ to depart.

מִישָׁאֵל [meeshāh-ēhl'], Mishael; who (is) what God (is). Compound of מִי who, שֶׁ that, what, abbreviated from אֲשֶׁר and אֵל God. Compare מִיכָאֵל and מִיכָיָה.

מֵישַׁךְ [mēhshakh'], Meshach; nimble, swift. Collated with the Arabic. The king's guest, collated with the Persic (Lorsbach quoted by Gesenius).

מֵישָׁע & מֵישַׁע [mēhshāhng'], Mesha; help, deliverance. From the Hiph. of יָשַׁע to help, deliver.

מַכְבֵּנָא [makhbēhnāh'], Machbena; band, i. q. כַּבּוֹן q. v. According to Gesenius (in Thes.), a cloak; from the Syriac כְּבַן to gird round, to put on, כְּבַנָא girdle, vestment; Talmudic מַכְבֵּינָא thin cloak.

מַכְבַּנַּי [makhbannah'y], Machbanai; doubtless allied in signification with the preceding. Gesenius (in Thes.) proposes, having on a cloak; but is himself undecided about it.

מָכִי [māhkhee'], Machi; pining, fainting. Participial of מוּךְ to pine, with adjectival י. giving it personality.

מָכִיר [māhkheer'], Machir; sold. Passive form of מָכַר to sell.

מָכִירִי [māhkheeree'], "of Machir." Patronymic of the same.

מִכְמָס [mikhmāhs'], Michmas; hid treasure, or, perhaps, a hiding-place. From כָּמַס to lay up, hide away.

מִכְמָשׁ & מִכְמָשׂ [mikhmāhsh'], Michmash; id. Compare Ezr. ii. 27 with Neh. vii. 31.

מִכְמָתָת [mikhm'thāhth'], Michmethah; *hiding-place*, i. q. כתם in the Arabic *to hide* (S.); whence the Hebrew כֶּתֶם *gold*, probably *what is hidden, laid up*.

מַכְנַדְבַי [makhnadvah'y], Machnadebai; *what* (is) *like the liberal?* Contracted for מָה כִּנְדָבַי, מָה *what*, and נָדָב *liberal*, compare Appellatives. Some copies read מִכְּנַדְבַי with compensative Dagesh in כ, compare מִן.

מְכֹנָה [m'khōhnāh'], Mekonah [better, Mechonah]; *foundation*. From כּוּן, compare Appellative מְכוֹנָה, of which this is written defectively.

מַכְפֵּלָה [makhpēhlāh'], Machpelah; *a doubling*. From כָּפַל *to double*.

מִכְרִי [mikhree'], Michri; *price of the Lord*. For מִכְרִיָה (G.), מֶכֶר *price* (compare Num. xx. 19) and יָהּ *the Lord*.

מְכֵרָתִי [m'khēhrāhthee'], Mecherathite; gentile noun from מְכֵרָה (perhaps *a mine*, from כּוּר *to dig*), the name of some unknown place.

מַכְתֵּשׁ [makhtēhsh'], Maktesh [better, Machtesh]; *a mortar*, from כָּתַשׁ. Compare Appellatives.

מַלְאָכִי [mal-āhkhee'], Malachi; *messenger of the Lord*. For מַלְאָכִיָה, from מַלְאָה *messenger*, and יָהּ *the Lord*.

מִלּוֹא [millōh'], Millo; *mound, rampart*. From מָלָא *to fill*, and *be filled*. From its being filled up with stones and earth, in the Chaldee מַלִּיתָא (S.).

מַלּוּךְ [mallookh'], Malluch; *reigning*, or, *counsellor*. From מָלַךְ *to reign*, or i. q. Syriac מַלּוּךְ (G.), compare Chaldee מְלַךְ *to counsel*.

מְלוּכִי [m'lookhee'], Kethib for מְלִיכוּ, probably id.

מַלּוֹתִי [mallōhthee'], Mallothi; *my fulness*. For מַלֹּאותִי, from the Piel Infinitive of מָלָא *to fill*, and *be filled*.

מְלַטְיָה [m'lat-yāh'], Melatiah; [whom] *the Lord delivers*. Pret. of מָלַט *to deliver*, and יָהּ *the Lord*.

מְלִיכוּ [m'leekhoo'], Melicu; probably i.q. מַלּוּךְ.

מֶלֶךְ [meh'lekh], Melech; *King*. Compare Appellatives.

מֹלֶךְ [mōh'lekh], Moloch; id., according to the Syriac dialect.

מִלְכָּה [milkāh'] Milcah; *queen*, i.q. Appellative מַלְכָּה, or *counsel*, from the Chaldee מְלַךְ *to counsel*, compare מַלּוּךְ.

מַלְכִּיאֵל [malkee-ēhl'], Malchiel; *king of God*, or *God* (is) *King*. From מֶלֶךְ *king*, and אֵל *God*, with י conjunctive between the two nouns.

מַלְכִּיאֵלִי [malkee-ēhlee'], Malchielite; patronymic of the preceding.

מַלְכִּיָה [malkiy-yāh'], Malchiah, Malchijah; *king of the Lord*, or, *the Lord* (is) *King*. From מֶלֶךְ and יָהּ *the Lord*, compare מַלְכִּיאֵל.

מַלְכִּיָהוּ [malkiy-yāh'hoo], id.

מַלְכִּי־צֶדֶק [malkee tzeh'dek], Melchizedek; *King of righteousness.* From מֶלֶךְ *king*, and צֶדֶק *righteousness.*

מַלְכִּירָם [malkeerāhm'], Malchiram ; *king of exaltation.* From מֶלֶךְ *king*, and רָם *exaltation*, from רוּם *to be high.*

מַלְכִּי־שׁוּעַ & מַלְכִּישׁוּעַ [malkeeshoo'ăng], Melchi-shua; *king of help.* From מֶלֶךְ *king*, and שׁוּעַ for יֵשׁוּעַ *help*, from יָשַׁע *to help, deliver.*

מַלְכָּם [malkāhm'], Malcham, and מִלְכֹּם [milkohm], Milcom; i. q. מֶלֶךְ, but the form is taken from מֶלֶךְ, with affixed ־ָם and ־ֹם; according to some, expressing intensity ; hence *great king.*

מֹלֶכֶת [mōhleh'keth], Hammoleketh (according as it occurs with the article הַ); *queen.* Strictly Part. fem. of מָלַךְ *to reign.*

מִלְלַי [mee-lălah'y], Milalai ; *eloquent* (G.), from מָלַל *to speak.*

מְמוּכָן [m'mookhāhn'], Memucan ; it is compared with an Arabic root מכן *to be able* (S.); hence, *having power, authority.*

מַמְרֵא [mamrēh'], Mamre; perhaps, *fatness*, from מרא, collated with the Arabic *to be full, well fed* (G.).

מָנוֹחַ [māhnōh'ăkh], Manoah ; *rest, quiet.* From נוּחַ *to rest.* Compare Appellatives.

מְנַחֵם [m'nah-khēhm'], Menahem ; *comforter.* Piel part. of נָחַם *to console, comfort.*

מָנַחַת [māhnah'khath], Manahath ;

rest, compare מָנוֹחַ; according to some, *gift, present*, from מָנַח, of which also מִנְחָה *a gift, offering*, is derived.

מְנִי [m'nee], " that number," marg. (Isaiah lxv. 12), Meni ; *fate, fortune* (fortuna), as the name of an idol, collated with the Arabic (G.)

מִנִּי [minnee'], Minni ; perhaps, *part, portion.* Compare Gesenius on the obsolete מנן; according to the Arabic *to divide out, to allot ;* whence the particle מִן *from*, is derived.

מִנְיָמִין [min-yāhmeen'], Miniamin ; i. q. מִיָּמִין, where נ is compensated by Dagesh in י.

מִנִּית [minneeth'], Minnith ; perhaps, *part, portion.* Compare מִנִּי.

מְנַשֶּׁה [m'nash-sheh'], Manasseh ; marg. (Gen. xli. 51) *forgetting;* better, *causing to forget.* Hiphil of נָשָׁה *to forget.*

מְנַשִּׁי [m'nash-shee'], Manassite ; patronymic of the same.

מַסָּה [massāh'], Massah ; margin (Ex. xvii. 7), *temptation* from נָסָה *to try.* Compare Appellatives.

מִסְפָּר [mispāhr'], Mispar ; *number*, from סָפַר *to number.* Compare Apellatives.

מִסְפֶּרֶת [mispeh'reth], Mispereth ; id.

מוֹסֵרוֹת see מֹסְרָה.

מַעֲדַי [mah-ngădah'y], Maadai ; *ornament of the Lord*, apoc. from the following.

מֽעֲדְיָה [mah-ngad-yāh'], Maadiah; *ornament of the Lord.* Compound of מַעַד *ornament,* from עָדָה *to adorn,* and יָה *the Lord;* but compare מוֹעַדְיָה.

מָעוֹךְ [māh-ngōhkh'], Maoch; *oppression.* From מָעַךְ *to press.*

מָעוֹן [māh-ngōhn'], Maon; *habitation, dwelling.* Compare Appellatives.

מְעוּנִים [m'ngooneem'], Meunim, Mehunim; *habitations.* Compare the preceding. As the name of a man, and also as a gentile noun of מָעוֹן, English version, *Mehunims.*

מְעוֹנֹתַי [m'ngōhnōhthah'y], Meonothai; *habitations of the Lord.* For מְעוֹנֹתְיָה (G.), plural of מְעוֹנָה.

מַעַזְיָה [mahngaz-yāh'], Maaziah; *consolation of the Lord.* Compound of מַעַז, from עזה, collated with the Arabic (S.) *to console,* and יָה *the Lord.*

מַעַזְיָהוּ [mahngaz-yāh'hoo], id.

מָעַי [māh-ngāh'y], Maai; *fountain of the Lord.* מֵע from מוּע, collated with the Syriac and Arabic *to flow* (S.), and יָ *the Lord.* Compare אָחִוַי.

מַעֲכָה [mah-ngăkhāh'], Maacha; *oppression,* from מָעַךְ *to press.*

מַעֲכָת [mah-ngăkhāhth'], Maachathites (probably *Maachath*); id.

מַעֲכָתִי [mah-ngăkāhthee'], Maachathite; gentile noun of the preceding מַעֲכָה.

מַעֲלֵה עַקְרַבִּים [mah-ngăleh' ngakrabbeem'], Maaleh-acrabbim, ascent of Akrabbim; *ascent of scorpions.* From מַעֲלָה *ascent,* of עָלָה *to ascend,* and the pl. of עַקְרָב *a scorpion.*

מַעַץ [mah'-ngats], Maaz; *wrath.* Collated with Arabic (G.)

מְעָרָה [m'ngāhrāh'], Mearah; *cave.* From עוּר. Compare Appellatives.

מְעָרַת [mahngărāhth'], Maarath; *place naked of trees* (G.), from עָרָה *to be naked.* Compare Appellatives.

מַעֲשַׂי [mahngăsah'y], Maasiai; *work of the Lord.* Apoc. of the following.

מַעֲשֵׂיָה [mah-ngăsēh-yāh'], Maaseiah; *work of the Lord.* Compound of מַעֲשֶׂה *work,* from עָשָׂה *to work,* and יָה *the Lord.*

מַעֲשֵׂיָהוּ [mahngăsēh-yāh'hoo], id.

מֹף [mōhph'], Memphis; this and English version *Noph,* are supposed to be derived from another Egyptian form of this name, signifying *full of the good* (ones), as a sepulchre for the good only.

מְפִיבֹשֶׁת [m'pheevōh'sheth], Mephibosheth; the signification of this name is difficult to determine. The supposition of Simonis, also adopted by Gesenius after him, that it stands for מַפְאֵי בֹשֶׁת *exterminating the idol,* is most improbable.

מֻפִּים [mooppeem'], Muppim; besides the uncertainty of the signification of this word, there is a discrepancy in the parallel passages (compare Gen. xlvi. 21 (מֻפִּים) with 1 Chr. vii. 12 and Num. xxvi. 39), and whatever has been suggested concerning it is of very little probability.

מָצְבְיָה [m'tsōhvāh-yāh'], Mesobaite; *assembly of the Lord*. From צוּב *to gather together*, collated with the Syriac (S.), and יָהּ *the Lord*. The name of an unknown place, used as a gentile noun.

מֹצָה [mōhtsāh'], Mozah; perhaps for מוֹצָא *fountain* (G.). Compare Appellatives.

מָצוֹר [māhtsōhr']; this word, in 2 Ki. xix. 24; Isa. xix. 6, xxxvii. 25; and, perhaps, Mic. vii. 12, where, in the English version, it is rendered by *besieged, fortified* (places, cities), *defence, fortress*, is by many taken as a p. n., and that as a paronomasia for מִצְרַיִם (Egypt). For its signification, *fortress*, compare Apellatives.

מִצְפֶּה [mitspeh'], Mizpeh; *watch-tower*. From צָפָה *to look about, to view*. Compare Appellatives.

מִצְפָּה [mitspāh'], Mizpah; id.

מִצְרִי [mitsree'], Egyptian; gentile noun of מִצְרַיִם.

מִצְרַיִם [mitsrah'-yim], Egypt (Egyptians), Mizraim; *straitness*. Dual of מֵצַר (compare Appellatives); hence, perhaps, *double straitness*, from צָרַר *to bind, to shut up*; according to which, it may also signify *fortification, fortress*, compare מָצוֹר. Gesenius, by a collation with the Syriac and Arabic, supposes the obsolete root מָצַר to signify the same from which this word may be derived.

מִצְרִית [mitsreeth'], Egyptian, Egyptian woman; feminine of מִצְרִי.

מַקֵּדָה [makkēhdāh'], Makkedah; *place of cattle-breeders*, or *shepherds*; from נָקֹד, hence Appellative נֹקֵד *a cattle-breeder*, or *shepherd*.

מַקְהֵלֹת [makhēhlōhth'], Makheloth; *assemblies*. From קָהַל *to call together*.

מִקְלוֹת [miklōhth'], Mikloth; *contempts*. Plural of מִקְלָה, from קָלָה i. q. קָלַל *to lightly esteem*.

מִקְנֵיָהוּ [miknēh-yāh'hoo], Mikneiah; *possession of the Lord*. From מִקְנֶה, of קָנָה *to possess, to buy*, and יָהּ *the Lord*.

מָקֵץ [māh-kats'], Makaz; *end*. From קָצַץ *to cut off*; after the form מָסַךְ (G.).

מָרָא [māhrāh'], Mara (marg. Ruth i. 20, *bitter*); *sad*. For מָרָה fem. of מַר *bitter, sad*, from מָרַר. Compare Appellatives.

מְרֹאדַךְ בַּלְאֲדָן [m'rōhdakh' balădāhn'], Merodach-baladan. For the first of these see מְרֹדָךְ, and for the second, compare בַּלְאֲדָן; hence Merodach is lord god.

מָרֵאשָׁה [māh-rēhshāh'], Mareshah; *what is at the head* (G.), denom. of רֹאשׁ *head*.

מֵרַב [mēhrav'], Merab; *increase*. From רָבַב *to become much, or many*.

מֶרֶד [meh'red], Mered; *rebellion*. From מָרַד *to rebel*, compare Apellatives.

מְרֹדָךְ [m'rōhdakh'], Merodach; the name of a Babylonian idol, supposed to be *Mars*; whom, says Gesenius (in

Thes.), as the bloody author of slaughter, the ancient Shemitic nations appeased by human sacrifices. The root מרד (ה_ being a Syriac and Chaldee formative) he compares with the German Morb, and the Latin *Mors*, which signify death and slaughter, which, he thinks, suits well the god of *slaughter* and *war*, since *Mars, Mavors*, and *Mors* seem to be of the same root. According to another opinion, by a collation with the Persic, this name is supposed to signify *the little man*, as an endearing appellation.

מָרְדְּכַי [*mor-d'khāh'y*], Mordecai; *the little man, or worshipper of Mars*, from מְרֹדָךְ (G.), compare the preceding. If the latter be the true signification, it can only be the name which that godly man was compelled to adopt at the Persian court.

מָרָה [*māhrāh'*], Marah; *bitterness*, or *what is bitter*. Feminine of מַר, from מָרַד to be bitter.

מֵרוֹז [*mēhrōhz'*], Meroz; *refuge, place of refuge*. For מְאֵרוֹז, from ארז, collated with the Arabic *to contract oneself*, also *to flee* (S.).

מֵרוֹם [*mēhrōhm'*], Merom; *height, high place*, i. q. מָרוֹם, from רום *to be raised, high*.

מָרוֹת [*māhrōhth'*], Maroth; *bitternesses, bitter fountains* (G.), plural of מָרָה q. v.

מְרִיב בַּעַל [*m'reev bah'-ngal*], Merib-baal; *contender against Baal*. מְרִיב from רִיב *to contend*.

מֵי מְרִיבָה see מְרִיבָה.

מְרִי בַעַל [*m'ree vah'-ngal*], Meribbaal; contracted for מְרִיב בַּעַל q. v.

מְרָיָה [*m'rāh-yāh'*], Meraiah; *rebellion*. From מָרָה *to rebel*.

מוֹרִיָה see מֹרִיָּה.

מְרָיוֹת [*m'rāh-yōhth'*], Meraioth; *rebellions*. Plural of מָרָה.

מִרְיָם [*mir-yāhm'*], Miriam; *rebellion*, i. q. מְרִי with formative ם, (G.). Compare Appellatives.

מִרְמָה [*mirmāh'*], Mirma; *deceit, fraud*. From רָמָה. Compare Appellatives.

מְרֵמוֹת [*m'rēhmōhth'*], Meremoth; *elevations*. From רום *to be raised, high*.

מֵרֹנֹתִי [*mēhrōhnōhthee'*], Meronothite; gentile noun of an unknown place. מֵרֹנֹת, perhaps contracted for מֵי רֹנוֹת *water of songs*.

מֶרֶס [*meh'res*], Meres; *worthy*, collated with the Sanscrit and Zendic (Benfey, by Gesenius).

מַרְסְנָא [*mar-s'nāh'*], Marsena; *worthy man*. By the same authority.

מַרְעֲלָה [*mar-ngălāh'*], Maralah; *a trembling*. From רָעַל *to shake, tremble*.

מְרָרִי [*m'rāhree'*], Merari, Merarite; *bitter*. From מָרַר *to be bitter*. The name of a man, and also as a patronymic.

מַרְאֵשָׁה [*mahrēhshāh'*], probably for מַרְאֵשָׁה q. v.

מְרָתַיִם [*m'rāh-thah'-yim*], Mera-

מרת (82) משל

thaim; *double rebellion.* Dual of מָרָה *rebellion.*

מַשָּׂא [*massāh'*], Massa; *burden.* From נָשָׂא *to bear.* Comp. Appellatives.

מִשְׂגָּב [*misgāhv'*], Misgab; *height, high place.* From שָׂגַב *to be lifted,* or *raised up.* Compare Appellatives.

מִשְׂרְפוֹת מַיִם [*mis-r'phōhth' mah'-yim*], Misrephoth-maim; *flowings of water.* שָׂרַף Ithpeal in the Chaldee, *to drop* (S.).

מַשְׂרֵקָה [*mas-rēhkāh'*], Masrekah; *place of noble vines.* Compare Appellatives שֹׂרֵק and שׂוֹרֵקָה.

מָשׁ [*mash*], Mash; the signification is uncertain.

מֵישָׁא [*mēhshāh'*], Mesha; perhaps i.q. מִישָׁא *retreat.*

מִשְׁאָל [*mish-āhl'*], Mishal; *entreaty.* From שָׁאַל *to ask, request, petition.*

מֹשֶׁה [*mōhsheh'*], Moses; (marg. Ex. ii. 10) *drawn out:* so it would appear from the tenor of that passage, because that Pharaoh's daughter says, " I drew *him* out of the water." But he (Moses) being the *object,* we naturally expect his name to have a *passive* signification; although from the verb מָשָׁה (to draw out) being used in such close connexion with it, we would, at first sight, be inclined to derive it immediately from it. But from the considerations, that, according to this derivation, the name has the form of an *active* participle, *drawing out,* instead of a *passive,* and that Pharaoh's daughter most likely spoke in the *Egyptian* tongue, the interpretation of Josephus (Antiq. ii. 9, § 6), with which the rendering of the Septuagint, Μωϋσῆς, fully agrees, is to be preferred, that its origin is Egyptian, signifying *drawn out of the water—* μω *water,* υσης *saved.* The verb מָשָׁה, in the sacred text, is then only to be considered as the nearest by which both the form of the name and its signification (from the Egyptian) could be expressed at once in the Hebrew.

מְשׁוֹבָב [*m'shōhvāhv'*], Meshobab; *brought back, restored.* Pual part. of שׁוּב *to return.*

מְשֵׁיזַבְאֵל [*m'shēhzav-ēhl'*], Meshezabeel; *delivered of God.* Aphel part. pass. of שׁזב in the Chaldee *to free, deliver.* For the form compare Dan. vi. 28.

מֶשֶׁךְ [*meh'shekh*], Meshech; *possession.* From מָשַׁךְ *to draw,* also *to lay hold, to hold.*

מָשָׁל [*māhshāhl'*], Mashal; once (1 Chr. vi. 59(74)) for מִשְׁאָל. Compare Josh. xxi. 30.

מְשֻׁלָּם [*m'shullāhm'*], Meshullam; *befriended.* Pual part. of שָׁלַם *to be at peace, in friendship with* any one.

מְשִׁלֵּמוֹת [*m'shillēhmōhth'*], Meshillemoth; *retributions, compensations.* From the Piel of שָׁלַם *to requite, recompense.*

מְשֶׁלֶמְיָה [*m'sheh-lem-yāh'*], Meshelemiah; (whom) *the Lord repays.* For מְשֶׁלֶמְיָה, Piel part. of שׁלם *to requite, repay,* and יָהּ *the Lord.*

מְשֶׁלֶמְיָהוּ [*m'sheh-lem-yāh'hoo*], id.

מְשַׁלֵּמִית [m'shillēhmeeth'], Meshillemith; *retribution, compensation.* Compare מְשִׁלֵּמוֹת, for which it stands, 1 Chr. ix. 12. Compare Neh. xi. 13.

מְשֻׁלֶּמֶת [m'shoolleh'meth], Meshullemeth; *befriended.* Feminine of מְשֻׁלָּם q. v.

מִשְׁמַנָּה [mishmannāh'], Mishmannah; *fatness.* From שָׁמֵן *to be,* or *become fat.* Compare Appellative מִשְׁמָן.

מִשְׁמָע [mishmāhng'], Mishma; *a hearing.* Perhaps, *obedience.* From שָׁמַע *to hear.* Compare Appellatives.

מִשְׁעָם [mish-ngāhm'], Misham; perhaps, *a cleansing.* Compare Appellative מִשְׁעִי.

מִשְׁרָעִי [mishrāh-ngee'], Mishraite; gentile noun of an unknown place. מִשְׁרָע *slippery place;* like the Chaldee משׁרועיתא.

מֶתֶג הָאַמָּה [meh'theg hāh-ammāh'], Metheg-ammah; (marg. 2 Sa. viii. 1, *bridle of Ammah*); both words are best taken as Appellatives, and rendered *the bridle of the mother-city;* i. e., (subdued) the metropolis. אַמָּה i. q. אֵם *mother.*

מְתוּשָׁאֵל [m'thooshāh-ēhl'], Methusael; *man of God.* מְתוּ *man,* as the construct state of מַת (from which the plural מְתִים *men* only is extant), [after the form רְעוּ אֵל (friend of God), from רֵעַ], אֲשֶׁר=שֶׁ sign of the genitive, and אֵל *God* (G.).

מְתוּשֶׁלַח [m'thoosheh'lakh], Methuselah; *man of darts* (G.). Compare the preceding. שֶׁלַח *dart.* Compare Appellatives.

מַתָּן [māttahn'], Mattan; *gift.* From נָתַן *to give.* Compare Appellatives.

מַתָּנָה [mattāhnāh'], Mattanah; id. Feminine of the same.

מַתְּנַי [matt'nah'y], Mattenai; *gift of the Lord.* Contracted from מַתַּנְיָה q. v.

מִתְנִי [mithnee'], Mithnite; gentile noun of some unknown place. מִתְנָה *gift,* from תָּנָה *to give gifts.*

מַתַּנְיָה [mattan-yāh'], Mattaniah; *gift of the Lord.* From מַתָּן *gift.* See above, and יָהּ *the Lord.*

מַתַּנְיָהוּ [mattan-yāh'hoo], id.

מִתְקָה [mithkāh'], Mithcah; *sweetness.* From מָתַק *to be,* or *become sweet.*

מִתְרְדָת [mithr'dāhth'], Mithredath; *given by Mithra.* Mithra, *the sun* (an object of worship among the Persians), collated with Persic (S.).

מַתַּתָּה [mattattāh'], Mattathah; contracted from מַתִּתְיָה q. v.

מַתִּתְיָה [mattath-yāh'], Mattithiah; *gift of the Lord.* From מָתַת *gift,* from נָתַן *to give,* and יָהּ *the Lord.* Compare Appellatives.

נ

נֹא [nōh'], No; *habitation,* or, *possession.* Either for נָאוֹ *habitation,* from נָאָה, or, according to Jablonski, by a collation with the Coptic, *possession.*

נֹא אָמוֹן [nōh āhmōhn], populous No (marg. Nah. iii. 8, *No-Amon*);

habitation, or, possession of Amon. Compare the preceding. אָמוֹן is the name of the chief Egyptian deity, compared with Jupiter. The signification of the word is uncertain, and therefore variously interpreted from the Egyptian, as, *father, pastor, drawing out, the light, glory*, &c.

נֹב [nōhv'], Nob; perhaps, *height, hill*. From נבה, collated with Arabic *to be high* (S.).

נְבוֹ [n'vōh'], Nebo; according to Gesenius, the planet *Mercury*, which the Chaldeans (Isa. xlvi. 1) and ancient Arabs worshipped. He derives the word from נָבָא; hence נְבוֹ for נְבוֹא i. q. נָבִיא *interpreter of the gods*.

נְבוּזַרְאֲדָן [n'voozarădāhn'], Nebuzaradan; *of Nebo chief* [and] *lord*, i. e., chief whom Mercury favours. Compounded of נְבוֹ (see the preceding, שַׂר=זַר *chief*, and אֲדָן i. q. אָדוֹן *Lord* (G.)

נְבוּכַדְנֶאצַּר [n'vookhadnēhtstsar'], and נְבוּכַדְרֶאצַּר [n'vookhadretstsar'], Nebuchadnezzar, Nebuchadrezzar; *of Mercury, the god, prince*, i. e., prince of god Mercury. Compounded of נְבוֹ q. v. *chodna*, or, *chodan*, according to the Persic *god*, and *zar*, prince (G.). But, according to others, quoted by Gesenius, *Nebo* (is) *the prince of the gods*; or, *Nebo* (is) *the god of fire*.

נְבוּשַׁזְבָּן [n'vooshazbāhn'], Nebushasban; *adorer of Mercury*, collated with the Persic (G.).

נָבוֹת [nāhvōht'], Naboth; *produce, fruit*. From נוב *to come forth, to sprout*; whence Appellatives נִיב and תְּנוּבָה *produce, fruit*.

נֹבַח [nōhvakh'], Nobah; *a barking*. From נבח *to bark*.

נִבְחַז [nivkhaz'], Nibhaz; perhaps, *lord of darkness* (G.).

נְבָט [n'vāht], Nebat; *aspect*. From נבט *to look, behold*.

נְבָיוֹת [n'vāh-yōhth'], Nebaioth, Nebajoth; *heights, hills*. From נָבָה *to be high*. Compare נֹב.

נָבָל [nāhvāhl'], Nabal; *faded, weak, foolish*, or, *impious*. From נבל *to fade, to faint, to act foolishly, wicked*. Compare Appellatives.

נְבַלָּט [n'vallāht'], Neballat; the signification is obscure.

נִבְשָׁן [nivshāhn'], Nibshan; *level and soft* (soil), collated with Arabic (S.).

נֹגַהּ [nōh'gah], Nogah; *splendour*. From נגה *to shine*. Compare Appellatives.

נָדָב [nāhdāhv'], Nadab; *liberal*, or, *noble*. Compare Appellative נָדִיב.

נְדַבְיָה [n'dav-yāh'], Nedabiah; *liberal*, or, *noble of the Lord*. Compare the preceding. According to Gesenius, (whom) *the Lord impels*.

נַהֲלֹל [nāh-hălōhl'], Nahalol; *a pasture*. From נהל *to lead*, spoken of leading of cattle; hence a place whither cattle is led for pasture.

נַהֲלָל [nah-hălāhl'], Nahalal; id.

נוּבַי [noovah'y], Kethib; perhaps, i. q. נֵיבַי Keri.

נוד (85) נטו

נוֹד [nōhd'], Nod ; *a wandering.* From נוּד *to wander.* Compare Appellatives.

נוֹדָב [nōhdāhv'], Nodab; *liberality.* From נָדַב. Compare נָדָב.

נוֹחָה [nōhkhāh'], Nohah ; *rest.* From נוּחַ *to rest.*

נְוָיֹת [n'vāh-yōhth'], Naioth ; *habitations.* According to Kethib, plural of Appellative נָוָה *habitation.*

נוּן [noon'], Nun ; *offspring,* i. q. Appellative נִין *offspring.* According to Gesenius, *fish;* as in the Chaldee and Syriac.

נוֹן [nōhn'], Non ; once (1 Chr. vii. 27) for נוּן.

נוֹעַדְיָה [nōh-ngad-yāh'], Noadiah; *the Lord meets with* (him). Niph. of יָעַד *to meet together,* and יָהּ *the Lord.*

נֹחַ [nōh'ăkh], Noah ; *rest, quiet.* From נוּחַ *to rest.*

נַחְבִּי [nakhbee'], Nahbi; *hidden.* Niphal of חָבָה *to hide.* Perhaps for נַחְבִּיָה *hidden,* i. e., *protected of the Lord.*

נַחוּם [nakhoom'], Nahum; *consolatory.* From נָחַם, in the Piel, *to comfort, console.* Comp. רחום, from רָחַם.

נְחוּם [n'khoom'], Nehum ; *comforted.* Compare the preceding.

נָחוֹר [nāhkhōhr'], Nahor; *snorting.* From an obsolete נחר, whence Appellative נַחַר *a snorting.*

נְחַלִיאֵל [nahkhălee-ēhl'], Nehaliel; *valley of God.* According to others, *brook of God.* From נַחַל *a valley,* or, *brook,* and אֵל *God.*

נֶחֱלָמִי [nehkhělāhmee'], Nehelamite ; *patronymic of some unknown* נֶחֱלָם *strengthened.* Niphal of חָלַם *to be strong.*

נַחַם [nah'kham], Naham ; *consolation.* From נָחַם, in the Piel, *to console, comfort.*

נְחֶמְיָה [n'khem-yāh'], Nehemiah ; (whom) *the Lord comforts.* Compare the preceding.

נַחֲמָנִי [nahkhămāhnee'], Nahamani; *consolatory.* From נָחַם. Compare Appellative רַחֲמָנִי.

נַחֲרַי [nahkhăray'], and נַחְרַי [nakhray'], Naharai ; *snorer.* From נָחַר *to snort, snore,* with adjectival יִ.

נָחָשׁ [nāhkhāhsh'], Nahash ; *serpent.* Compare Appellatives.

נַחְשׁוֹן [nakhshōhn'], Nahshon, Naashon ; *enchanter.* From נָחַשׁ, in Piel, *to practise enchantment.* Compare Appellative נַחַשׁ *enchantment.*

נְחֻשְׁתָּא [n'khooshtāh'], Nehushta ; *brass.* Compare Appellative נְחֹשֶׁת.

נְחֻשְׁתָּן [n'khooshtāhn'], Nehushtan; (marg. 2 Ki. xviii. 4) *a piece of brass.* Commonly taken as an adjective, *brasen,* i. e., *brasen serpent;* denom. of נְחֹשֶׁת *brass.*

נַחַת [nah'khath], Nahath ; *rest, quiet.* From נוּחַ *to rest,* or נָחַת.

נְטוֹפָתִי see נְטֹפָתִי.

נִיבַי [nēhvah'y], Nebai; perhaps, bearing fruit (G.). Compare Apellative נִיב produce, fruit.

נָיוֹת [nāh-yōhth'], Naioth; habitations. From נָוָה i. q. נָוֶה habitation.

נִינְוֵה [neen'vēh'], Nineveh. Commonly supposed to stand for נִין נָוֶה habitation of Ninus; according to Greek writers, the builder of Nineveh; and, on account of Gen. x. 8 (compare marg.), some try to find the name Ninus again in the word נִמְרֹד, which is indeed devoid of all probability.

נְכֹה [n'khōh'], Necho; as the name of an Egyptian king, its signification ought doubtless to be looked for in the Egyptian tongue.

נָכוֹן [nāhkhōhn'], Nachon; established. Niph. part. of כּוּן to stand, be erect.

נְמוּאֵל [n'moo-ēhl'], Nemuel; found Num. xxvi. 12; and, for Num. xxvi. 12, we find in Gen. xlvi. 12, Ex. vi. 15, and 1 Chr. iv. 24, יְמוּאֵל, which see; so that it is very likely that both are alike in signification.

נְמוּאֵלִי [n'moo-ēhlee'], Nemuelite; patronymic of the same.

נִמְרָה [nimrāh'], Nimrah; Num. xxxii. 3. For the fuller name, בֵּית נִמְרָה Num. xxxii. 36, and Josh. xiii. 27, q. v.

נִמְרֹד & נִמְרוֹד [nimrōhd'], Nimrod; perhaps, rebel. According to some, let us revolt! From מָרַד to rebel. Compare also נִינְוֵה.

נִמְרִים [nimreem'], Nimrim; perhaps, better Nimrites; as gentile noun of בֵּית נִמְרָה, or, בֵּית נִ׳.

נִמְשִׁי [nimshee'], Nimshi; drawn out, saved. For נִמְשֶׁה (G.), Niphal of מָשָׁה to draw out.

נִסְרֹךְ [nisrōhkh'], Nisroch; great eagle (G.).

נֹחַ [nōh-ngāh'], Noah; motion, or, quaking. From נוּעַ to move.

נֵעָה [neh-ngāh'], Neah; id.

נְעִיאֵל [n'ngee-ēhl'], Neiel; a shutting up of God; i. e., a place shut up of God, greatly fortified, for נְעִיל אֵל, from נָעַל to bolt, or bar (S.). According to others, for נְעִים אֵל pleasantness, favour of God.

נַעַם [nāh'-ngam], Naam; pleasantness. From נָעֵם to be pleasant.

נַעֲמָה [nah-ngămāh], Naamah; pleasant. Compare the preceding.

נָעֳמִי [no-ngŏmee'], Naomi; my pleasantness (G.). From נֹעַם pleasantness, with suffix.

נַעֲמִי [nah-ngămee'], Naamite; patronymic of the following.

נַעֲמָן [nah-ngămahn'], Naaman; pleasant. From נָעֵם to be pleasant, with adjectival וָ׳.

נַעֲמָתִי [nah-ngămāhthee'], Naamathite; gentile noun of some unknown place, נַעֲמָה pleasantness.

נַעֲרָה [nah-ngărāh'], Naarah; maiden. Compare Appellatives.

נַעֲרַי [nah-ngăray'], Naarai; *youthful*. From נַעַר *a youth*.

נְעַרְיָה [n'ngar-yāh'], Neariah; *servant of the Lord*. For נַעַרְיָה, from נַעַר *youth, boy, servant*, and יָה *the Lord*.

נַעֲרָן [nah-ngărāhn'], Naaran; *juvenile* (G.). Compare the preceding.

נֹף [nohph], Noph; see מֹף.

נֶפֶג [neh'pheg], Nepheg; *sprout*. From נָפַג, according to the Arabic, *to come forth* (S.).

נְפוּסִים [n'phooseem'], Nephusim; *expansions*. From נָפַס, in the Syriac and Chaldee, *to expand* (G.).

נֹפַח [nōh'phakh], Nophah; *blast*. From נָפַח *to blow*.

נְפִיסִים [n'pheeseem'], Kethib for נְפוּסִים.

נָפִישׁ [nāhpheesh'], Naphish; *increased*. From נפשׁ, in the Chaldee, *to increase*. According to the Syriac use of the word, *recreation* (G.), from נָפַשׁ, in the Niphal, *to take breath*.

מֵי נִפְתּוֹחַ see נִפְתּוֹחַ.

נַפְתֻּחִים [naphtookheem'], Naphtuhim; gentile noun of נַפְתֻּחַ, the name of some region no where occurring in Scripture.

נַפְתָּלִי [naphtāhlee'], Naphtali; (marg. Gen. xxx. 8) *my wrestling*. From פָּתַל, in the Niphal, *to wrestle*.

נְצִיב [n'tseev'], Nezib; *station, post*.

From *to set, put, place*. Compare Appellatives.

נְצִיחַ [n'tsee'ăkh], Neziah; *conquered*. A passive form of נָצָה, in the Hebrew not used in Kal; according to Syriac, *to conquer*. Compare Chaldee נְצָה.

נֶקֶב [neh'kev], Nekeb; *cavern*. From נָקַב *to hollow out, excavate, bore*.

נְקוֹדָא [n'kōhdāh], Nekoda; *marked*. Compare Appellative נָקֹד *marked with spots, spotted*.

נֵר [nēhr'], Ner; *light, lamp*. From נוּר. Compare Appellatives.

נֵרְגַל [nēhrgal'], Nergal; according to Gesenius, by a collation with the Arabic, *Mars, the god of war*.

נֵרְגַל שַׁרְאֶצֶר [nēhrgal shar-ēh'tser], Nergal-sharezer; *Mars, prince of fire*. Compare the preceding, and שַׁרְאֶצֶר.

נֵרִיָה [nēhriy-yāh'], Neriah; *light*, or, *lamp of the Lord*. Compounded of נֵר *light*. Compare Appellatives, and יָה *the Lord*.

נֵרִיָהוּ [nēhriy-yāh'hoo], id.

נָתָן [nāhthāhn'], Nathan; *given*, i. e., *gift*. From נָתַן *to give*. For the passive signification, compare חָלָל and שָׁלָל.

נְתַן־מֶלֶךְ [n'than meh'lekh], Nathan-melech; *gift of the king*. Compare the preceding, and מֶלֶךְ.

נְתַנְאֵל [n'than-ēhl'], Nethaniel; *gift of God*. Compare נָתַן and אֵל.

נְתַנְיָה [n'than-yāh'], Nethaniah; gift of the Lord.

נְתַנְיָהוּ [n'than-yāh'hoo], id.

ס

סְבָא [s'vāh'], Seba; perhaps, *man*. Collated with the Æthiopic (G.).

סְבָאִים [s'vāheem'], Sabeans; gentile noun of the preceding.

סִבְּכַי [sibb'khah'y], Sibbechai; *sambuca-player*. From סַבְּכָא, in the Chaldee, *a sambuca*, a stringed instrument of music.

סִבְרַיִם [sivrah'-yim], Sibraim; *two-fold hope*. Dual of סֵבֶר, from סבר, in the Chaldee, *to hope*.

סַבְתָּה & סַבְתָּא [savtāh'], Sabtah; *a striking*, i. e., *terror*. From סבת, in the Arabic, *to strike*; also, *to be astonished* (S.).

סַבְתְּכָא [savt'khāh'], Sabtechah; *great terror* (S.). Compare the preceding, of which the first part of the word consists, כָּא, from כָּאָה, supposed to be i. q. נָכָה *to strike, smite*.

סְדֹם [s'dōhm'], Sodom; its proper signification is not well ascertained.

סוֹא [sōh'], So; *sublime. lifted up*. Collated with the Hebrew נָשָׂא and the Coptic (S.).

סוֹדִי [sōhdee'], Sodi; *confidant*. Compare Appellative סוֹד *familiar intercourse, a secret*. According to Gesenius, for סוֹדִיָה *confidant of the Lord*.

סוּחַ [soo'ăkh], Suah; perhaps, *sprout*, i. q. Appellative שִׂיחַ.

סוֹתַי [sōhtah'y], Sotai; *departure*. From שׂוּט i. q. שׂטה and שָׁמָה *to give way, turn away, depart*. Or, perhaps, *departure of the Lord*, י., the Lord. Compare אֲחֻזִי.

סְוֵנֵה [s'vēhnēh'], Syene; (marg. Eze. xxix. 10) Seveneh; *opening, key*. Collated with the Coptic (Champollion by Gesenius).

סוּסִי [soosee'], Susi; *horseman*. Compare Appellative סוּס *a horse*. According to others, *joyous*; סוּס for שׂוּשׂ.

סוּף [sooph], Red sea (Deu. i. 1). Marg. Suph; *reed, rush*. Compare Appellatives.

סִיחוֹן [seekhōhn'], Sihon; *sweeping away*; i. e., warrior sweeping all before him (G.). From סוּחַ *to sweep away*.

סִין [seen], Sin; *mire*, i. q. Chaldee סִין.

סִינַי [seenah'y], Sinai; *miry*. Compare the preceding.

סִינִי [seenee'], Sinite; the name of a people, from סִין, probably the same in signification as above.

סִיסְרָא [sees'rāh'], Sisera; *battle-array*. Collated with the Syriac (G.).

סִיעָא [see-ngāh'], Sia; *company, assembly*. Thus in the Syriac (S.).

סִיעֲהָא [see-ngăhāh'], Siaha; id. The הָא, Simonis supposes to be the Persic plural form.

סֻכּוֹת [sookkōhth'], Succoth; *booths*. Plural of Appellative סֻכָּה.

סֻכּוֹת בְּנוֹת [sookkōhth' b'nōhth'], Succoth-benoth; *booths of the daughters*. Plural of סֻכָּה and בַּת. Compare Appellatives. See 2 Ki. xvii. 30. *Tents*, in which their *daughters* prostituted themselves.

סֻכִּיִּים [sookkiy-yeem'], Sukkiims; *dwellers in tents*. Denom. of סֻכָּה a *tent*.

סְכָכָה [s'khāhkhāh'], Secacah; *enclosure, fence*. From סָכַךְ *to hedge, fence*.

סִלָּא [sillāh'], Silla; *a way, raised way*. From סָלַל *to cast up* (as a way). Compare Appellative מְסִלָּה.

סֶלֶד [seh'led], Seled; either, *exultation, hardness, burning*, or, *supplication*, according as it may be derived either from the Arabic, Chaldee, or Rabbinic. Nor is the signification of the verb סָלַד, from which this name is to be derived, in its only occurrence of Job vi. 10, quite certain, as it has been variously interpreted, according to these different significations.

סָלוּא [sāhloo'], Salu; *elevated*. Part. pass. of סָלָא *to lift up*.

סָלֻא, סָלוּ & סַלּוּא [salloo'], Sallu; *elevation*. Compare the preceding.

סַלַּי [sallay'], Sallai; *elevated, exalted*. From סָלָה *to lift up, raise*.

סַלְכָה [salkhāh'], Salcah; perhaps, *a wandering*. Compare Gesenius under the obsolete סלך. According to the Arabic, *to move along, move about, to go*.

סֶלַע [seh'lang], Sela, Selah; *rock*. Compare Appellatives.

סֶלַע הַמַּחְלְקוֹת [seh'lang hammakhl'kōhth'], Sela-hammahlekoth; (marg. 1 Sa. xxiii. 28) *rock of division*. Compare the preceding, and Appellative מַחֲלֹקֶת *division*.

סַמְגַּר־נְבוּ [samgar-n'voo'], Samgar-nebo; perhaps, *sword of Mercury*. The first of these words is collated with the Persic, and the second is i. q. נְבוֹ q. v. (G.).

סְמַכְיָהוּ [s'makh-yāh'hoo], Semachiah; (whom) *the Lord sustains*. Pret. of סָמַךְ *to uphold, sustain*, and יְהוֹ *the Lord*.

סְנָאָה [s'nāh-āh'], Senaah, Hassenaah; *high, exalted*. Collated with the Arabic (S.). Or, perhaps, *thorny* (spinosa), סָנָא i. q. סָנָה (Gesen. in Thes.).

סְנֻאָה see סְנוּאָה.

סַנְבַלָּט [sanvallāht'], Sanballat; collated with the Persic, *praised by the army*; but with the Sanscrit, *giving strength to the army* (Bohlen, by Gesenius, in Thes.).

סֶנֶה [seh'neh], Seneh; *thorn-bush*. Compare Appellative סְנֶה; but here (1 Sa. xiv. 4) it is סֶנֶה, as occurring in pause. Compare מֶרִי, in pause.

סְנֻאָה & סְנוּאָה [s'noo-āh'], Senuah; *hated*. Part. pass. of סָנָא, probably i. q. שָׂנֵא *to hate*. Compare also סְנָאָה above, as there is doubtless some connection between *to be thorny*, and, *to be hated*, or, *hateful*.

סַנְחֵרִיב [sankhēhreev'], Sennacherib ; *conqueror of armies.* Collated with the Sanscrit (Bohlen, by Gesenius in Thes.).

סַנְסַנָּה [*sansannāh'*], Sansannah ; *palm-branch.* Compare Appellative סַנְסִנִּים *palm-branches.*

סִסְמַי [*sismay'*], Sisamai ; its signification is obscure.

סַף [*saph'*], Saph ; *threshold.* Compare Appellatives. According to Simonis, *extended, long, tall.* Collated with Æthiopic.

סִפַּי [*sippay'*], Sippai ; stands, 1 Chr. xx. 4, for the preceding סַף, 2 Sa. xxi. 18.

סְפָר [*s'phāhr'*], Sephar ; *conspicuous.* Collated with the Arabic, a mountain in Arabia, from which the city (Gen. x. 30) takes its name (S.). According to the Hebrew, *a numbering, census.* Compare Appellatives.

סְפָרַד [*s'phāhrad'*], Sepharad ; *separated tract,* or, *region.* From סְפָר, in the Chaldee, *tract of country,* and פרד *to separate* (S.). But compare the preceding.

סְפָרְוַיִם [*s'pharvah'-yim*], Sepharvaim ; according to Hiller, by Simonis, for סְפַר פַּרְוַיִם, i. e., *mount Sephar,* which is bordering on *Parvaim,* an Arabian region. Compare פַּרְוַיִם.

סְפָרְוִים [*s'pharveem'*], Sepharvites ; gentile noun of the preceding.

סְפָרִים [*s'phahreem'*], in Kethib (Eng. version, in 2 Ki. xvii. 31, *Sepharvaim,* according to Keri) ; perhaps, a gentile noun of סְפָר.

סֹפֶרֶת [*sōhpheh'reth*], Sophereth ; *scribe.* Part. fem. of סָפַר. Compare Appellatives.

סַרְגּוֹן [*sargōhn'*], Sargon ; perhaps, *prince of the sun,* collated with the Persic. Thus, Gesenius in his Manuale, but he abandons this interpretation in his Thesaurus. According to Simonis, *just and merciful prince ;* from סַר *prince,* and Syriac גנא *justice, clemency.*

סֶרֶד [*seh'red*], Sered ; *fear.* From שרד, in the Syriac, *to fear, to tremble* (G.).

סַרְדִּי [*sardee'*], Sardite ; patronymic of the preceding.

סְרָה [*seerāh'*], Sirah ; *a going back, retiring.* From סור *to turn away,* or, *back, to depart.*

סִתּוּר [*s'thoor'*], Sether ; *hidden.* Passive form of סָתַר *to hide.*

סִתְרִי [*sithree'*], Zithri ; *protection of the Lord,* סִתְרִיָה (G.). From סֵתֶר *a hiding, covering, protection.* Compare Appellatives.

ע

עֶבֶד [*ngeh'ved'*], Ebed ; *servant.* Compare Appellatives.

עַבְדָּא [*ngavdāh'*], Abda ; id., in a Chaldee form.

עֹבֵד אֱדוֹם [*ngōhvēhd' ĕdōbm'*], Obed-edom ; *serving Edom.* The first word as a Participle of עָבַד *to work, to serve.*

עַבְדְּאֵל [*ngavd'ēhl'*], Abdeel ; *ser-*

vant of God. From עֶבֶד and אֵל. Compare Appellatives.

עַבְדּוֹן [ngavdōhn'], Abdon; servile. Adj. of עָבַד to work, to serve.

עַבְדִּי [ngavdee'], Abdi; servant of the Lord, for עַבְדִיָה, from עֶבֶד and יָה. Compare Appellative.

עַבְדִּיאֵל [ngavdee-ēhl'], Abdiel; servant of God. Compare the preceding.

עֹבַדְיָה [ngōhvad-yāh'], Obadiah; servant of the Lord. Compounded of עָבַד, part. of עָבַד to serve, and יָה the Lord.

עֹבַדְיָהוּ [ngōhvad-yāh'hoo], id.

עֶבֶד מֶלֶךְ [ngeh'ved meh'lekh], Ebed-melech; servant of the king. Compare Appellatives.

עֶבֶד נְגוֹ & עֲבֵד נְגוֹ [ngăvēhd' n'gōh'], Abed-nego; servant of Nego. עֶבֶד Chaldee for Hebrew עֶבֶד, and נְגוֹ the name of a Chaldean divinity, supposed to be i. q. נְבוֹ Mercury.

עֵבֶר [ngēh'ver], Eber; a passing over, passage, or, a region on the other side. Compare Gen. xi. 2 and x. 24, 25. From עָבַר to pass over. Compare Appellatives.

עִבְרִי [ngivree'], Hebrew; patronymic (according to some gentile noun) of עֵבֶר.

עִבְרִיָה [ngivriy-yāh'], Hebrewess, Hebrew woman; fem. of the preceding.

עֲבָרִים [ngăvāhreem'], Abarim; regions on the other side. Compare עֵבֶר.

עֶבְרוֹן [ngevrōhn'], Hebron; passage. From עָבַר to pass over.

עַבְרֹנָה [ngavrōhnāh'], Ebronah; id.

עֶגְלָה [ngeglāh'], Eglah; heifer. Compare Appellative.

עֶגְלוֹן [ngeglōhn'], Eglon; vitulinus (of, or, belonging to a calf), denom. of Appellative עֵגֶל, or עֶגְלָה (G.).

עָדָה [ngahdāh'], Adah; ornament, in the verb, to adorn.

עִדּוֹ & עִדּוֹא [ngiddōh'], Iddo; timely. Compare Gesenius on the Appellative עִדִּים.

עֲדִיאֵל [ngădee-ēhl'], Adiel; ornament of God. Compare Appellative עֲדִי, from עָדָה to adorn, and אֵל God.

עֲדָיָה [ngădāh-yāh'], Adaiah; (whom) the Lord has adorned. Pret. of עָדָה, compare the preceding.

עֲדָיָהוּ [ngădāh-yāh'hoo], id.

עָדִין [ngāhdeen'], Adin; tender, delicate. From עָדַן, compare Appellatives.

עֲדִינָא [ngădeenāh'], Adina; id.

עֲדִינוֹ הָעֶצְנִי [ngădeenōh' hāh-ngeznee'], Adino the Eznite; according to the rendering of the English version, 2 Sa. xxiii. 8, the first would be a proper name, and the second, a patronymic of עֶצֶן; but, according to some, both would form one patronymic, i. e., the Adino-eznite, from עֲדִינוֹ עֶצֶן whose pleasure (is) the spear. For עָדִין (with suff.), comp. עָדַן, and the latter word is collated with the Arabic. But, on account of the parallel passage, 1 Chr. xi. 11, where, instead of these words, we find עוֹרֵר אֶת חֲנִיתוֹ *lifted up his spear*, Simonis takes these as appellatives, and reading with the Kethib (הָעֶצְנוֹ), he renders it, *whose striking with his spear* (was) against, &c. The sense of the first of these words he derives from the Arabic.

עֲדִיתַיִם [*ngădeethah'-yim*], Adithaim; *double ornament*. Dual of עֲדִית i. q. Appellative עֲדִי.

עַדְלִי [*ngadlah'y*], Adlai; *justice of the Lord*. For עֲדַלְיָה ,עָדָל *justice*, collated with the Arabic (S.).

עֲדֻלָּם [*ngădoollāhm'*], Adullam; *justice of the people*. For עָדָל עָם (G.), compare the preceding.

עֲדֻלָּמִי [*ngădoollāhmee'*], Adullamite; gentile noun of the preceding.

עֵדֶן & עֶדֶן [*ngeh'den*], Eden; *delight, pleasure*. Compare Appellative.

עַדְנָא [*ngadnāh'*], Adna; id.

עַדְנָה [*ngadnāh'*], Adnah; id.

עַדְעָדָה [*ngadngāhdāh'*], Adadah; *festival*, like the Syriac (G.).

עֶדֶר & עֵדֶר [*ngeh'der*], Eder, and Ader (from the pause in the Hebrew); *flock*. Compare Appellatives.

עַדְרִיאֵל [*ngadree-ēhl'*], Adriel; *flock of God*. From עֵדֶר and אֵל, compare Appellatives.

עַוָּא [*ngavvāh'*], Ava; *an overturning*, i. q. Appellative עַוָּה.

עוֹבֵד [*ngōhvēhd'*], Obed; *serving*, or, *worshipping*. Part. of עָבַד *to serve*, also, *to worship*.

עוֹבָל [*ngōhvāhl'*], Obal; *stripped of foliage*. From עָבַל, collated with the Arabic (G.).

עוֹג [*ngōhg'*], Og; perhaps, contracted for עָנֶב, עֲנָק, i. e. *long-necked in stature, gigantic*. Compare עֲנָק (G.).

עוֹדֵד [*ngōhdēhd'*], Oded; *setting up again, restoring*. For מְעוֹדֵד Part. Piel of עוּד.

עִוָּה [*ngivvāh'*], Ivah; *overturning*, i. q. Appellative עַוָּה.

עַוִּים [*ngavveem'*], Avites, Avim, Avims; gentile noun of the preceding, and also with the article ה the name of a town, in which latter it may have the signification of *ruins*.

עַוִּית [*ngăveeth'*], Avith; *ruins*, lit. overturned, from עָוָה *to bend*; and compare Appellative עַוָּה.

עוֹלָם [*ngōhlāhm'*], in Kethib, *long duration*. Compare Appellatives, where the Keri is עֵילָם q. v.

עוֹפַי [*ngōhphah'y*], in Kethib for עֵיפַי in Keri.

עוּץ [*ngoots'*], Uz; *counsel*. Either from עוּץ i. q. יָעַץ *to counsel*; or, from the latter, עוּץ standing for יְעוּץ. Thus as the name of man (Gen. x. 23; xxii. 21; xxxvi. 28). But Gesenius only having regard to this word as the name of a country, gives it signification, by collation with the Arab. *light sandy soil*.

עוּתַי [*ngoothah'y*], Uthai; (whom)

the Lord succours. For עוּתְיָה עוּתִיָה, from עוּת i.q. עוּשׁ to hasten, to hasten to one's assistance, to succour (G.).

עֻזָּא [ngoozzāh'], Uzza; strength. From עָזַז to be strong.

עַזְבּוּק [ngazbook'], Azbuk; strength (is) exhausted. עַז strength, from עָזַז to be, or, become strong; בּוּק emptied, exhausted, as part. pass. of בּוּק.

עַזְגָּד [ngazgāhd'], Azgad; strong in fortune. עַז here as an adjective. Compare Appellatives, and גָּד.

עַזָּה [ngazzāh'], Gazah, Azzah; strong, fortified. Adj. f. of עַז, compare Appellatives.

עֻזָּה [ngoozzāh'], Uzzah, Uzza; strength, i. q. עֻזָּא.

עֲזוּבָה [ngăzoovāh'], Azubah; left, forsaken. Part. pass. fem. of עָזַב to leave, forsake.

עַזּוּר [ngazzoor'], Azur, Azzur; helper. From עָזַר to help.

עֲזָז [ngāhzāhz'], Azaz; strong. From עָזַז to be, or, become strong.

עֲזַזְיָהוּ [ngăzaz-yāh'hoo], Azaziah; (whom) the Lord strengthens. From עָזַז, here translated to strengthen abbreviated from יְהוָֹה the Lord. יהו

עֻזִּי [ngoozzee'], Uzzi; might of the Lord. Abbreviated from עֻזִּיָה. Or, perhaps, simply, strong.

עֻזִּיָּא [ngoozziy-yāh'], Uzzia; might of the Lord, for עֻזִּיָה.

עֲזִיאֵל [ngazzee-ēhl'], Aziel; might of God.

עֻזִּיאֵל [ngoozzee-ēhl'], Uzziel; might of God. עֹז strength, might; אֵל God. Compare Appellatives.

עָזִּיאֵלִי [ngozzee-ēhlee'], Uzzielite; patronymic of the preceding.

עֻזִּיָּה [ngoozziy-yāh'], Uzziah; might of the Lord. From עֹז strength, might. Comp. Appellatives, and יָהּ the Lord.

עֻזִּיָּהוּ [ngoozziy-yāh'hoo], id.

עֲזִיזָא [ngăzeezāh'], Aziza; strong. From עָזַז to be, or, become strong.

עַזְמָוֶת [ngazmāh'veth], Azmaveth; strong (as) death. From עַז and מָוֶת, compare Appellatives. As the name of a man, and also the name of a place, for which latter it is also found (Neh. vii. 28).

*בֵּית עַזְמָוֶת [Beth-ngazmāh'veth], Beth-azmaveth, i.e., house, or, dwelling of Azmaveth.

עַזָּן [ngazzāhn'], Azzan; strong. From עַז, with formative ן, for וֹ.

עֲזֵקָה [ngăzēhkāh'], Azekah; a field dug over, broken up. From עָזַק to dig up, or, over (G.).

עֶזֶר & עֵזֶר [ngēh'zer], Ezer; help. From עָזַר to help. Comp. Appellatives.

עֶזְרָא [ngezrāh'], Ezra; id.

עֲזַרְאֵל [ngăzar-ēhl'], Azareel; (whom) God has helped, or, help of God. Either Pret. of עָזַר to help, or, construct. עֶזֶר help, and אֵל God.

---

* This is noticed here on account of its being omitted in its proper order, under בּ.

עֶזְרָה [ngezrāh'], Ezra; *help*. Compare Appellatives, and also the preceding.

עֶזְרִי [ngezree'], Ezri; *help of the Lord*, abbreviated from עֲזַרְיָה, from עֵזֶר *help*, and יָהּ *the Lord*.

עַזְרִיאֵל [ngazree-ēhl'], Azriel; *help of God*. From עֵזֶר *help*, and אֵל *God*.

עֲזַרְיָה [ngăzar-yāh'], Azariah; (whom) *the Lord has helped*, or, *help of the Lord*. Compare עֲזַרְאֵל.

עֲזַרְיָהוּ [ngăzar-yāh'hoo], id.

עַזְרִיקָם [ngazreekāhm'], Azrikam; *the helper is risen*. From עֵזֶר *help*, often used as a concrete *helper* (compare Psa. xxxiii. 20; lxx. 6, &c.), and קָם, Pret. or Part. of קוּם *to arise*. According to others, *help against the enemy*, קָם *one arising* in a hostile manner, compare Psa. xviii. 40.

עַזָּתִי [ngazzāhthee'], Gazathite, Gazite; gentile noun of עַזָּה.

עֲטָרָה [ngătahrāh'], Atarah; *crown*. From עָטַר *to surround*. Compare Appellatives.

עֲטָרוֹת [ngătāhrōhth'], Ataroth; *crowns*; perhaps, *circumvallations*. Plural of the preceding.

עַטְרוֹת אַדָּר [ngatrōhth' addāhr'], Ataroth-addar, Ataroth-adar; *crowns*, perhaps, *circumvallation of Adar*, probably the builder of the same. See the preceding, and אַדָּר.

עַטְרוֹת בֵּית יוֹאָב [ngatrōhth' bēhth yōh-āhv'], Ataroth the house of Joab (marg. 1 Chr. ii. 54), *crowns*, perhaps, *circumvallation of the house of Joab*. Compare the preceding, Appellative בַּיִת, and proper name יוֹאָב.

עַטְרוֹת שׁוֹפָן [ngatrōhth' shōhphāhn'], Atroth, Shophan (as two different names); *crowns*, perhaps, *circumvallations of Shophan*. שׁוֹפָן probably, *a bruising*, from שׁוּף.

עַי [ngah'y], Ai, Hai; *heap of ruins*, i. q. Appellative עִי *a heap*, from עָוָה in the Piel, *to overturn, destroy*.

עַיָּא [ngay-yāh'], Aija; id.

עֵיבָל [ngēhvāhl'], Ebal; *stripped of foliage*. From עָבַל, collated with the Arabic, *to strip a tree of its leaves* (G.).

עִיּוֹן [ngiy-yōhn'], Ijon; *ruin*. Compare עִי.

עַיּוּת [ngay-yooth'], id. only in Kethib, 1 Chron. i. 46, for עֲוִית.

עֵיטָם [ngēhtāhm'], Etam; *place of ravenous beasts*. From עַיִט *a ravenous beast*, with adjectival ם.

עִיִּים [ngiy-yeem'], Iim; *heaps of ruins*. Plural of Appellative עִי, compare עַי above.

עִיֵּי הָעֲבָרִים [ngiy-yēh hāh-ngăvāhreem'], Ije-abarim (marg. Num. xxxiii. 44, *heaps of Abarim*); compare the preceding, and עֲבָרִים above, the name of a mountain.

עִילַי [ngeelay'], Ilai; *supreme*. i. q. Chaldee Appellative עִלַּי (G.).

עֵילָם [ngēhlāhm'], Elam; *long duration*. i. q. Appellative עוֹלָם (S.). Compare עֵילוֹם, 2 Chron. xxxiii. 7.

עַיִן [ngah-'yin], Ain; fountain. Compare Appellatives.

עֵין גְּדִי [ngēhn g'dee'], En-gedi; fountain of the kid. Compare the preceding, and Appellative גְּדִי.

עֵין גַּנִּים [ngēhn ganneem'], En-gannim; fountain of gardens. See עַיִן above, and Appellative גַּן a garden.

עֵין דֹּר & עֵין דּוֹר, עֵין דֹּאר [ngēhn dōhr'], En-dor; fountain of (the place) Dor, or, fountain of the dwelling. Compare דּוֹר.

עֵין הַקּוֹרֵא [ngēhn hakkōhrēh'], En-hakkore (marg Jud. xv. 19, *the well of him that called*, or, *cried*). Compare עַיִן; the second is a participle of קָרָא to call, cry.

עֵין חַדָּה [ngēhn khaddāh'], En-haddah; sharp, i. e., quick fountain Compare עַיִן above, and Appellative חַד sharp.

עֵין חָצוֹר [ngēhn khāhtsōhr'], En-hazor; fountain of Hazor, or, near Hazor. Compare עַיִן & חָצוֹר.

עֵין חֲרֹד [ngēhn khărōhd'], well of Harod (Jud. vii. 1), or, fountain near Harod. Compare עַיִן & חֲרֹד.

עֵינַיִם [ngēhnah'-yim], the way side; (marg. Gen. xxxviii. 21, Enajim); two fountains. This is by most taken, not as an Appellative, but as the name of a place, supposed to be the same with the following.

עֵינָם [ngēhnāhm'], Enam; id. As a contracted Dual of the preceding.

עֵין מִשְׁפָּט [ngēhn mishpāht'], En-mishpat; fountain of judgment. Compare Appellatives.

עֵינָן [ngēhnāhn'], Enan; (oculatus) having eyes (G.). עַיִן eye, with adjectival ן; but this word in the compound חֲצַר עֵינָן, as the name of a place, stands as contracted Dual, for עֵינַיִן fountains, see under חֲצַר.

עֵין עֶגְלַיִם [ngēhn ngeglah'-yim], En-eglaim; fountain of two calves. Compare Appellatives עַיִן & עֵגֶל.

עֵין רֹגֵל [ngēhn rōhgēhl'], En-rogel; fuller's fountain. From עַיִן fountain, and רֶגֶל, Part. of רָגַל to tread, as garments with the feet, denom. of רֶגֶל a foot.

עֵין רִמּוֹן [ngēhn rimmōhn'], En-rimmon; fountain of (i. e. near) the pomegranates. Compare עַיִן & רִמּוֹן.

עֵין שֶׁמֶשׁ [ngēhn sheh'mesh], En-shemesh; fountain of the sun. Compare Appellatives.

עֵין תַּנִּים [ngēhn tanneem'], dragon-well (Neh. ii. 13); according to other, fountain of jackals. Compare Appel.

עֵין תַּפּוּחַ [ngēhn tappoo'ăkh], En-tappuah; fountain of (i. e. near) Tappuah. Compare תַּפּוּחַ.

עֵיפָה [ngēhphāh'], Ephah; weariness. From עוּף to faint, be weary.

עֵיפַי [ngēhphay'], Ephai; weary. Compare the preceding.

עִיר [ngeer'], Ir; city. Compare Appellatives.

עִירָא [ngeerāh'], Ira; id.

עִירָד [*ngeerāhd'*], Irad; perhaps i.q. Appellative עָרוֹד *wild ass, onager.*

עִירוּ [*ngee'roo*], Iru; its signification is doubtful.

עִירִי [*ngeeree'*], Iri; *citizen.* From עִיר *city.*

עִירָם [*ngeerāhm'*], Iram; id.

עִיר הַמֶּלַח [*ngeer hammeh'lekh*], city of Salt (Jos. xv. 62); compare Appellatives. This ought doubtless to have been given as a proper name.

עִיר נָחָשׁ [*ngeer nāhkhāhsh'*], Irnahash; *city of serpents.* Compare Appellatives.

עִיר שֶׁמֶשׁ [*ngeer sheh'mesh*], Irshemesh; *city of the sun.* Compare Appellatives.

עַיָּת [*ngay-yāhth'*], Aiath; *heap of ruins.* Compare עִי.

עַכְבּוֹר [*ngakhbōhr'*], Achbor; *mouse.* Compare Appellative עַכְבָּר.

עַכּוֹ [*ngakkōh'*], Accho; *sand heated by the sun.* Collated with the Arabic (G.).

עֵמֶק עָכוֹר see ע׳.

עָכָן [*ngahkhāhn'*], Achan; *troubler.* From עָכַן, probably i.q. עָכַר *to trouble,* compare Jos. vii. 1 with 1 Chr. ii. 7.

עַכְסָה [*ngakhsāh'*], Achsah; *ankle-chain.* i.q. Appellative עֶכֶס an ornament fastened upon the ankles of females, rendered in the English Version, Isa. iii. 18, *tinkling ornaments.*

עָכָר [*ngāhkhāhr'*], Achar; *troubler.* From עָכַר *to afflict, trouble.*

עָכְרָן [*ngokhrāhn'*], Ocran; *troubled, afflicted.* Compare the preceding.

עֻלָּא [*ngoollāh'*], Ulla; *yoke.* For עֻלָּה, from the masculine עֹל.

עַלְוָה [*ngalvāh'*], Alvah, Aliah; *exaltation,* perhaps for concrete *exalted.* From עָלָה *to ascend, rise, increase.*

עַלְוָן [*ngalvāhn'*], Alvan; *exalted.* Compare the preceding.

עֵלִי [*ngēhlee'*], Eli; *foster-child of the Lord* (S.). For עֲלִיָּה, from עוּל *to suckle, nourish.*

עַלְיָה [*ngalyāh'*], Aliah, in Kethib (1 Chron. i. 51) for עַלְוָה, probably of the same signification, q. v.

עַלְיָן [*ngalyāhn'*], Alian; *exalted,* i.q. עַלְוָן above.

עַלְמוֹן [*ngalmōhn'*], Almon; *concealment.* From עָלַם *to hide, conceal.*

עַלְמוֹן־דִּבְלָתַיְמָה [*ngalmōhn divlāhthahymāh'*], Almon-diblathaim; *Almon towards Diblathaim.* For the first, see the preceding; and for the second, בֵּית דִּבְ׳.

עַלֶּמֶת [*ngalleh'meth*], Alemeth; stands, 1 Chron. vi. 45(60) for עַלְמוֹן Jos. xxi. 18.

עָלֶמֶת [*ngāhleh'meth*], Alemeth, Alameth; *a covering.* From עָלַם *to hide.*

עֻמָּה [*ngoommāh'*], Ummah; *conjunction.* From עָמַם, of which the derivatives עַם *with*, and the construct עֲמַת *with, by, near*, &c.

עַמּוֹן [*ngammōhn'*], Ammon ; i q. בֶּן־עַמִּי, compare Gen. xix. 38, viz. *son of my people, son of my kindred*, i. e. born of incest; from the noun עַם, with the syllable וֹן added, as קַדְמוֹן, from קֶדֶם, רִאשׁוֹן, from רֹאשׁ (Gesenius in Manuale).

עַמּוֹנִי [*ngammōhnee'*], Ammonite ; gentile noun of the same.

עַמּוֹנִית [*ngammōhneeth'*], Ammonitess, woman of Ammon ; feminine of the preceding.

עָמוֹס [*ngāhmōhs'*], Amos ; *bearer, carrier*. From עָמַס *to bear, carry*.

עָמוֹק [*ngāhmōhk'*], Amok ; *deep*. From עָמַק *to be deep*.

עַמִּיאֵל [*ngămmee-ēhl'*], Ammiel ; (of) *the people of God*. Compounded of עַם and אֵל, compare Appellatives.*

---

* In this compound and those following, Gesenius renders the word עַם by *kindred;* and this he again explains to mean *servant,* and all this because עַם is not only spoken of *a people and tribe,* but also of the *family race,* lineage of any one. For this he quotes Lev. xxi. 1, 4 ; xix. 16. But in neither of these passages does the word עָמָיו necessarily express any of the above significations, but rather the word *people* seems to be the most suitable. And, supposing the word meant here *family,* and then *kindred* in a collective sense, would it not be conjecturing too far to suppose it to mean in the end *a single kindred,* or *relative*—so as to interpret עַמִּינָדָב *kindred of the Giver,* עַמִּיאֵל *kindred of God,* i. e., servant or worshipper of God, and עַמִּישַׁדַּי *kindred,* i.e. servant *of the Almighty ?* Fürst (in Conc. Heb) gives *individuum* as the primary meaning of עַם;

עַמִּיהוּד [*ngammeehood'*], Ammihud ; (of) *the people of glory*. Compounded of עַם *people*, and הוֹד i. q. הוֹד *majesty, splendour,* compare Appellatives. According to Gesenius, for עַמִּי יְהוּד *kindred of Judah*, i. e., one of the tribe of Judah. Compare also אֲבִיהוּד, which Gesenius considers to be a similar contraction.

עַמִּיזָבָד [*ngammeezāhvāhd'*], Ammizadab ; (of) *the people of the Giver,* i. e., belonging to Him, who is the God of providence. From עַם *people,* זָבַד *to give, present with, endow*.

עַמִּינָדָב [*ngammeenāhdāhv'*], Amminadab ; (of) *the people of the liberal Giver,* i. e., of the Lord who gives liberally. Compare the preceding, and Appellative נָדִיב *giving willingly, liberally,* נָדָב here doubtless the same in signification.

עַמִּישַׁדַּי [*ngammeeshaddah'y*], Ammishadai ; (of) *the people of the Almighty*. Compare the preceding compounds, and שַׁדַּי.

עָמָל [*ngāhmāhl'*], Amal ; *labour, trouble*. Compare Appellatives.

עֲמָלֵק [*ngămāhlēhk'*], Amalek; the signification is not ascertained.

---

for a proof of which he brings the Talmudic עַם הָאָרֶץ (idiota, unus (?) ex plebe). But though this is used for a single individual, it is probably nothing else than a misusage of its primary collective sense, *people of the country* for *the common illiterate people*. He then thinks to find the same in these compound proper names, so that both evidently had an eye to the difficulty of these names, and thus tried to evade it in this unwarrantable way.

עֲמָלֵקִי [ngămāhlĕhkee'], Amalekite; gentile noun of the preceding.

עִמָּנוּאֵל [ngimmāhnoo-ēhl'], Immanuel; *God with us.* Compound of עִם with suff. and אֵל *God.*

עֲמַסְיָה [ngămas-yāh'], Amasiah; (whom) *the Lord bears.* Pret. of עָמַס *to bear,* and יָהּ *the Lord.* According to others, *burden of the Lord.*

עֲמָעָד [ngamngāhd'], Amad; *people of duration.* Compare Appellatives עַם and עַד.

עֵמֶק בְּרָכָה [ngēh'mek b'rāhkhāh'], *valley of Berachah* (marg. 2 Chr. xx. 26, *blessing*). Compare Appellatives.

עֵמֶק הַמֶּלֶךְ [ngēh'mek hammeh'lekh], *the king's dale* (Gen. xiv. 17; 2 Sa. xviii. 18). Compare Appellatives.

עֵמֶק עָכוֹר [ngēh'mek ngāhkhōhr'], *valley of Achor; the valley of him that causeth affliction.* עָכוֹר from עָכַר *to trouble, afflict.* Compare Josh. vii. 26.

עֵמֶק קָצִיץ [ngēh'mek k'tzeetz'], *valley of Keziz; valley of cutting off,* or, *of a person of that name.* From קָצַץ *to cut off.* According to others, for עֵ' קְצִיעָ *valley of cassia,* compare קְצִיעָה.

עֵמֶק רְפָאִים [ngēh'mek r'phāh-eem'], *valley of giants, valley of Rephaim;* the latter is doubtless the best rendering. *Rephaim* is the name of a people of gigantic stature, compare רְפָאִים.

עֲמֹרָה [ngămōhrāh'], Gomorrah; *abundance of water* (S.); probably, *immersion* (Gesenius in Thes.). Collated with the Arabic עמר *the water covered, there was much water.*

עָמְרִי [ngomree'], Omri; for עָמְרִיָה *servant of Jehovah,* from עמר, in the Arabic, *to serve.* Thus Gesenius in Manuale; but, in his Thesaurus, he proposes, "tiro Jova" *a novice with Jehovah,* also collated with the Arabic.

עַמְרָם [ngamrāhm'], Amram; (of) *the exalted people.* From עָם *people,* and רָם, participle of רוּם, *to be high.* According to Gesenius, *kindred of the High,* i.e., God. See note under עַמִּיאֵל.

עַמְרָמִי [ngamrāhmee'], Amramite; patronymic of the same.

עֲמָשָׂא [ngămāhsāh'], Amasa; *burden,* from עָמַשׂ i. q. עָמַס *to bear.*

עֲמָשַׂי [ngămāhsah'y], Amasai; *burdensome.* Compare the preceding.

עֲמַשְׂסַי [ngămashsah'y], Amashai; perhaps id.

עֲנָב [ngănāhv'], Anab; *cluster of grapes,* i. q. Appellative עֵנָב.

עֲנָה [ngănāh'], Anah; *answer,* sc. of prayer (G.), from עָנָה *to answer.*

עָנוּב [ngāhnoov'], Anub; *bound together.* Participle pass. of עָנַב, according to the Chaldee, *to bind together.*

עֲנוֹק [ngănōhk'], Anak; *long-necked, gigantic,* i. q. עֲנָק.

עֻנִּי [ngoonnee'], Unni; *depressed.* For מְעֻנֶּה (G.) Pual part. of עָנָה *to be depressed, afflicted.*

עֲנִי (99) עֶצֶם

עֲנָיָה [ngănāh-yāh'], Anaiah; (whom) the Lord answers. Pret. of עָנָה to answer, and יָהּ the Lord.

עָנִים [ngāhneem'], Anim; contracted for עֲיָנִים fountains.

עֲנֵם [ngāhnēhm'], Anem; two fountains. Supposed to be contracted for עֲנָיִם=עֵינַיִם two fountains.

עֲנָמִים [ngănāhmeem'], Anamim; the name of an unknown people, from עֲנָם or עָנָם. According to Simonis, as the name of a place, plenty of herds, collated with the Arabic.

עֲנַמֶּלֶךְ [ngănammeh'lekh], Anammelech; sheep-king. Compare the preceding.

עָנָן [ngāhnāhn'], Anan; cloud. Compare Appellatives.

עֲנָנִי [ngănāhnee'], Anani; apoc. for the following עֲנַנְיָה.

עֲנַנְיָה [ngănan-yāh'], Ananiah; (whom) the Lord covers, i. e., protects (G.). From עָנַן to cover, kindred with בָּנַן.

עֲנָק [ngănāhk'], Anak; long-necked, gigantic. Collated with the Arabic (G.).

עֲנָקִים [ngănāhkeem'], Anakim; patronymic of the same.

עָנֵר [ngāhnēhr'], Aner; the signification is uncertain.

עֲנָת [ngănāhth'], Anath; answer, sc. to prayer, from עָנָה to answer.

עֲנָתוֹת [ngănāhthōhth'], Anathoth; answers. Plural of the preceding.

עֲנְתֹתִי [nganthōhthee'], and עֲנַתֹּתִי [nyan-n'thōhthee'], of Anathoth, Antothite, Anethothite, Anetothite; gentile noun of the preceding.

עֲנְתֹתִיָּה [nganthōhthiy-yāh'], Antothijah; answer of the Lord. From עֲנָתוֹת above, and יָהּ the Lord.

עֹפֶל [ngōh'phel], Ophel; hill. Compare Appellatives.

עָפְנִי [ngophnee'], Ophnee; only Josh. xviii. 24, where it ought to be taken as a gentile noun, and rendered with the preceding words, כְּפַר הָעַמּוֹנִי וְהָעָפְנִי ('כ) the village of the Ammonite, and (the village) of the Ophnite. עָפֵן, in the Arabic and Syriac, to become mouldy.

עֵפֶר [ngūch'pher'], Epher; calf, young animal. Collated with the Arabic (G.).

עָפְרָה [ngophrāh'], Ophrah; female fawn. Feminine of Appellative עֹפֶר.

עֶפְרוֹן [ngephrōhn'], Ephron; vitulinus (of a calf). Compare עֵפֶר (G.).

עֶפְרַיִן [ngephrāh'-yin], Ephrain; two calves. Dual of עֵפֶר above.

עֶצְיוֹן גֶּבֶר [ngetz-yōhn' geh'ver], Ezion-geber; back-bone of a man. עֶצְיוֹן i. q. Appellative עָצֶה back-bone, and גֶּבֶר a man. Compare Appellatives.

עֶצֶם [ngeh'tzem], Ezem, Azem; strength, or, bone. Compare Appellatives, and the verb עָצַם to be strong.

עַצְמוֹן [ngatzmōhn'], Azmon; strong. Compare the preceding.

עָקוּב [ngakkoov'], Akkub; probably, *supplanter*. Compare יַעֲקוֹב.

עָקָן [ngăkāhn'], Akan (marg. Gen. xxxvi. 27, *Jaakan*); stands for יַעֲקָן, 1 Chr. i. 42, compare also Num. xxxiii. 1; Deu. x. 6.

עֵקֶר [ngēh'ker], Eker; *root, or, a sprout.* Compare Appellatives.

עֶקְרוֹן [ngekrōhn'], Ekron; *eradication.* From עָקַר *to root out*.

עֶקְרוֹנִי [ngekrōhnee'], Ekronite; gentile noun of the same.

עִקֵּשׁ [ngikkēhsh'], Ikkesh; *perverse.* From עָקַשׁ *to pervert.* Compare Appellatives.

עָר [ngāhr'], Ar; *city.* i. q. Appellative עִיר.

עֵר [ngēhr'], Er; *waking.* Participle of עוּר *to awake.*

עֲרָב [ngărāhv'], Arabia; *dry, sterile.* From עָרַב i. q. חָרַב, hence עֲרָבָה *a desert*, and חֲרָבָה *dry land*.

עֲרָבִי [ngărāhvee'], Arabian; gentile noun of the preceding.

עַרְבִי [ngarvee'], Arabian; id.

עַרְבָתִי [ngarvāhthee'], Arbathite; gentile noun of בֵּית הָעֲרָבָה.

עֲרָד [ngărāhd'], Arad; *wild ass, onager.* i. q. Appellative עָרוֹד.

עַרְעֵר & עֲרוֹעֵר [ngăroh-ngēhr'], Aroer; *ruins.* From עָרַר *to be naked*, in Poel, *to lay bare* as a foundation.

עֵרִי [ngēhree'], Eri; *watchful.* Participle of עוּר *to wake, watch*, with constructive י. According to Gesenius, for עֵרִיָה *watching*, i. e., *worshipping the Lord.*

עֵרָן [ngēhrāhn'], Eran; *watchful.* Compare the preceding.

עֵרָנִי [ngēhrāhnee'], Eranite; patronymic of the same.

עַרְעוֹר [ngar-ngōhr'], Aroer; i. q. עֲרוֹעֵר *ruins.*

עַרְעֹרִי [ngărōh-ngēhree'], Aroerite; gentile noun of עֲרוֹעֵר.

עָרְפָּה [ngorpāh'], Orpah; *a hind, or, fawn.* According to Simonis, for עָפְרָה above.

עַרְקִי [ngarkee'], Arkite; gentile noun of a city. עָרַק *flight*, from עָרַק *to flee.*

עֲשָׂהאֵל [ngăsāh-ēhl'], Asahel; *(whom) God created.* From עָשָׂה *he made, created* אֵל *God.*

עֵשָׂו [ngēhsāhv'], Esau; *hairy, rough.* From עָשָׂה, collated with the Arabic, *to be hairy, rough* (G.). Compare Gen. xxv. 25.

עֲשִׂיאֵל [ngăsee-ēhl'], Asiel; *created of God.* From עָשִׂי *created*, a passive form (compare דָּוִד), and אֵל *God.*

עֲשָׂיָה [ngăsāh-yah'], Asaiah, Asahiah; *(whom) the Lord created.* Compare the preceding, and עֲשָׂהאֵל.

עֵשֶׂק [ngēh'sek], Esek; *strife, quarrel.* From עָשַׂק *to strive, quarrel.* Compare Gen. xxvi. 20.

עֲשָׁוֵת [ngashvāhth'], Ashvath; the signification is not evident.

עָשָׁן [ngāhshāhn'], Ashan; *smoke.* Compare Appellatives.

עֵשֶׁק [ngēh'shek], Eshek; *oppression.* From עָשַׁק *to oppress.*

עַשְׁתֹּרֶת [ngashtōh'reth], Ashtoreth; *star* (collated with the Persic by Gesenius), specially the star of Venus, *the goddess of love and fortune, prof. Astarte.*

עַשְׁתָּרוֹת [ngashtāhrōhth'], Ashtaroth; plural of the preceding, sc. *images,* or, *statues of Astarte,* and, as such, it is also the name of a city.

עַשְׁתְּרוֹת קַרְנַיִם [ngasht'rōhth' karnah'yim], Ashtaroth-karnaim; *Astarte with two horns.* The name of a city, only Gen. xiv. 5, for the preceding simple *Ashteroth.* קֶרֶן קַרְנַיִם, Dual of *horn.*

עֶשְׁתְּרָתִי [ngasht'rāhthee'], Ashterothite; gentile noun of עַשְׁתָּרוֹת.

עַתַּי [ngattah'y], Attai; perhaps, *opportune,* i. q. Appellative עִתִּי q. v. (G.).

עֲתָיָה [ngăthāh-yāh'], Athaiah; perhaps, i. q. עֲשָׂיָה (whom) *the Lord created.* עָתָה i. q. עָשָׂה (G.).

עָתָךְ [ngăthāhkh'], Athach; *lodging-place.* Collated with the Arabic (S.).

עַתְלַי [ngathlah'y], Athlai; apoc. for the following עֲתַלְיָה.

עֲתַלְיָה [ngăthal-yāh'], Athaliah; (whom) *the Lord afflicts.* From עתל, according to the Arabic, *to treat with violence* (G.), and יָהּ *the Lord.*

עֲתַלְיָהוּ [ngăthal-yāh'hoo], id.

עָתְנִי [ngothnee'], Othnee; *lion of the Lord.* From עֹתֶן, collated with the Arabic, *a lion* (S.), and then apoc. for עָתְנִיָה.

עָתְנִיאֵל [ngothnee-ēhl'], Othniel; *lion of God.* Compare the preceding.

עֵת קָצִין [ngēhth' kāhtzeen'], Ittahkazin (Josh. xix. 13); *time of the judge.* Compare Appellatives. The translators have mistaken the ה local (*unto*) of עִתָּה קָ, when they rendered it *Ittah,* and it ought to have been, *to Ethkazin.* Compare פַּדֶּנָה אֲרָם (Gen. xxviii. 2, 5, 6), from פַּדַּן אֲ.

עֶתֶר [ngeh'ther], Ether; *abundance.* From עָתַר *to be rich, abundant.*

פ

פָּארָן [pāhrāhn'], Paran; *abounding in caverns.* From פאר, according to the Arabic, *to dig, to bore* (S.).

פַּגְעִיאֵל [pag-ngee-ēhl'], Pagiel; *event, incident from God.* From Appellative פֶּגַע *event, incident, chance,* and אֵל *God.*

פְּדָהאֵל [p'dah-ēhl'], Pedahel; (whom) *God redeemed.* Pret. of פָּדָה *to redeem,* and אֵל *God.* Comp. פְּדָיָה.

פְּדָהצוּר [p'dāhtzoor'], Pedahzur; (whom) *the Rock* (God) *redeemed.* From פָּדָה *to redeem,* and צוּר *rock.* Compare Appellatives.

פָּדוֹן [*pāhdōhn'*], Padon; *deliverance, redemption*. Comp. the preceding.

פְּדָיָה [*p'dāh-yāh'*], Pedaiah; (whom) *the Lord redeemed*. Compare פְּדָהאֵל.

פְּדָיָהוּ [*p'dāh-yāh'hoo*], id.

פַּדָּן [*paddāhn'*], Padan; *field, plain*. Compare Appellatives.

פַּדַּן אֲרָם [*paddan' ărāhm'*], Padanaram; *plain*, or, *level region of Syria*. Compare the preceding, and אֲרָם.

פּוּאָה [*pooāh'*], Puah; *mouth*. Collated with the Arabic (G.).

פֻּוָּה [*poovāh'*], Phuvah, Pua; found Gen. xlvi. 13, and Num xxvi. 23, for פוּאָה, 1 Chr. vii. 1.

פּוּט [*poot'*], Put, Phut, Libyans, Libya; probably, *afflicted*. Compare the following.

פּוּטִיאֵל [*pootee-ēhl'*], Putiel; *afflicted of God*. פּוּט, according to the Syriac in Aphel, *to despise, to afflict* (G.), and אֵל *God*.

פּוֹטִיפַר [*pōhteephar'*], Potiphar; abbreviated for the following.

פּוֹטִי פֶרַע [*pōhtee pheh'rang*], Potiphera; *who is of the sun*, i. e., very near, consecrated to the sun. Collated with the Egyptian (G.).

פּוּל [*pool'*], Pul; *elephant*, i. q. Chaldee פִּיל.

פּוּנִי [*poonee'*], Punite; patronymic of an unknown person. פּוּן probably, *distracted*. Compare אָפוּנָה, Psa. lxxxviii. 16(15).

פּוּנֹן [*poonōhn'*], Punon; *darkness*. From פּוּן, collated with the Arabic, *to set*, spoken of the sun, *to become dark* (G.).

פּוּעָה [*poo-ngāh'*], Puah; *splendour*. For יְפוּעָה, from יָפָה *to be bright*, *to shine* (S.).

פּוֹרָתָא [*pōhrāh'thāh*], Poratha; *gift, portion*. Collated with Persic (S). Gesenius (in Thes.) suspects it to be a contraction from פּוּרְדָתָא *given as a lot*, since LXX. read, according to Cod. Vat., Φαραδαθά; Alex., Βαρδαθά, otherwise, Φαρδαθά.

פּוּתִי [*poothee'*], Puhite; patronymic of an unknown person. פּוּת, perhaps, *open, open-hearted*. פּוּת i. q. פָּתָה (cogn. with פָּתַח) *to be open*; whence Part. פֹּתֶה *simple, foolish*, one easily persuaded, seduced.

פַּחַת מוֹאָב [*pakhath' mōh-āhv'*], Pahath-moab; *prefect of Moab*. פַּחַת construct state of Appellative פֶּחָה.

פִּי־בֶסֶת [*pee-veh'seth*], Pi-beseth; the name of a city (Vulg. *Bubastus*), signifying, according to Gesenius (in Thes.), *the Diana*; *Pasht, Basht*, being the name of Diana, and *pi* the article in the Egyptian.

פִּי הַחִירֹת [*pee hakheerōhth'*], Pi-hahiroth; according to the Hebrew, *mouth of caverns*. פִּי const. state of פֶּה *mouth*; חִירֹת plur. of חִירָה, i. q. Appellative חוֹר *hole, cavern*. But, collated with the Egyptian, *place of green grass*, or, *sedge* (G.).

פִּיכֹל [*peekhōhl'*], Phichol; *mouth of all* (S.), i. e., all-commanding. Compare Appellatives פֶּה and כֹּל.

פִּינְחָס [peen'khāhs'], Phinehas; *mouth of brass.* Compounded of פִּי. Compare the preceding, and נְחָס, collated with the Arabic, i. q. Heb. נְחֹשֶׁת, *brass* (G.).

פִּינֹן [peenohn'], Pinon; i. q. פּוּנֹן *darkness.*

פִּישׁוֹן [peeshōhn'], Pison; *overflowing.* From פּוּשׁ *to diffuse itself.*

פִּיתוֹן [peethōhn'], Pithon; *enlargement.* For פִּתְיוֹן, from פתח, in the Chaldee, *to be wide, extended.*

פֹּכֶרֶת הַצְּבָיִים [pōhkheh'reth hatsts'vāh-yeem'], Pochereth of Zebaim; *retarding,* i. e., getting a-head of, *the gazelles.* פֹּכֶרֶת Part. act. of פכר, in the Syriac Pah., *to retard;* צְבָיִים plural Appellative צְבִי q. v. (S.). The translators have taken the second word as the name of a place.

פַּלֻּאִי [palloo-ee'], Palluite; patronymic of פַּלּוּא.

פְּלָאיָה [p'lāh-yāh'], Pelaiah; (whom) *the Lord distinguishes.* From the Pret. of פָּלָא *to separate, to distinguish,* and יָהּ *the Lord.*

פֶּלֶג [peh'leg], Peleg; *division.* From פָּלַג *to divide.*

פִּלְדָּשׁ [pildāhsh'], Pildash; the etymology of this word is obscure.

פַּלּוּא [palloo'], Pallu; *distinguished.* From פָּלָא *to separate, to distinguish.*

פְּלוֹנִי [p'lōhnee'], Pelonite; gentile noun of an unknown place. פָּלוֹן *distinguished,* from פָּלָה *to be separate, to be distinguished.*

פִּלְחָא [pilkhāh'], Pileha; according to the Hebrew, *slice;* according to the Chaldee, *worship,* from פלח, Hebrew, *to cleave;* Chaldee, *to serve, worship.*

פֶּלֶט [peh'let], Pelet; *deliverance.* From פָּלַט *to escape.*

פַּלְטִי [paltee'], Palti, Paltite; *deliverance of the Lord,* for פְּלַטְיָה, compare the preceding (G.). It occurs also as a gentile noun, probably of בֵּית פֶּלֶט.

פִּלְטַי [piltah'y], Piltai; apoc. from פְּלַטְיָה.

פַּלְטִיאֵל [paltee-ēhl'], Paltiel; *deliverance of God.* Compare פֶּלֶט and פַּלְטִי.

פְּלַטְיָה [p'lat-yāh'], Pelatiah; (whom) *the Lord delivers.* Pret. of פָּלַט, only here transitive, *to deliver,* and יָהּ *the Lord.*

פְּלַטְיָהוּ [p'lat-yāh'hoo], id.

פְּלָיָה [p'lāh-yāh'], Pelaiah; i. q. פְּלָאיָה (whom) *the Lord distinguishes.*

פָּלָל [pāhlāhl'], Palal; *judge.* From פָּלַל *to judge.*

פְּלַלְיָה [p'lal-yāh'], Pelaliah; (whom) *the Lord judges.* From פָּלַל *to judge,* and יָהּ *the Lord.*

פְּלֶשֶׁת [p'leh'sheth], Philistia, Palestina, Palestine, Philistines; *sojourning.* From פלשׁ, in the Ethiopic, *to rove, wander* (S.).

פְּלִשְׁתִּי [p'lishtee'], Philistine; gentile noun of the preceding.

פֶּלֶת [peh'leth], Peleth; *swiftness.* פלת collated with the Arabic (G.).

פְּנוּאֵל [p'noo-ēhl'], Penuel; *face of God.* A sing. פְּנוּ for פָּנִים (face). Compare מְתוּ plur. מְתִים (G.). Compare also Gen. xxxii. 32.

פְּנִיאֵל [p'nee-ēhl'], Peniel; id.

פְּנִנָּה [p'ninnāh'], Peninnah; *coral,* or, *pearl,* as there are differences of opinion regarding the Appellative פְּנִינִים.

פִּסְגָּה [pisgāh'], Pisgah; *piece, part,* i. q. Chaldee פִּסְגָא, from פְּסַג *to cut up, to divide* (G.).

פַּס דַּמִּים [pas dammeem'], Pasdammim; stands, 1 Chr. xi. 13, for אֶפֶס דַּמִּים, 1 Sa. xvii. 1, doubtless the same in signification, *a ceasing from blood,* or, *bloodshed.* פס from פָּסַם *to cease.*

פָּסֵחַ [pāhsēh'ăkh], Paseah, Phaseah; *lame.* Compare Appellative פִּסֵּחַ.

פָּסַךְ [pāhsakh'], Pasach; *He cut off,* thus according to the Chaldee.

פִּסְפָּה [pispāh'], Pispah; *dispersion,* for פִּסְפָּסָה, from פספס, in the Chaldee and Syriac, *to scatter, disperse* (S.).

פָּעוּ [pāh'ngoo], Pau; *a bleating, lowing.* From פָּעָה, in the Syriac and Chaldee, פעא *to bleat, to bellow.*

פְּעוֹר [p'ngōhr'], Peor; *gap,* or, *opening of a mountain.* From פָּעַר *to open wide the mouth, to gape.*

פָּעִי [pāh-ngee'], Pai; stands, 1 Ch. i. 50, for פָּעוּ, Gen. xxxvi. 39.

פְּעֻלְּתָי [p'ngooll'thah'y], Peulthai; *wages of the Lord.* From פְּעֻלָּה *wages,* compare Appellatives, and יְ_ *the Lord.* Compare אֲחֻזַי.

פַּעֲרַי [pāh-ngărah'y], Paarai; only, 2 Sa. xxiii. 35, for נַעֲרַי, 1 Chr. xi. 37.

פְּקוֹד [p'kōhd'], Pekod; only Jer. l. 21, ought rather to be taken as an allegorical name for Babylon, signifying *visitation,* from פָּקַד *to visit.*

פֶּקַח [peh'kakh], Pekah; *open-eyed, seeing.* Compare Appellative פִּקֵחַ.

פְּקַחְיָה [p'kakh yāh'], Pekahiah; *the Lord has opened* sc. *his eyes.* From פָּקַח *to open,* spoken of the eyes, and יָהּ *the Lord.*

פִּרְאָם [pir-āhm'], Piram; *swift, wild.* Compare פֶּרֶא *wild ass,* so called from its fleetness.

פָּרָה [pāhrāh'], Parah; with ה art., הַפָּרָה *the heifer.* Comp. Appellatives.

פֻּרָה [poorāh'], Phurah; *bough,* for פֻּאָרָה. See Appellatives.

פְּרֻדָא [p'roo-dāh'], Peruda; *kernel.* Compare Appellative פְּרֻדוֹת *grains, kernels.*

פָּרוּחַ [pāhroo'ăkh], Paruah; *blossoming.* Part. pass. of פָּרַח *to flourish.*

פַּרְוַיִם [parvāh'yim], Parvaim; *fertile.* Dual of פֶּרוּ, from פָּרָה *to bear fruit.* Gesenius compares it with the Sanscrit pûrva *prior, anterior, oriental;* hence here *oriental regions.*

פְּרִזִּי [p'rizzee'], Perizzites; *villager.* Compare Appellative פְּרָזִי.

פְּרִידָא [p'reedāh'], Perida; *kernel.* i. q. פְּרוּדָא, for which it stands, compare Ezra ii. 54 with Neh. vii. 57.

פַּרְמַשְׁתָּא [parmashtāh'], Parmashta; *strong-fisted.* Collated with the Persic (S.).

פַּרְנָךְ [parnāhkh'], Parnach; *brisk, swift.* Probably for פַּנָּךְ, the ר being inserted instead of doubling the נ (compare דַּרְמֶשֶׂק for דַּמֶּשֶׂק), from פנך, in the Chaldee, *to leap.* Others compare it with the name *Pharnaces,* in the Persic, *august, Augustus.*

פָּרַס in pause פָּרָס [pāh-rāhs'], Persia, Persians; *horse,* or, *horseman.* i. q. Appellative פָּרָשׁ. Others compare it with the Zend, pârs, *pure.*

פַּרְסִי [parsee'], Persian; gentile noun from the preceding.

פַּרְסָיָא [parsāh-yāh'], Persian; the Chaldee emph. of פַּרְסִי, gentile noun from פרס.

פַּרְעֹה [par-ngōh'], Pharaoh; *prince,* or, *king.* Either from the Hebrew פֶּרַע *leader, prince,* with the termination ה–, or from the Egyptian, pouro, *king.*

פַּרְעֹה חָפְרַע [par-ngōh' khophrang'], Pharaoh-hophra; *prince,* or, *king Hophra,* see the preceding. חָפְרַע, according to Jablonsky, collated with the Coptic, *priest of the sun.*

פַּרְעֹה נְכֹה [par-ngōh' n'khōh'], Pharaoh-nechoh; *prince,* or, *king Necho.* Compare פַּרְעֹה. The word נכה, according to the Hebrew, *hurt, injured.* By the testimony of Abulpharius, Pharaoh Necho was *lame.*

פַּרְעֹשׁ [par-ngōhsh'], Parosh; *flea.* Compare Appellatives.

פִּרְעָתוֹן [peer-ngāhthōhn], Pirathon; *principal, chief.* Compare Appellative פֶּרַע *prince.*

פִּרְעָתוֹנִי [peer-ngāhthōhnee'], Pirathonite; gentile noun from the preceding.

פַּרְפַּר [parpar'], Pharphar; *swift.* From פרר, collated with the Arabic, *to run* (G.).

פֶּרֶץ [peh'-rets], Pharez, Perez *breach,* or, *breaking forth.* Compare Appellatives.

פַּרְצִי [partsee'], Pharzites; patronymic of the preceding.

פֶּרֶץ עֻזָּא [peh'rets ngoozzāh'], Perez-uzzah; *breach of Uzzah.* See proper names פֶּרֶץ and עֻזָּא. Compare 2 Sa. vi. 8.

פֶּרֶשׁ [peh'-resh], Peresh; *separation.* But compare Appellatives.

פַּרְשַׁנְדָּתָא [parshandāhthāh'], Parshandatha; *interpreter of the law.* פַּרְשָׁן from פָּרַשׁ *to explain,* for דָּתָא. Compare Appellative דָּת.

פְּרָת [p'rāhth], Euphrates; perhaps, *bursting forth.* From פרת i. q. פרץ (G.).

פַּשְׁחוּר [pash-khoor'], Pashur; *prosperity round about.* Compounded from פשׂה, Arabic, *to be wide, ample,* and סָחוֹר *round about.* Appellative מָגוֹר מִסָּבִיב, compare Jer. xx. 3 (G.).

פְּתוּאֵל [p'thoo-ēhl'], Pethuel;

enlargement of God. From פָּתָה, in the Hiphil, to enlarge, compare יֶפֶת. According to some, for פָּתוּעַ אֵל set free by God. From פתע, in the Samaritan, i. q. פָּתָה; compare Gesenius on this obsolete root. Compare also פְּתַחְיָה.

פְּתוֹר [p'thōhr'], Pethor; interpretation of dreams, i. q. Appellative פִּתְרוֹן, from פָּתַר to interpret.

פְּתַחְיָה [p'thakh-yāh'], Pethahiah; (whom) the Lord sets free. From פָּתַח to open, to set free, and יָהּ the Lord.

פִּתֹם [peethōhm'], Pithom; narrow place, i. e., shut up by mountains. Collated with the Egyptian (G.).

פַּתְרוֹס [pathrōhs'], Pathros; region of the south. Collated with the Egyptian.

פַּתְרֻסִים [pathrooseem'], Pathrusim; gentile noun of the preceding.

צ

צַאֲנָן [tsah-ănāhn'], Zanaan; place of flocks. From Appellative צֹאן flocks.

צְבָאִים [ts'vōh-eem'], Zeboim; gazelles, i. q. Appellatives צְבָאִים.

צֹבֵבָה [tsōhvēhvāh'], Zobebah; with ה, article, the slow-moving. Participle of צבב, cognate with דָבַב, to move gently.

צִבְיָא [tsiv-yāh'], Zibia; gazelle. Feminine of Appellative צְבִי.

צִבְיָה [tsiv-yāh'], Zibiah; id.

צְבֹיִים & צְבֹיִם [ts'vōh-yeem'], Zeboiim, Zeboim; i. q. צְבָאִים, compare plural of Appellative צְבִי.

צִבְעוֹן [tsiv-ngōhn'], Zibeon; versicolour. Compare Appellative צֶבַע.

צְבֹעִים [ts'vōh-ngeem'], Zeboim; hyenas. Compare Appellative צָבוּעַ.

צְדָד [ts'dāhd'], Zedad; side, sc. of a mountain. i. q. Appellative צַד, from צדד.

צָדוֹק [tsāhdōhk'], Zadok; just. From צָדַק to be just, righteous.

צִדִּים [tsiddeem'], Ziddim; with ה article, the sides.

צִדֹנִיֹּת [tsēhdniy-yōhth'], Zidonians; feminine gentile noun of צִידוֹן.

צִדְקִיָּה [tsidkiy-yāh'], more frequently, צִדְקִיָּהוּ [tsidkiy-yāh'hoo], Zedekiah, Zidkijah; righteousness of the Lord. From צֶדֶק=צָדַק to be just, righteous, and יָהּ the Lord.

צוֹבָה & צוֹבָא [tsōhvāh'], Zoba, Zobah; station. For נְצוּבָה=נָצַב to set, put, place (G.).

צוֹעַר, more frequently צֹעַר, [tsōhngāhr'], Zoar; smallness. From צָעַר to be small.

צוּעָר [tsoo-ngāhr'], Zuar; id.

צוּף [tsooph'], Zuph; honeycomb. Compare Appellatives.

צוֹפַח [tsōhphakh'], Zopha; cruse. Compare Appellative צַפַּחַת cruse.

צוֹפַי [tsōhphah'y], Zophai; honeycomb, i.e., sweet gift *of the Lord*, for צוֹפִיָה ; צוֹף i.q. צוּף above.

צוֹפַר [tsōhphar'], Zophar; *exultation*. From צפר, according to the Arabic, *to dance* (S.).

צוֹר, more frequently צֹר, [tsōhr'], Tyre, Tyrus; *rock*, i. q. צוּר.

צוּר [tsoor'], Zur; *rock*. Compare Appellatives.

צוּרִיאֵל [tsooree-ēhl'],Zuriel; (whose) *rock is God*. From the preceding, and אֵל *God*.

צוּרִישַׁדָּי [tsooreeshaddah'y], Zurishaddai; (whose) *rock is the Almighty*. From צוּר *rock*, and שַׁדַּי *Almighty*.

צֹחַר [tsōh'khar], Zohar; *whiteness*. Compare Appellative צַחַר *whiteness*.

צִיבָא [tseevāh'], Ziba; *plant*. For נצב=נְצִיבָה, Chaldee, Syriac, and Arabic, *to plant*.

צִידוֹן [tseedōhn'], Zidon, Sidon; *prey*. From צוּד *to hunt, catch*. According to Justin, the city of the same name is so called from the *abundance of fish* (S.); as the word, according to him, signified *fish* in the Phœnician.

צִידוֹנִי [tseedōhnee'], Zidonian; gentile noun of the preceding.

צִיחָא & צִיהָא [tseekāh'], Ziha; *dryness*. Compare Appellative צִחֶה *dry, thirsty*.

צִיּוֹן [tsiy-yōhn'], Zion; *dry place, dry mountain*. Compare Appellatives צִיָּה *dryness*, צִיּוֹן *dry land*. According to some, *top, summit*. Compare Appellative צִיּוּן *pillar, column*.

צִיעֹר [tsee-ngōhr'], Zior; *smallness*. From צָעַר *to be small*.

צִיף [tseeph'], Zuph; in Kethib, 1 Chr. vi. 20(35), for צוּף; in Keri, perhaps the same in signification, *honeycomb*.

צִיץ [tseets'], Ziz; with the ה article, *the flower*. From צוּץ *to flower, flourish*. Compare Appellatives.

צִיקְלַג, צִיקְלָג, but more frequently צִקְלָג [tseeklāhg'], Ziklag; *outpouring of a fountain*. Which Simonis considers to stand for יַצִּיק גַּל, from יָצַק; but not necessarily, as צִיק may be derived from צוּק *to pour out;* and, to avoid the concurrence of two palatal letters, לג קג stands, by transposition, for גל.

צִלָּה [tsillāh'], Zillah; *shade*. i. q. Appellative צֵל.

צְלֶלְפּוֹנִי [ts'lelpōhnee'], vers. with ה article, Hazelelponi; *the shadow looketh upon me*. From צֵלָל *shadow*, and Part. פּוֹנָה with suff., from פָּנָה *to turn one's face towards* any thing, *to look upon*.

צַלְמוֹן [tsalmōhn'],Zalmon, Salmon; *shadow*, or, *shady*. Comp. צֶלֶם *shadow*.

צַלְמֻנָּע [tsalmunnāhng'], Zalmunna; *shadow is removed, departed*. Contracted for צַלְמוֹן נָע. Compare the preceding, and נָע, Preterite of נוּעַ *to move, to wander*.

צֶלַע [tsēhlāhng'], Zelah; *side*. Compare Appellatives.

צָלַף [tsāhlāhph'], Zalaph; *fracture, wound.* From צָלַף, Syriac, *to break, wound.*

צְלָפְחָד [ts'lophkhāhd'], Zelophehad; *first rupture*, i. e., first-born. From צָלַף=צְלוּף *to break.* See the preceding, חָד *one, first.* In the Chaldee, i. q. Hebrew אֶחָד.

צֶלְצַח [tseltsakh'], Zelzah; *shadow from the sun.* From צֵל *shadow*, and צח, collated with the Arabic, *the sun* (S.).

צֶלַע [tseh'lek], Zelek; *fissure.* From Chaldee צְלַע *to cleave.*

צִלְּתַי [tsill'thah'y], Zilthai; *shadow*, i. e., protection *of the Lord.* For צַלַת יָהּ, compare צִלָּה above, and יָהּ *the Lord.*

צְמָרִי [ts'māhree'], Zemarite; gentile noun, probably, of the following.

צְמָרַיִם [ts'māhrah'-yim], Zemaraim; according to Simonis, from צָמַר *hot.* From the Chaldee צָמַר *to be hot.*

צִן [tsin'], Zin; *thorn.* i. q. Appellative צִנָּה. According to others, i. q. Talmudic, צִין *a low palm tree.*

צְנָן [ts'nāhn'], Zenan; perhaps, *place of flocks.* Contracted for צַאֲנָן above.

צָעִיר [tsāhngeer'], Zair; *small.* Compare Appellatives.

צֹעַן [tsōh'ngan], Zoan; *low region.* Collated with the Egyptian (G.).

צַעֲנִים [tsahngănah'-yim], Zaanaim; *two removals.* Dual of צַעַן, compare

the following, for which this stands in Kethib, Jud. iv. 11.

צַעֲנַנִּים [tsahngănanneem'], Zaananim; *removals.* Plural of צַעַן=צָעַן, collated with the Arabic, *to remove* (S.).

צְפוֹ [ts'phōh'], Zepho; *expectation, hope.* From צָפָה *to look out for, to wait.*

צָפוֹן [tsāhphōhn'], Zaphon; *north.* Compare Appellatives.

צְפוֹן [ts'phōhn'], Zephon; *expectation, hope.* Compare צְפוֹ above. It stands, Num. xxvi. 15, for צְפִיוֹן, Gen. xlvi. 16.

צְפוֹנִי [ts'phōhnee'], Zephonite; patronymic of the preceding.

צִפּוֹר [tsippōhr'], Zippor; *bird.* Compare Appellatives.

צְפִי [ts'phee'], Zephi; i. q. צְפוֹ (Gen. xxxvi. 11), for which this is found, 1 Chr. i. 36.

צִפְיוֹן [tsiph-yōhn'], Ziphion; *expectation, hope.* From צָפָה *to look out for, to wait.*

צֹפִים [tsōhpheem'], Zophim; *watchmen.* Part. pl. of צָפָה *to look about.*

צְפַנְיָה [ts'phan-yāh'], Zephaniah; (whom) *the Lord hides*, i. e., *protects.* From צָפַן *to hide*, and יָהּ *the Lord.*

צְפַנְיָהוּ [ts'phan-yāh'hoo], id.

צָפְנַת פַּעְנֵחַ [tsāhph'nath pahngănēh'ăkh], Zaphnath-paaneah; by collation with the Egyptian, the meaning is supposed to be, *saviour of the age.*

צִפֹּרָה [tsippōhrāh'], Zipporah; *bird.* Compare צִפּוֹר above.

צְפָת [ts'phāhth'], Zephath; *watchtower.* From צָפָה *to look about.*

צֵר [tsēhr'], Zer; *strait.* From צוּר *to straiten, to press.*

צְרֵדָה [ts'rēhdāh'], Zeredah; *a cooling.* From צָרַד, collated with the Arabic, *to be cool.*

צְרוּיָה [ts'roo-yāh'], Zeruiah; *balmy, odoriferous.* From צְרִי *balsam.*

צְרוּעָה [ts'roo-ngāh'], Zeruah; *leprous.* Compare Appellative צָרוּעַ Part. pass.

צְרוֹר [ts'rōhr'], Zeror; *bundle.* Compare Appellatives.

צֹרִי [tsōhree'], Tyrian; gentile noun of צוֹר.

צְרִי [ts'ree'], Zeri; stands, 1 Chr. xxv. 3, for יִצְרִי ver. 11.

צָרְעָה [tsor-ngāh'], Zorah; *hornet's town.* i. q. צִרְעָה *hornet* (G.).

צָרְעִי [tsor-ngee'], Zorite; gentile noun of the preceding.

צָרְעָתִי [tsor-ngāhthee'], Zareathite, Zoreathite; id.

צֹרְפִי [tsōhr'phee'], *goldsmith* (Neh. iii. 31); ought to have been rendered as a proper name, Zorphi, or, as it is with ה article, Hazzorphi; as an Appellative, it ought simply to have been הַצֹּרֵף, Part. of צָרַף *to melt, smelt.*

צָרְפַת [tsāhr'phath'], Zarephath; *a melting, smelting.* From צָרַף *to melt, smelt.*

צְרֵרָה [ts'rēhrāh], Zererath; stands, Jud. vii. 22, for צְרֵדָה.

צֶרֶת [tseh'reth], Zereth; perhaps for צִהֲרָה *splendour* (S.), from צָהַר *to shine, glitter.* Comp. the following.

צֶרֶת הַשַּׁחַר [tseh'reth hashshah'khar], Zareth-shahar; *splendour of the dawn.* Compare the preceding and Appellative שַׁחַר.

צָרְתָן [tsāhr'thāhn'], Zaretan, Zarthan, Zartanah; the etymology is obscure.

ק

קַבְצְאֵל [kavts'ēhl'], Kabzeel; stands for יְקַבְצְאֵל q. v.

קִבְצַיִם [kivtsah'yim], Kibzaim; *two heaps* (G.). Dual of קָבַץ=קְבָץ *to gather, to collect.*

קִבְרוֹת הַתַּאֲוָה [kivrōhth hattah-ăvāh'], Kibroth-hattaavah; *graves of lust.* Compare Appellatives, and Nu. xi. 34.

קֵדְמָה [kēh'd'māh], Kedemah; *eastward.* From קֶדֶם *east,* with ה local.

קְדֵמוֹת [k'dēhmōhth'], Kedemoth; *beginnings.* Plural of קְדֵמָה i. q. Appellative קַדְמָה.

קַדְמִיאֵל [kadmee-ēhl'], Kadmiel; *one before, in the presence of God,* i. e., *minister of God* (G.). From קֶדֶם i. q. Chaldee קֳדָם, as a preposition, *before,* and אֵל *God.*

קַדְמֹנִי [kadmōhnee'], Kadmonite; oriental. Compare Appellatives.

קֵדָר [kēhdāhr'], Kedar; dark skinned. From קָדַר to be dark coloured.

קִדְרוֹן [kidrōhn'], Kidron; turbid. From קָדַר, collated with the Arabic, to be turbid (G.).

קָדֵשׁ [kāhdēhsh'], Kadesh; consecrated, sc., to Astarte, or Venus. Compare Gesenius on the Appellative of this form. From קָדַשׁ to be holy, sacred.

קֶדֶשׁ [keh'desh], Kedesh; sanctuary. From קָדַשׁ to be holy, sacred.

קָדֵשׁ בַּרְנֵעַ [kāhdēhsh' barnēh'ăng], Kadesh-barnea; Kadesh of Barnea, of a desert of that name, only occurring in connection with קָדֵשׁ. Barnea, according to Simonis, desert of wandering, sc. of the Israelites. בַּר, from the Chaldee, Syriac, and Arabic, a desert, and נֵעַ wandering; from נוּעַ to move to and fro, to wander. According to Hiller, contracted for בְּאֵר נָע cistern of the fugitive. Others again, son of wandering; hence Kedesh of the Nomades.

קְהֵלָה [k'hēhlāh'], with paragogic קְהֵלָתָה [k'hēhlāh'thāh], Kehelathah; convocation. From קָהַל to convoke.

קְהָת [k'hāhth'], Kohath; assembly. From obsolete קָהָה, in the Chaldee, to assemble.

קְהָתִי [k'hāhthee'], Kohathite; patronymic of the preceding.

קֹהֶלֶת, once קוֹהֶלֶת, [koh-heh'leth], preacher (Eccl. i. 1, &c.); a masculine proper name with feminine termination, as designating office. Literally, the convoker, for preacher, from his gathering an assembly around him. Part. fem. of קָהַל to convoke.

קוֹלָיָה [kōhlāh-yāh'], Kolaiah; voice of the Lord. For קוֹל יָהּ (G.).

קוֹץ [kōhts'], Koz, and with ה art., Hakkoz, Koz, Coz; the thorn. Compare Appellatives.

קוֹרֵא, once קֹרֵא, [kōhrēh'], Kore; partridge. Compare Appellative קָרָא, properly, the crier, caller. Part. from קָרָא to cry, to call.

קוּשָׁיָהוּ [kooshāh-yāh'hoo], Kushaiah; bow of the Lord, i. e., rainbow. From קוּשׁ, in the Arabic, to be curved, bent, as a bow (G.).

קְטוּרָה [k'toorāh'], Keturah; incense. i. q. Appellative קְטוֹרָה.

קָטָן [kāhtāhn'], with the ה article, Hakkatan; the little, or, younger. Compare Appellatives.

קִטְרוֹן [kitrōhn'], Kitron; small. Collated with the Appellative קְטָרוֹת, Eze. xlvi. 22, which the Vulgate, Syriac, and Arabic render small. It is found, Jud. i. 30, instead of which it is קַטָּת in Jos. xix. 15.

קַטָּת [kattāhth'], or better as other copies read, קַטַּת [kattath], Kattath; small. Supposed to be contracted for קְטַנָּה. Compare the preceding.

קַיִן [kah'-yin], Cain; acquisition, possession. From קוּן, or קִין, probably i. q. קָנָה to get, acquire. Compare Gen. iv. 1.

קִינָה [keenāh'], Kinah; *lamentation.* From קוּן, in Piel, *to lament.*

קֵינִי & קֵינִּי [kēhnee'], Kenite; *gentile noun of* קַיִן. Compare Nu. xxiv. 22, and Jud. iv. 11.

קֵינִים [keeneem'], Kenites; id.

קֵינָן [kēhnāhn'], Cainan, Kenan; perhaps i. q. קִנְיָן *possession* (G.), but compare קַיִן.

קִיר [keer'], Kir; *wall.* Compare Appellatives.

קִיר חֶרֶשׂ [keer kheh'res], Kir-heres, Kir-haresh; *wall of tiles.* Compare Appellatives.

קִיר חֲרֶשֶׂת [keer khăreh'seth], Kir-hareseth; id.

קֵרֹס & קֵירֹס [kēhrōhs'], Keros; from the Chaldee, *weaver's comb* (G.).

קִישׁ [keesh], Kish; *a snaring.* From קוֹשׁ *to lay snares.*

קִישׁוֹן [keeshōhn'], Kishon; *winding.* From קוֹשׁ, collated with the Arabic, *to be curved, bent* (G.).

קִישִׁי [keeshee'], Kishi; stands, 1 Chr. vi. 29 (44), for קוּשָׁיָהוּ xv. 17.

קַלַּי [kăllah'y], Kallai; *swift,* sc., *servant of the Lord.* Perhaps for קַלְיָה (G.), from קָלַל *to be light, swift.*

קְלָיָה [kēhlāh-yāh'], Kelaiah; *assembly of the Lord.* Contracted from קְהֵלַת יָה (S.) for קְהִלָה יָה, from קָהַל *to convoke.* It stands, Ezr. x. 23, for the following.

קְלִיטָה [k'leetāh'], Kelitah; id., from קָלַט, in the Chaldee, *to gather together.* Compare the preceding, especially Ezr. x. 23.

קְמוּאֵל [k'moo-ēhl'], Kemuel; *assembly of God.* קמא or קמי, in the Arabic, *to gather together,* and אֵל *God* (S.).

קָמוֹן [kāhmōhn'], Camon; *standing firm.* From קוּם *to stand.*

קָנָה [kāhnāh'], Kanah; *reed, reeds,* i. e., *place of reeds.* Compare Appellative קָנֶה *reed.*

קְנַז [k'naz']. Kenaz; *a hunting.* קנז, collated with the Arabic, *to hunt.*

קְנִזִּי [k'nizzee'], Kenizzite; patronymic and gentile noun of קְנַז, as the signification for the latter it is, *hunter.*

קְנָת [k'nāhth'], Kenath; *possession.* From קָנָה *to acquire, possess.*

קְעִילָה [k'ngeelāh'], Keilah; *fortress, refuge.* Collated with the Arabic (S.).

קְצִיעָה [k'tsee-ngāh'], Kezia; *cassia.* Compare Appellative.

עֵמֶק קְצִיץ see ק׳.

קוֹרֵא see קֹרֵא.

קָרֵחַ [kāhrēh'ăkh], Kareah; *baldhead.* Compare Appellative קָרְחָה.

קֹרַח [kōh'rakh], Korah; *ice.* Compare Appellative.

קָרְחִי [korkhee'], Korahite, Korhite,

Korathite; patronymic of the preceding.

קְרִיּוֹת [k'riy-yōhth'], Kerioth; cities. Plur. of קִרְיָה i. q. קִרְיָה.

קִרְיַת אַרְבַּע [kir-yath' arbang'], Kirjath-arba; city of Arba, one of the Anakims. Compare Appellative קִרְיָה and proper name אַרְבַּע.

קִרְיַת בַּעַל [kir-yath' bah'-ngal], Kirjath-baal; city of Baal. Compare Appellative קִרְיָה and pr. name בַּעַל.

קִרְיַת חֻצוֹת [kir-yath' khootsōhth'], Kirjath-huzoth; city of streets. Compare Appellatives קִרְיָה & חוּץ.

קִרְיָתַיִם [kir-yāhthah'-yim], Kirjathaim; double city. Dual of קִרְיָה, compare Appellatives.

קִרְיַת יְעָרִים [kir-yath' y'ngāhreem'], Kirjath-jearim; city of woods. Compare Appellatives קִרְיָה & יַעַר.

קִרְיַת סַנָּה [kir-yath' sannāh'], Kirjath-sannah; city of palms. Compare Appellative סַנְסִנִּים (G.).

קִרְיַת סֵפֶר [kir-yath' sēh'pher], Kirjath-sepher; city of writing, or, books; i. e., learning. Compare Appellatives.

קִרְיַת עָרִים [kir-yath' ngāhreem'], Kirjath-arim; contracted for קִרְיַת יְעָרִים.

קֶרֶן הַפּוּךְ [keh'ren happookh'], Keren-happuch; splendour (lit. rays) of carbuncle. But as this meaning for the second word is uncertain, others render it horn of paint, i. e., eye-paint, stibium. Compare Appellatives.

קָרֵס. see קֵירֹס.

קַרְקַע [karkang'], Karkaa; floor, pavement. Compare Appellatives.

קַרְקֹר [karkōhr'], Karkor; an undermining. From קוּר. Compare Isa. xxii. 5.

קַרְתָּה [kartāh'], Kartah; city. i. q. Appellative קֶרֶת.

קַרְתָּן [kartāhn'], Kartan; two cities. Dual after the Chaldee or Arabic (S.), elsewhere קִרְיָתַיִם q. v.

קִשְׁיוֹן [kish-yōhn'], Kishion, Kishon; hardness. From קָשָׁה to be hard.

ר

רֹאֶה [rōh-eh'], with the article, Haroeh; the beholding, regarding, sc. God, Part. of רָאָה to see, behold, regard. It stands, 1 Chr. ii. 52, for רְאָיָה (the Lord regards him); see ch. iv. 2.

רְאוּבֵן [r'oovēhn'], Reuben; See, a son! רְאוּ Imper. pl. of רָאָה and בֵּן a son. See Gen. xxix. 32, where the words "for she said, Surely the Lord hath looked upon my affliction," &c. are not to be understood as the cause why she (Leah) gave him this name, but why she thus joyfully exclaimed, "See, a son!" And though this fact is not expressly stated, it is most probable, from the plain signification of the name.

רְאוּבֵנִי [r'oovēhnee'], Reubenite; patronymic of the same.

רְאוּמָה [r'oomāh'], Reumah; *raised, high.* Part. pass. of רָאַם *to be high.*

רְאָיָה [r'āh-yāh'], Reaiah; *the Lord has regarded* (him). From רָאָה *to see, behold, regard,* and יָהּ *the Lord.*

רָאמוֹת and רָמוֹת [rāhmōhth'], Ramoth; *heights.* From רָאַם *to be high.*

רָאמַת־נֶגֶב [rāhmath' neh'gev], Ramath of the south (Jos. xix. 8); *height, high place of the south.* Comp. the preceding and the Appellative נֶגֶב.

רֹאשׁ [rōhsh'], Rosh; *head.* Compare Appellatives.

רַבָּה [rabbāh'], Rabbah; *great,* sc. great city, metropolis. Fem. of רַב *great,* from רָבַב *to become much,* or, *many.*

רַבִּית [rabbeeth'], Rabbith; *multitude.* From רָבַב *to become great,* or, *many.*

רִבְלָה [rivlāh'], Riblah; *fertility.* From רָבַל, according to the Arabic, *to be much, fertile, abundant* (G.).

רֶבַע [reh'vang], Reba; *the fourth.* From אַרְבַּע *four.*

רִבְקָה [rivkāh'], Rebekah; *binding,* hence perhaps *fascinating.* From רָבַק, comp. Lex. on this obsolete root.

רַבְשָׁקֵה [ravshāhkēh'], Rab-shakeh; *chief cupbearer.* רַב *great, chief,* compare Appellatives, and שָׁקָה participle of שָׁקָה. Compare Gesenius on this obsolete root.

רֹגְלִים [rōhg'leem'], Rogelim; *fullers'-place.* Participle of רָגַל *to tread,* sc. garments in washing (G.). Compare עֵין רֹגֵל.

רֶגֶם [reh'gem], Regem; *friend.* Collated with the Arabic (S.).

רֶגֶם מֶלֶךְ [reh'gem meh'lekh], Regem-melech; *friend of the king.* Compare the preceding.

רַדַּי [raddah'y], Raddai; *the Lord subdues.* For רְדָיָה, preterite of רָדָד *to subdue,* and יָהּ *the Lord.*

רַחַב [rah'hav], Rahab; *pride.* Compare Appellative.

רָהְגָּה [rohgāl'], Rohgah; *outcry, clamour.* From רחג, collated with the Arabic, *to cry out* (G.). This is the reading according to Keri, but רוֹהֲנָה according to Kethib.

רוּמָה [roomāh'], Rumah; *lofty.* From רום *to be high.*

רוֹמַמְתִּי עֶזֶר [rōhmam'tee ngēh'zer], Romamti-ezer; *I have exalted* (his) *help.* Piel of רום *to be raised, to be high,* and עֶזֶר *help.* Compare Appellatives.

רוּת [rooth], Ruth; *appearance, beauty.* Contracted from רְאוּת. Compare Appellative.

רְזוֹן [r'zōhn'], Rezon; *prince,* i. q. רֹזֵן (G.), which latter is a participle of רזן. See Gesenius on this root.

רָחָב [rākhhāhv'], Rahab; *enlargement.* From רָחַב *to be,* or, *become wide, large.*

רְחֹבוֹת [r'khōhvōhth'], Rehoboth; *wide places, ample room.* From רָחַב, compare the preceding, also Gen. xxvi. 22.

Q

רְחַבְיָה [*r'khav-yāh'*], Rehabiah; *enlargement of the Lord.* Compare רָחָב above, and יָהּ *the Lord.*

רְחַבְיָהוּ [*r'khav-yāh'hoo*], id.

רְחַבְעָם [*r'khavngāhm'*], Rehoboam; *enlargement of the people.* Compare רָחָב above, and Appellative עָם.

רְחוֹב [*r'khōhv'*], Rehob; *street.* Compare Appellatives.

רְחוּם [*r'khoom'*], Rehum; *beloved.* Participle passive form of רָחַם *to love.*

רָחֵל [*rāhkhēhl'*], Rachel; *ewe, sheep.* Compare Appellatives.

רַחַם [*rah'kham*], Raham; *love, compassion.* From רָחַם *to love, to have compassion.*

רְחֻם see רָחוּם.

רִיבַי [*reevah'y*], Ribai; i. q. יְרִיבַי *adversary.*

רִיפַת [*reephath'*], Riphath; the etymology is obscure.

רֵכָב [*rēhkhāhv'*], Rechab; *rider.* From רָכַב *to ride.*

רֵכָבִי [*rēhkhāhvee'*], Rechabite; patronymic of the same.

רֵכָה [*rēhkhāh'*], Rechah; *side.* For יְרֵכָה. Compare Appellatives.

רָכָל [*rāhkhāhl'*], Rachal; *traffic.* From רָכַל, from which רֹכֵל *a trader, merchant.*

רָם [*rāhm'*], Ram; *high.* From רוּם *to be high.*

רָמָה [*rāhmāh'*], Ramah; *height, high place.* From רוּם *to be high.*

רִמּוֹן [*rimmōhn'*], Rimmon; *pomegranate.* Compare Appellatives.

רָמוֹת [*rāhmōhth'*], Ramoth; *heights.* i. q. רָאמוֹת q. v.

רָמוֹת גִּלְעָד [*rāhmōhth' gil-ngāhd'*], Ramoth-gilead; *Ramoth in Gilead.* Compare the preceding, and גִּלְעָד.

רַמְיָה [*ram-yāh'*], Ramiah; *the Lord is exalted.* Pret. of רָמַם *to be high, exalted,* and יָהּ *the Lord.*

רַמִּים [*rammeem'*], Syrians; with article הָרַמִּים for הָאֲרַמִּים.

רְמַלְיָהוּ [*r'mal-yāh'hoo*], Remaliah; (whom) *the Lord decks, adorns.* From רָמַל according to the Arabic, *to deck with gems* (G.).

רִמּוֹן פֶּרֶץ [*rimmōhn peh'rets*], Rimmon-parez; *pomegranate-cleft.* Compare רִמּוֹן above, and פֶּרֶץ *a breach.*

רֶמֶת [*reh'meth*], Remeth; *height.* i. q. רָמָה.

רָמַת הַמִּצְפֶּה [*rāhmath' hammitspeh*], Ramath-mizpeh; *height of the watch-tower.* Comp. רָמָה and מִצְפֶּה.

רָמָתִי [*rāhmāhthee'*], Ramathite; gentile noun of רָמָה.

רָמַת לֶחִי [*rāhmath' l'khee'*], Ramath-lehi; *height of the jaw-bone.* Compare רָמָה and appellative לְחִי.

רָמָתַיִם צוֹפִים [*rāhmahthah'-yim tsōhpheem'*], Ramathaim-zophim; *two heights of the Zophites,* or, *the watchmen.*

Dual of רָמָה *height*, and the part. of צָפָה *to look about, to watch.*

רִנָּה [*rinnāh'*], Rinnah; *rejoicing.* From רָנַן *to shout.* Compare Appellatives.

רִסָּה [*rissāh'*], Rissah; *dew.* From רָסַס *to moisten, sprinkle.* Collated with the Chaldee, Arabic, and Sanscrit (G.).

רֶסֶן [*reh'sen*], Resen; *bridle.* Compare Appellatives.

רְעוּ [*r'ngoo'*], Reu; *friend,* sc. of God (G.). From רָעָה *to delight in one, to be his companion.* For this form compare פְּנוּאֵל.

רְעוּאֵל [*r'ngoo-ēhl'*], Reuel; *friend of God.* Compare the preceding and אֵל *God.*

רֵעִי [*rēh-ngee'*], Rei; *friendly, social.* Denom. of רֵעַ *companion, friend* (G.).

רְעֵלָיָה [*r'ngēhlāh-yāh'*], Reelaiah; *trembling,* i. e. *terror of the Lord.* From רָעַל *to shake, tremble,* and יָה *the Lord.*

רַעְמָה [*rangmah'*], Raamah; *trembling,* or, *thundering.* From רָעַם *to tremble, thunder.*

רַעַמְיָה [*rāh-ngam-yāh'*], Raamiah; *terror of the Lord.* Compare the preceding, and רְעֵלָיָה (Ezra ii. 2), for which this stands in Neh. vii. 7.

רַעְמְסֵס [*rangm'sēhs'*], Rameses, and רַעַמְסֵס [*rah-ngamsēhs'*], Raamses; the first form, according to the Coptic, is composed of *man, pastor,* i. e. *shep-*herd, and the second, *field of the sun* (Jablonski by Simonis).

רָפָא [*rāhphāh'*], Rapha (only 1 Chr. viii. 2), elsewhere rendered *giant* (xx. 4, 6, 8); i. q. רָפָה *giant,* q. v.

רְפָאִים [*r'phāh-eem'*], Rephaims; *giants,* gentile noun from רָפָא *giant.* Compare 1 Chr. ii. 4, 6, or רָפָה (2 Sa. xxi. 18, 20).

רְפָאֵל [*r'phāh-ēhl'*], Rephael; (whom) *God heals.* For רָפָא אֵל, preterite of רָפָא *to heal,* and אֵל *God.*

רָפָה [*rāhphāh'*], Rapha (1 Chr. viii. 37), *giant* (2 Sa. xx. 16, 18, 21, 22); *giant.* From רפה *to cast down, let fall,* hence this word signifies *a casting down, overthrowing,* i. e. *hero, champion, giant* (G.). But in 1 Chr. viii. 37, it has most likely the signification of *healing,* as in ix. 23, רְפָיָה (whom) *the Lord heals,* stands instead of it.

רָפוּא [*rāhphoo'*], Raphu; *healed.* Participle passive of רָפָא *to heal.*

רֶפַח [*reh'phakh*], Rephah; *rich.* From רָפַח according to the Arabic, *to be rich* (S.).

רְפִידִים [*r'pheedeem'*], Rephidim; *beds, couches.* Passive form of רָפַד *to strew, to spread out a bed.* Compare יָצִיעַ, יָצוּעַ *bed, couch,* from יָצַע.

רְפָיָה [*r'phāh-yāh'*], Rephaiah; (whom) *the Lord heals.* For רָפָא יָה, preterite of רָפָא *to heal,* and אֵל *God.* Compare רְפָאֵל.

רִצְיָא [rits-yāh'], Rizia; *delight.* From רָצָה *to delight in* anything.

רְצִין [r'tseen'], Rezin; probably i. q. *prince,* q. v.

רֶצֶף [reh'tseph], Rezeph; *pavement,* i. q. Appellative רִצְפָה.

רִצְפָּה [ritspāh'], Rizpah; *hot coal,* probably *hot stone,* used for roasting or baking. Compare Appellative. Or perhaps *flame,* רָצַף for רָשַׁף *to inflame, kindle,* whence רֶשֶׁף q. v.

רַקּוֹן [rakkōhn'], Rakkon; perhaps (situate) *on the shore.* Compare רַקַּת.

רֶקֶם [reh'kem], Rekem; *variegated.* From רָקַם *to variegate.* Hence, collated with the Arabic (S.) *a flower garden.*

רַקַּת [rakkath'], Rakkath; *shore.* In the Chaldee רַקְתָּא *shore.*

רֶשֶׁף [reh'sheph], Resheph; *flame.* Compare Appellatives.

רִתְמָה [rithmāh'], Rithmah; i. q. רֹתֶם, according to some, *juniper.* According to Gesenius *genista, broom,* a shrub growing in the deserts of Arabia.

שׂ

שְׂבָם [s'vāhm'], Sevam; *fragrance.* Transposed for בשׂם (S.), *coolness,* collated with the Arabic (G.).

שִׂבְמָה [sivmāh'], Sibmah; id.

שְׂגוּב [s'goov'], Segub; *elevated.* Passive form of שָׂגַב *to be lifted up, to be raised.*

שְׂגִיב [s'geev], Segub; id. Thus according to Kethib, 1 Ki. xvi. 34.

שִׂדִּים [siddeem'], Siddim; *plains.* Plural of שַׂד or שָׂדָה from שָׂדַד *to be straight, even* (G.).

שׂוֹכֹה, שׂוֹכוֹ [sōhkhōh'], Sochoh, Shochoh, Socoh, Shocho, Socho, Soco; *hedge, enclosure.* From שׂוּךְ *to hedge, hedge in,* or, *about.*

שׂוּכָתִים [sookhāhtheem'], Suchathites; gentile noun from an unknown place שׂוּכָה *hedge, enclosure.* Compare the preceding.

שִׂטְנָה [sitnāh'], Sitnah; *opposition, hatred.* From שָׂטַן *to be an adversary.* Compare Gen. xxvi. 21.

שִׂיאוֹן [see-ōhn'], Sion; *elevated.* For נְשִׂיאוֹן from נָשָׂא *to lift up, to raise.*

שֶׂכוּ [sēh'khoo], Sechu; *watchtower.* From שָׂכָה i. q. Chaldee שְׂכָא *to look, view,* whence Chaldee סְכוּת *watch-tower.*

שָׂכָר [sāhkhār'], Sacar; *hire, wages.* From שָׂכַר *to hire.* Compare Appellatives.

שַׂלְמָה, שַׂלְמָא [salmāh'], Salma; *garment.* Compare Appellative שַׂלְמָה.

שַׂלְמוֹן [salmōhn'], Salmon; *clothed.* From שַׂלְמָה *a garment.*

שַׂלְמַי [salmah'y], Shalmai; stands for שַׁלְמַי Ez. ii. 46, which reading the English version proposes also here Neh. vii. 48.

שִׂמְלָה [samlāh'], Samlah; garment, i. q. Appellative שִׂמְלָה.

שְׂנִיר [s'neer'], Senir; coat of mail (S.).

שֵׂעִיר [sēh-ngeer'], Seir; hairy, i. q. Appellative שָׂעִיר.

שְׂעֹרִים [s'ngōhreem'], Seorim; barley. Compare Appellative שְׂעֹרָה.

שִׂפְמוֹת [siphmōhth'], Siphmoth; according to other copies שִׂפְמוֹת, which see under ש.

שָׂרָה [sāhrāh'], Sarah; princess. Feminine of שַׂר prince. Compare Appellatives. Or perhaps as a Pret. שָׂרָה she is become princess, she has prevailed. In reference both to the past event regarding Hagar, and the promise which the Lord was about to bestow upon her immediately. Compare Gen. xvii. 15, 16.

שְׂרוּג [s'roog], Serig; shoot, tendril, i. q. Appellative שָׂרִיג.

שֶׂרַח [sēh'rakh], Serah; abundance, i. q. Appellative סָרַח (G.), from סָרַח to be superfluous, redundant.

שָׂרַי [sāhrah'y], Sarai; perhaps for שָׂרְיָה the Lord reigns, literally has dominion. Pret. of שׂוּר to be prince, to have dominion, to reign.

שָׂרִיד [sāhreed'], Sarid; remainder. From שָׂרַד to flee, to escape, hence Appellative שָׂרִיד one escaped, left.

שְׂרָיָה [s'rāh-yāh'], Seraiah; the Lord has dominion, reigns. From שָׂרָה i. q. שׂוּר and שָׂרַר. Compare שָׂרַי and יָהּ the Lord. This word, besides its numerous occurrences, is also found in 2 Sa. viii. 17, as the name of David's scribe. But in every other parallel passage a different word is found instead, so שְׁוָא in Keri, and שְׁיָא Kethib, 2 Sa. xx. 25, שִׁישָׁא 1 Ki. iv. 2, שַׁוְשָׁא 1 Chr. xviii. 16. Simonis, who considers these to refer to one and the same person, prefers to read in 2 Sa. viii. 17, שְׂרָיָה habitation of the Lord, from the Chaldee שְׁרָא or שְׁרָה to dwell. And in agreement with this, by collations with the Arabic, Syriac, and Chaldee, he tries to prove that the other words, שְׁוָא or שְׁיָא, שַׁוְשָׁא and שִׁישָׁא, signify habitation, sc. of the Lord.

שְׂרָיָהוּ [s'rāh-yāh'hoo], id.

שִׂרְיוֹן [sir-yōhn'], Sirion; coat of mail, i. q. Appellatives סִרְיוֹן and שִׂרְיוֹן.

שַׂרְסְכִים [sars'kheem'], Sarsechim; prince of the Scythians. From שַׂר prince, and סְכִים answering to Σακαι of Herodot. Lib. VII. as the Persian name for the Scythians (S.).

שָׂרָף [sāhrāhph'], Saraph; perhaps noble, prince. Compare Gesenius on the root שׂרף, which according to the Arabic may signify to be noble, of high birth.

שׂוֹרֵק [sōhrēhk'], Sorek; shoot, tendril. Compare Appellatives.

ש

שָׁאוּל [shāh-ool'], Saul; asked for, obtained by entreaty. From שָׁאַל to ask, request.

שָׁאוּלִי [shāh-oolee'], Shaulite; patronymic of the same.

שְׁאָל [sh'āhl'], Sheal; petition. From שָׁאַל to ask, request.

שְׁאַלְתִּיאֵל [sh'altee-ehl'], Shealtiel, Salatiel; *I have asked* (him) *of God*, or *petition of God*, the abstract for the concrete, *asked for of God*. שָׁאַלְתִּי either the participle or a noun, שְׁאֵלַת with conjunctive י, from שָׁאַל to ask, request, and אֵל God.

שְׁאֵרָה [shēh-ĕrāh'], Sheerah; *blood-relationship, kindred*, concr. *kinswoman*, i.q. Appellative שְׁאֵרָה (G.).

שְׁאָר יָשׁוּב [sh'āhr' yāhshoov'], Shear-jashub; *a remnant shall return*. For the first compare Appellatives, and יָשׁוּב future of שׁוּב to return.

שְׁבָא [sh'vāh'], Sheba, Sabeans; *man*. Collated with the Ethiopic (G.).

שְׁבָאִים [sh'vāh-eem'], Sabeans; gentile noun of the same.

שְׁבוּאֵל [sh'voo-ēhl'], Shebuel; *captivity of God*, perhaps for concr. *captive of God*. שְׁבוּ Chaldee form for שְׁבוּת *captivity* (compare מַלְכוּ and מַלְכוּת), and אֵל God.

שֹׁבַי [shōhvah'y], Shobai; *captor, one who takes captive*. Participle of שָׁבָה to take, or, lead captive.

שׁוֹבִי [shōhvee'], Shobi; id.

שִׁבְיָה [shov-yāh'], Shachiah; this is the reading of some copies, but others read שִׁכְיָה which the English version has followed.

שֶׁבְנָה & שֶׁבְנָא [shevnāh'], Shebna; *approach, access*. From an Arabic root *to draw near*, whence, according to others, *confidence, trust*, for concr. *confidant*.

שְׁבַנְיָה [sh'van-yāh'], Shebaniah; perhaps *confidant of the Lord*. Compare the preceding.

שְׁבַנְיָהוּ [sh'van-yāh'hoo], id.

שֶׁבַע [sheh'vang], Sheba; *oath*. As the name of a place, compare Gen. xxi. 14, 31, and xxvi. 33. But it being also the name of a man, compare 2 Sa. xx. 1, 2; it may signify *seven*, compare Appellatives.

שִׁבְעָה [shiv-ngāh'], Shebah; *oath*. Compare Gen. xxvi. 33.

שֶׁבֶר [sheh'ver], Sheber; *breach*, or, *fracture*. From שָׁבַר to break. Compare Appellatives.

שְׁבָרִים [sh'vāhreem'], Shebarim; *breaches*, plural of שֶׁבֶר. Compare the preceding.

שַׁבְּתַי [shabb'thah'y], Shabbethai; *Sabbath of the Lord*, for שַׁבְּתִיָה, i. e. *Sabbath-born*. Compare Appellative שַׁבָּת.

שַׁגֵא [shāhgēh'], Shage; *erring*. Participial form of שָׁגָא i.q. שָׁגָה *to err*.

שְׁדֵיאוּר [sh'dēh-oor'], Shedeur; *darting of fire*. שָׁדָא in the Chaldee *to cast, shoot*, and אוּר *fire*. Compare Appellatives (S.).

שַׁדְרַךְ [shadrakh'], Shadrach; *rejoicing in the way*. Collated with the Persic (Bohlen by Gesenius).

שֹׁ֫הַם [shōh'ham], Shoham; *onyx*. Compare Appellatives.

שְׁוָא [sh'vāh'] Keri, but שְׁיָא [sh'yāh'] Kethib, Sheva; see שְׁרָיָה.

שׁוּבָאֵל [shoovāh-ēhl'], Shubael; stands twice by transposition for שְׁבוּאֵל. Compare 1 Chr. xxiv. 20, xxv. 20, with xxv. 4, xxvi. 24.

שׁוֹבָב [shōhvāhv'], Shobab; *rebellious, apostate*. From שׁוּב in Piel, *to turn away, to depart*. Compare Appellative.

שׁוֹבָךְ [shōhvakh'], Shobach; probably i. q. שׁוֹפָךְ *effusion*. שָׁבַד i. q. שָׁפַךְ *to pour out*.

שׁוֹבָל [shōhvāhl'], Shoval; perhaps *increase*. From שָׁבַל *to go up, rise, to grow*. Compare Gesenius on this obsolete verb.

שׁוֹבֵק [shōhvēhk'], Shobek; *forsaking*. Part. of שׁבק, in the Ch., *to leave*.

שָׁוֵה [shāh-vēh'], Shaveh; *plain*. From שָׁוָה *to be even, level*.

שָׁוֵה קִרְיָתַיִם [shāhvēh' kir-yāhthah'-yim], Shaveh-kirjathaim; *Shaveh* (near) *kirjathaim*. Compare the preceding and קִרְיָתַיִם.

שׁוּחַ [shoo'ăkh], Shuah; *bowed down*. From the verb שׁוּחַ *to be bowed down*.

שׁוּחִי [shookhee'], Shoohite; patron. and gentile noun of the preceding.

שׁוּחָם [shookhāhm'], Shuham; probably by transposition for חוּשָׁם; it stands Num. xxvi. 42, instead of חוּשִׁים Gen. xlvi. 23.

שׁוּחָמִי [shookhāhmee'], Shuhamite; patronymic of the preceding.

שׁוּלַמִּית [shoolammeeth'], Shulamite; *peaceful*. From שָׁלַם *to be at peace, enjoying peace*.

שׁוֹמֵר & שֹׁמֵר [shōhmēhr'], Shomer; *keeper*. From שָׁמַר *to watch, to keep*.

שׁוּנִי [shoonee'], Shuni, Shunite; *quiet*. From שׁוּן probably i. q. שָׁאַן *to be quiet*, as the name of a man, and as a patronymic.

שׁוּנֵם [shoonēhm'], Shunem; perhaps *two resting-places*. For שׁוּנַיִם, compare עֲנָם for עֵינַיִם. (G.).

שׁוּנַמִּית [shoonammeeth'], Shunammite; f. gentile noun of the preceding.

שׁוּעַ [shoo'ăng], Shuah; *riches*. Compare Appellatives. Or perhaps for יְשׁוּעָה *help*.

שׁוּעָא [shoo-ngāh'], Shua; *riches*. Compare the preceding.

שׁוּעָל [shoo-ngāhl'], Shual; *fox*. Compare Appellatives.

שׁוֹפָךְ [shōhphakh'], Shophach; *effusion*, i. e., *profusion*. From שָׁפַךְ *to pour out*.

שׁוּפָמִי [shoophāhmee'], Shuphamite; patronymic of שְׁפוּפָם.

שׁוּר [shoor], Shur; *wall*. Compare Appellatives.

שַׁוְשָׁא [shavshāh'], Shavsha; compare שְׂרָיָה.

שׁוּשַׁן [shooshan'], Shushan; *lily*. Compare Appellatives.

שׁוּשַׁנְכָיֵא [shooshankhāh-yēh'], Shusanchites; Chaldee gentile noun of שׁוּשַׁן.

שׁוּשַׁק [shooshak'], Kethib for שִׁישַׁק.

שׁוּתֶלַח [shootheh'lakh], Shuthelah; the etymology is obscure. According to Gesenius, for שְׁאוּתְלַח crack of tearing in pieces; שְׁאוּ from שָׁאָה to make a noise, and תְלַח from תָלַח Aram. to break, or, tear in pieces.

שַׁחֲצוֹם [shahkhătsōhm'] in Kethib, שַׁחֲצִים [shahkhătseem'] in Keri, Shahazimah; high place, or, high places. From שחץ according to the Arabic to lift up, or, raise oneself (G.).

שָׁחוֹר & שָׁחֹר, see שׁוֹחוֹר.

שְׁחַרְיָה [sh'khar-yāh'], Shehariah; (whom) the Lord seeks. From שָׁחַר to seek, and יָהּ the Lord.

שַׁחֲרַיִם [shahkhărah'-yim], Shaharaim; dawns. Probably two dawns. Dual of שַׁחַר dawn, morning. Compare Appellatives עַרְבַּיִם, צָהֳרַיִם.

שִׁטִּים [shitteem'], Shittim; acacia-trees. Plural of שִׁטָּה. Compare Appellatives.

שִׁטְרַי [shitrah'y], according to Kethib, Shitrai; writer. From שָׁטַר in the Arabic, to write (G.).

שִׂיָא [sh'yāh'] according to Kethib; see שְׂרָיָה.

שִׁיאוֹן [shee-ōhn'], Shihon; destruction. From שׁוֹא; compare the Appellative of this form and שׁוֹאָה.

שִׁיזָא [sheezāh'], Shiza; perhaps love. From שׁיז according to the Arabic to love.

שִׁיחוֹר [sheekhōhr'], Shihor; black. From שָׁחַר to be black.

שִׁילֹה (only Gen. xlix. 10, which ought to be taken as an Appellative), שִׁילוֹ, שִׁלֹה and שִׁילֹה [sheelōh'], Shiloh; place of rest, or, peace. From שָׁלָה to be tranquil, at rest.

שִׁלֹנִי & שִׁילוֹנִי [sheelōhnee'], Shilonite; gentile noun of the preceding, and also 1 Chr. ix. 5, of שֵׁלָה.

שִׁימוֹן [sheemōhn'], Shimon; perhaps for יְשִׁימוֹן desert, from יָשַׁם to be laid waste.

שִׁישָׁא [sheeshāh'], Shisha; see שְׂרָיָה.

שִׁישַׁק [sheeshak'], Shishak; the etymology is obscure.

שְׁכֶם [sh'khem'], Shechem, Sichem; shoulder, or, portion. Compare Appellatives.

שֶׁכֶם [sheh'khem], Shechem; id.

שִׁכְמִי [shikhmee'], Shechemite; patronymic of the preceding.

שְׁכַנְיָה [sh'khan-yāh'], Shechaniah; the Lord abides (with him). From שָׁכַן to abide, dwell, and יָהּ the Lord.

שְׁכַנְיָהוּ [sh'khan-yāh'hoo], id.

שִׁכְּרוֹן [shikk'rōhn'], Shichron; drunkenness. From שָׁכַר to be drunken. Compare Appellative שִׁכָּרוֹן.

שֵׁלָה [shēhlāh'], Shelah; petition.

contr. for שְׁאֵלָה, from שָׁאַל to ask, request.

שָׁלֹם & שָׁלוֹם [shalloom'], Shallum; retribution. From Piel of שָׁלַם to requite, recompense. Compare Appellatives שָׁלֹם & שָׁלוֹם.

שַׁלּוּן [shalloon'], Shallum; quiet. From שָׁלָה to be tranquil, quiet.

שֶׁלַח [sheh'lakh], Shelah, Salah, Siloah; shoot, sprout. Compare Appellatives.

שִׁלֹחַ [sheelōh'ăkh], Shiloah; prop. a sending of water, i. e., conduit, aqueduct. Compare שֶׁלַח, Ps. civ. 10 (G.).

שִׁלְחִי [shilkhee'], Shilhi; armed. Compare Appellative שֶׁלַח weapon.

שִׁלְחִים [shilkheem'], Shilhim; armed men. Compare the preceding.

שַׁלֶּכֶת [shalleh'kheth], Shallecheth; a casting down, overthrow. From שָׁלָה to cast, throw.

שָׁלֵם [shāhlēhm'], Shalem, Salem; peaceable. Compare Appellative.

שִׁלֵּם [shillēhm'], Shillem; retribution. Compare Appellatives, and שָׁלוֹם above.

שְׁלֹמֹה [sh'lōhmōh'], Solomon; peaceable. From שָׁלַם to be safe, enjoying peace. Compare 1 Ch. xxii. 9.

שְׁלֹמוֹת [sh'lōhmōhth'], Shelomoth; prosperity, prosperous state. Fem. pl. of שָׁלוֹם as a substantive, compare Appellative נָעִים, whence נְעִימִים & נְעִימוֹת.

שְׁלֹמִי [sh'lōhmee'], Shelomi; peaceable. i. q. Appellative שָׁלוֹם with constructive י.

שִׁלֵּמִי [shillēhmee'], Shillemite; patronymic of שָׁלֵם.

שַׁלְמַי [shalmah'y], Shalmai; retribution of the Lord. Contr. for שֶׁלֶמְיָה. Compare the following.

שְׁלֻמִיאֵל [sh'loomee-ēhl'], Shelumiel; friend of God. Part. pass. of שָׁלַם to be at peace, in friendship with any one. Compare 2 Sa. xx. 19, and אֵל God.

שֶׁלֶמְיָה [shehlem-yāh'], Shelemiah; retribution of the Lord. From שָׁלַם in the Piel, to requite, recompense, and יָהּ the Lord.

שֶׁלֶמְיָהוּ [shehlem-yāh'hoo], id.

שְׁלֹמִית [sh'lōhmeeth'], Shelomith; peaceable. Fem. שְׁלֹמִי q. v. as the name of a female; but as the name of a man, it may be a substantive, peaceableness, prosperity. Compare the use of שָׁלוֹם as an adjective and as a substantive.

שַׁלְמַן [shalman'], Shalman; apoc. from the following.

שַׁלְמַנְאֶסֶר [shalman-eh'ser], Shalmanezer; the etymology is obscure.

שֵׁלָנִי [shēhlāhnee'], Shelanite; patronymic of שֵׁלָה.

שֶׁלֶף [sheh'leph], Sheleph; a drawing out. From שָׁלַף to draw out.

שָׁלֵשׁ [shēh'lesh], Shelesh; triad (G.). From שָׁלוֹשׁ three.

שָׁלֹשׁ

שְׁלִשָׁה [shilshāh'], Shilshah; id.

שְׁלִשָׁה [shāhleeshāh'], Shalishah; triangle. From שָׁלוֹשׁ three.

שַׁלְתִּיאֵל [shaltee-ēhl'], Shealtiel; contracted from שְׁאַלְתִּיאֵל.

שֵׁם [shēhm'], Shem; name. Compare Appellatives.

שַׁמָּא [shammāh'], Shamma; i. q. שַׁמָּה astonishment. From שָׁמַם to be astonished, amazed.

שְׁמֵאָבֶר [shemēh'ver], Shemeber; soaring on high, for שַׂמְאָבֶר, prop. in the abstract, lofty flight, from שָׂמָה =שָׁם (whence שָׁמַיִם heaven) height, and אֵבֶר (G.), prop. pinion.

שִׁמְאָה [shim-āh'], Shimeah; astonishment. According to Simonis, for שְׁמָמָה. Compare שַׁמָּה. According to Gesenius, i. q. שִׁמְעָא fame.

שִׁמְאָם [shim-āhm'], Shimeam; stands instead of the preceding. Compare 1 Chr. ix. 32 with 38.

שַׁמְגַּר [shamgar'], Shamgar; its signification is not ascertained.

שַׁמָּה [shammāh'], Shammah; astonishment. From שָׁמַם to be astonished, amazed. Compare Appellatives.

שַׁמְהוּת [shamhooth'], Shamhuth; probably id. It stands for the preceding, compare 2 Sa. xxiii. 25 with 1 Chr. xxvii. 18.

שְׁמוּאֵל [sh'moo-ēhl'], Shemuel, Samuel; heard of God, i. e., given of God in answer to prayer. Compare 1 Sa. i. 20. Contracted from שְׁמוּעַ

שָׁמֵעַ

part. pass. of שָׁמַע to hear; also, to hear and answer prayer, and אֵל God.

שַׁמּוּעַ [shammoo'ăng], Shammua; renowned. From שָׁמַע to hear.

שָׁמוּר [shāhmoor'], Shamir; in Kethib, 1 Chr. xxiv. 24, for שָׁמִיר in Keri.

שַׁמּוֹת [shammōhth'], Shammoth; i. q. שַׁמָּה astonishment, for which it stands. Compare 2 Sa. xxiii. 25 with 1 Chr. xi. 27. Compare also this Infinitive form in Eze. xxxvi. 3.

שַׁמַּי [shammah'y], Shammai; astonished. From שָׁמַם to be astonished, amazed.

שְׁמִידָע [sh'meedāhng'], Shemida; fame of wisdom. Compounded of שֵׁם name, with conjunctive י, and דֵּעַ i. q. Appellative דַּעַ knowledge, wisdom, from יָדַע to know.

שְׁמִידָעִי [sh'meedāh-ngee'], Shemidite; patronymic of the same.

שָׁמִיר [shāhmeer'], Shamir; diamond. Compare Appellatives.

שְׁמִירָמוֹת [sh'meerāhmōhth'], Shemiramoth; of great renown, properly, name of exaltations. From שֵׁם name, with conjunctive י, and רָמוֹת, from רוּם to be high.

שַׁמְלַי [shamlah'y], Shalmai; in Kethib, for שַׁלְמַי, Ezr. ii. 46.

שָׁמָע [shāhmāhng'], Shama; obedient. From שָׁמַע to hear.

שֶׁמַע [sheh'mang], Shema; fame. From שָׁמַע to hear. Compare Appellative שֹׁמַע fame, שֵׁמַע sound.

שֶׁמַע (123) שִׁמְעָא

שִׁמְעָא [shim-ngāh'], Shimea, Shimei; fame. From שָׁמַע to hear. Compare the preceding.

שִׁמְעָה [shim-ngāh'], Shimeah; id.

שְׁמָעָה [sh'māh-ngāh'], Shemaah; with ה article, the hearing, sc. the answer of prayer. From שָׁמַע to hear, also, to hear and answer prayer, spoken of God.

שִׁמְעוֹן [shim-ngōhn'], Simeon; a hearing, sc. answer of prayer. Compare the preceding, and Gen. xxix. 33.

שִׁמְעוֹנִי [shim-ngōhnee'], Simeonite; patronymic of the same.

שִׁמְעִי [shim-ngee'], Shimei; Shimite; renowned. From שָׁמַע to hear, compare שֶׁמַע above. The patronymic from this name retains this same form.

שְׁמַעְיָה [sh'mang-yāh'], Shemaiah; (whom) the Lord hears. Pret. of שָׁמַע to hear; and יָהּ the Lord.

שְׁמַעְיָהוּ [sh'mang-yāh'hoo], id.

שִׁמְעָת [shim-ngāhth'], Shimath; i. q. שִׁמְעָה fame.

שִׁמְעָתִי [shim-ngāhthee'], Shimeathite; patronymic of שִׁמְעָה.

שֶׁמֶר [sheh'mer], Shemer, (in pause) Shamer; keeping, preserving. From שָׁמַר to keep, to watch.

שֹׁמֵר see שׁוֹמֵר.

שֹׁמְרוֹן [shōh-m'rōhn'], Samaria; pertaining to a watch, watch-height (G.). Compare the preceding.

שִׁמְרוֹן [shimrōhn'], Shimron; watch-guard (custodia). From שָׁמַר to keep watch, guard.

שִׁמְרוֹן מְרֹאוֹן [shimrōhn' m'rōhn'], Shimron-meron; the etymology of the second word is unknown.

שִׁמְרִי [shimree'], Shimri; watchful. From שָׁמַר to watch.

שְׁמַרְיָה [sh'mar-yāh'], Shemariah; (whom) the Lord keeps. From שָׁמַר to keep, watch, and יָהּ the Lord.

שְׁמַרְיָהוּ [sh'mar-yāh'hoo], id.

שָׁמְרַיִן [shāhm'rah'-yin], Samaria; the Chaldee form for שֹׁמְרוֹן.

שִׁמְרִית [shimreeth'], Shimrith; watchful. Fem. of שִׁמְרִי, for which it stands. Compare 2 Ki. xii. 22 with 2 Chr. xxiv. 26.

שֹׁמְרֹנִי [shōhm'rōhnee'], Samaritan; gentile noun of שֹׁמְרוֹן.

שִׁמְרֹנִי [shimrōhnee'], Shimronite; patronymic of שִׁמְרוֹן.

שִׁמְרָת [shimrāhth'], Shimrath; watch, guard. From שָׁמַר to keep, to watch.

שִׁמְשׁוֹן [shimshōhn'], Samson; sun-like (G.), from שֶׁמֶשׁ the sun.

שִׁמְשַׁי [shimshah'y], Shimshai; sunny, id.

שַׁמְשְׁרַי [shamsh'rah'y], Shamsherai; the etymology is not evident.

שֻׁמָתִי [shoomāhthee'], Shumathite; patronymic of an unknown person.

שָׁמָה perhaps i. q. Appellative שׁוּם garlic.

שֵׁן [shēhn'], Shen; cliff. Compare Appellative שֵׁן tooth, also, sharp rock, cliff.

שִׁנְאָב [shin-āhv'], Shinab; perhaps, the father's rest, quiet. Contracted from שָׁאַן, as a verb, to rest, be quiet, and אָב father. Others, father's tooth, compare the preceding.

שֶׁנְאַצַּר [shen-ats-tsar'], Shenazar; the signification is not known.

שְׁנִיר [sh'neer'], Shenir; most copies read שְׂנִיר q. v.

שִׁנְעָר [shin-ngāhr'], Shinar; the etymology is obscure.

שַׁעַלְבִים [shah-ngah-l'veem'], Shaalbim, and

שַׁעֲלַבִּים [shah-ngălabbeem'], Shaalabbin; foxes, sc. place of foxes. תעלב, in the Arabic, a fox (G.).

שַׁעַלְבֹנִי [shah-ngalvōhnee'], Shaalbonite; gentile noun of the preceding.

שַׁעֲלִים [shah-ngăleem'], Shalim; foxes, sc. region of foxes. Plural of שָׁעָל, i. q. שׁוּעָל fox.

שַׁעַף [shah'ngaph], Shaaph; balsam. i. q. Chaldee שְׁעִיף (S.).

שְׁעַרְיָה [sh'ngar-yāh'], Sheariah; (whom) the Lord estimates. From שָׁעַר, collated with the Arabic, to estimate (G.), and יָה the Lord.

שַׁעֲרַיִם [shah-ngărah'-yim], Shaaraim; two gates. Dual of שַׁעַר a gate, compare Appellatives.

שַׁעַשְׁגַּז [shah-ngashgaz'], Shaashgaz; servant of the beautiful. Collated with the Persic (G.).

שְׁפוֹ [sh'phōh'], Shepho; nakedness, baldness, from שָׁפָה to scrape, to scrape, or, pare off; in Aram. to make smooth, bald (G.).

שְׁפוּפָם [sh'phoophāhm'], Shupham; perhaps, i. q. שְׁפִיפוֹן serpent, from שָׁפַף, collated with the Syriac, to creep (G.).

שְׁפוּפָן [sh'phoophāhn'], Shephuphan; id.

שָׁפָט [shahphāht'], Shaphat; judge. From שָׁפַט to judge.

שְׁפַטְיָה [sh'phat-yāh'], Shephatiah; (whom) the Lord judges. Preterite of שָׁפַט to judge, and יָה the Lord.

שְׁפַטְיָהוּ [sh'phat-yāh'hoo], id.

שִׁפְטָן [shiphtāhn'], Shiphtan; judicial. From שָׁפַט to judge.

שְׁפִי [sh'phee'], Shephi; i. q. שְׁפִי nakedness, for which it stands, compare Gen. xxxvi. 23 with 1 Chr. i. 40.

שֻׁפִּים [shooppeem'], Shuppim; perhaps, serpents. Compare שְׁפוּפָם (G.), but very unsuitable for the name of a man.

שַׁפִּיר [shāhpheer'], Shaphir; fair. i. q. Chaldee שַׁפִּיר from שָׁפַר to be polished; hence, to be fair.

שָׁפָם [shāhphāhm'], Shapham; perhaps, bald. From שָׁפָה, compare שְׁפוֹ.

שְׁפָם [sh'phāhm'], Shepham; bare-

שִׁפְמוֹת [shiphmōth'], Shiphmoth; perhaps, id.

שִׁפְמִי [shiphmee'], Shiphmite; gentile noun of שְׁפָם.

שָׁפָן [shāhphāhn'], Shaphan; *coney*, or, *rabbit*. Compare Appellatives.

שִׁפְעִי [shiph-ngee'], Shiphi; *abounding, having abundance*. From שפע, in the Chaldee, *to overflow*. Compare Appellative שֶׁפַע *abundance*.

שֶׁפֶר [sheh'pher], Shapher; *beauty*. From שָׁפַר *to be polished;* hence, *to be fair*. Compare שָׁפִיר.

שִׁפְרָה [shiphrāh'], Shiphrah; *beauty*. Compare the preceding.

שַׂרְאֶצֶר [shar-eh'tser], Sharezer; *prince of fire*. Collated with the Persic (G.).

שֵׁרֵבְיָה [shēhrēhv-yāh'], Sherebiah; *heat of the Lord*. From שָׂרַב *to be hot*. Compare Appellative שָׂרָב *heat*.

שָׂרוּחֶן [shāhrookhen'], Sharuhen; *pleasant lodging*. For שָׂרוּת *lodging*, from שָׂרָה i.q. Chaldee שְׁרָא *to put up for the night, to lodge* (comp. the forms מַלְכוּ Chaldee, and מַלְכוּת Hebrew), and חֵן *grace, favour, kindness, gracefulness;* here, *pleasantness*, compare Appellatives (G.).

שָׁרוֹן [shāhrōhn'], Sharon; *plain*. For יִשְׁרוֹן, from יָשַׁר *to be even, level*.

שָׁרוֹנִי [shāhrōhnee'], Sharonite; gentile noun of the preceding.

שִׁרְטַי [shirtah'y], Shirtai; thus, according to the Keri, in 1 Chr. xxvii. 29; but the Kethib, which reads שִׁמְרַי q. v., seems to be the more correct.

שָׂרַי [shāhrah'y], Sharai; perhaps, *liberator*. From שָׂרָה i.q. Chaldee שְׁרָא *to loose, to solve*.

שִׂרְיוֹן [shir-yōhn'], Sirion; *coat of mail*. Compare Appellatives.

שָׂרָר [shāhrāhr'], Sharar; *firm, muscular*. From שָׂרַר *to twist together, to be firm;* whence שְׂרִירִים *nerves, sinews*, שֹׂרֶר *navel*.

שֶׁרֶשׁ [sheh'resh], Sheresh; *root*. i. q. Appellative שֹׁרֶשׁ.

שֵׁשְׁבַּצַּר [shēhshbatstsar'], Sheshbazzar; *fire-worshipper*. Collated with the Arabic (G.).

שָׁשַׁי [shāhshah'y], Shashai; perhaps, *whitish*. From שוּשׁ, which probably signified, *to be white;* whence שֵׁשׁ *byssus*, and white marble; שַׁיִשׁ id., &c. (G.).

שֵׁשַׁי [shēhshah'y], Sheshai; id.

שֵׁשַׁךְ [shēhshakh'], Sheshach; *house of the prince*. Collated with the Persic (Bohlen, by Gesenius).

שֵׁשָׁן [shēhshāhn'], Sheshan; perhaps i. q. שׁוּשָׁן *lily* (G.).

שָׁשָׁק [shāhshak'], Shashak; *eagerness, longing*. For שַׁקְשָׁק, from שָׁקָה *to run to and fro, to be eager, to be greedy* (S.).

שֵׁת [shēhth'], Sheth, Seth; marg. (Gen. iv. 25), *appointed*, or, *put*. From

שׁוּת or שִׁית *to set, place*; here, *replace*, hence *replaced*.

שֻׁתַלְחִי [*shoothalkhee'*], Shuthalite; patronymic of שׁוּתֶלַח.

שֵׁתָר [*shēhthāhr'*], Shethar; *star*. Collated with the Persic (S.).

שְׁתַר בּוֹזְנַי [*sh'thar bōhz'nah'y*], Shethar-boznai; *shining star*, properly, *star of splendour* (S.).

ת

תַּאֲנַת שִׁלֹה [*tah-ănath' sheelōh'*], Taanath-shiloh; *approach to Shiloh*. From אָנָה *to approach*. See also שִׁלֹה.

תַּאְרֵעַ [*tahrēh'ăng*], Tarea; *cunning*. i. q. תַּחְרֵעַ q. v.

תָּבוֹר [*tāhvōhr'*], Tabor; *height, mount*. תבר i. q. טבר, whence Appellative טַבּוּר *high place*.

תִּבְנִי [*tivnee'*], Tibni; *like, resembling*. From בָּנָה *to construct, build*; whence Appellative תַּבְנִית *structure, pattern, likeness*.

תַּבְעֵרָה [*tav-ngēhrāh'*], Taberah; *a burning*. From בָּעַר *to burn up*. Compare Nu. xi. 3.

תֵּבֵץ [*tēhvēhts'*], Tebez; perhaps, *brightness*. From an obsolete יָבֵץ i. q. Arabic ובץ *to shine, to be bright* (G.).

תִּגְלַת פִּלְאֶסֶר [*tiglath pil-eh'ser*], and תִּגְלַת פְּלֶסֶר [*tiglath p'leh'ser*], *lord of the Tigris*. Collated with the Persic (G.).

תַּדְמֹר [*tadmōhr'*], Tadmor; *city of palm-trees*. Coll. with the Arab. (G.).

תִּדְעָל [*tid-ngāhl'*], Tidal; *fear, veneration*. From דעל, in the Samaritan, *to fear, venerate* (S.).

תֻּבַל, תּוּבַל [*tooval'*], Tubal; *issue, offspring*. From יָבַל *to flow*; whence יָבוּל *a stream*, *produce*.

תּוּבַל קַיִן [*tooval kah'-yin*], Tubal-cain; *issue of Cain*. Compare the preceding. According to Gesenius (scoriarum faber), *smith of dross*; dross prob. for *ore*. Coll. with the Arabic.

תּוֹגַרְמָה [*tōhgarmāh'*], Togarmah; the signification is not evident.

תּוֹחַ [*tōh'ăkh*], Toh; perhaps, *rest*. Properly, *a settling down*. חוח (according to Simonis, i. q. Arabic תאח) *to descend*. Compare Gesenius on the root נוח *to rest*; properly, *to settle down*; whence נַחַת *rest*. The person called תּוֹחַ in 1 Chr. vi. 19 is called נַחַת in ver. 11.

תּוֹלָד [*tōhlāhd'*], Tolad; *family, posterity*. From יָלַד *to bear, bring forth*. Compare Appellative תּוֹלְדָה *generation, family*, &c.

תּוּלוֹן [*toolōhn'*], in Kethib, Tilon; *gift*. From נָתַל, in Chaldee and Syriac, *to give* (S.).

תּוֹלָע [*tōhlāhng'*], Tola; *worm*. Compare Appellatives.

תּוֹלָעִי [*tōhlāh-ngee'*], Tolaite; patronymic of the preceding.

תּוֹמָן [*tōhmāhn'*], in Kethib, for תֵּימָן q. v.

תּוֹקַהַת [tōhkah'hath], in Kethib, Tikvath; *congregation*. From יָקָה, whence יִקְהָה, Gen. xlix. 10, which is also rendered *congregation* (S.).

תֹּחוּ [tōh'khoo], Tohu; stands, 1 Sa. xi. 1, for תּוֹחַ q v.

תַּחְכְּמֹנִי [takh-k'mōhnee'], Tachmonite; patronymic of an unknown תַּחְכְּמֹן *wisdom*, from חָכַם *to be wise*.

תַּחַן [tah'khan], Tahan; *station, camp*. From חָנָה *to encamp*.

תְּחִנָּה [t'khinnāh'], Tehinnah; *grace, favour*. From חָנַן *to be gracious*.

תַּחֲנִי [tah-khănee'], Tahanite; patronymic of תַּחַן.

תְּחַפְנְחֵס [t'khaph-n'khēhs'], Tehaphnehes, & תַּחְפַּנְחֵס [takhpankhēhs'], Tahpanhes; *head, or, beginning of the world*. Collated with the Egyptian (Jablonski, by Gesenius).

תַּחְפְּנֵיס & תַּחְפְּנֵס [takhp'nēhs'], Tahpenes; of the same signification.

תַּחְרֵעַ [takhrēh'ăng], Tahrea; *cunning*. From חרע, according to the Syriac; in the Æth., *to be cunning* (G.).

תַּחַשׁ [tah'khash], Tahash; *badger*. Compare Appellatives.

תַּחַת [tah'khath], Tahath; *place, station*. Compare Appellatives.

תֵּימָא & תֵּמָא [tēmāh'], Tema; *desert, uninhabited country*. Collated with the Arabic (G.).

תֵּימָן [tēmāhn'], Teman; *south*. Compare Appellatives.

תֵּימָנִי [tēmāhnee'], Temanite; patronymic of the preceding.

תֵּימְנִי [tēhm'nee'], Temeni; perhaps better *Temenite*, as a patronymic of תֵּימָן.

תִּילוֹן [teelōhn'], Tilon; *gift*. For נְתִילוֹן, from נָתַל, in the Chaldee and Syriac, *to give* (S.).

תִּיצִי [teetsee'], Tizite; a gentile noun of some unknown place. תִּיץ, perhaps for נְתִיץ *ruins*, from נָתַץ *to tear, break down, destroy*.

תִּירְיָא [teer'yāh'], Tiria; *fear*. By transposition for תִּירְאָה, from יָרֵא *to fear*.

תִּירָס [teerāhs'], Tiras; *desire*. Collated with the Arabic.

תֹּכֶן [tōh'khen], Tochen; *measure*. From תָּכַן *to make even, to level*. Compare Appellatives.

תֵּל אָבִיב [tēhl āhveev'], Tel-abib; *hill of corn-ears*. Comp. Appellatives.

תְּלַאשַּׂר & תְּלַשַּׂר [t'lassāhr'], Telasar, Thelasar; perhaps for תֵּל אַשֵּׁר *heap, or, hill of vow*. תֵּל *heap, or, hill*. Compare Appellatives אַשֵּׁר i.q. Appellative אָשַׁר.

תִּלְגַּת פִּלְנְאֶסֶר [tilgath piln'eh'ser], & תִּלְגַּת פִּלְנֶסֶר [tilgath pilnēh'ser], Tilgath-pilneser; by transposition for תִּגְלַת פְּלְאֶסֶר.

תֶּלַח [teh'lakh], Telah; *breach*. From תָּלַח, according to the Syriac and Chaldee, *to break* (S.).

תֵּל חַרְשָׁא [tēhl kharshāh'], Tel-harsha; *hill of the forest.* For the first, compare Appellatives. חָרְשָׁא i.q. חֹרֶשׁ and Chaldee חוּרְשָׁא *a wood, forest.*

תַּלְמַי [*talmah'y*], Talmai; *full of furrows.* From Appellative תֶּלֶם *a furrow* (G.).

תֵּל מֶלַח [*tēhl meh'lekh*], Tel-melah; *hill of salt, salt-hill.* Compare Appellatives.

תַּמּוּז [*tammooz'*], Tammuz; perhaps, *fear.* For תָּמִוּז, from מזז, in the Chaldee, *to flow down, melt with fear* (G.).

תֶּמַח [*teh'makh*], Tamah; *laughter.* Collated with the Samaritan (S.).

תֵּמָן see תֵּימָן.

תִּמְנָה [*timnāh'*], Timnah; *portion.* From מָנָה *to divide out, allot, appoint.*

תִּמְנִי [*timnee'*], Timnite; gentile noun of the preceding.

תִּמְנָע [*timnāhng'*], Timna; *restraint.* From מָנַע *to restrain.*

תִּמְנָתָה [*timnāh'thāh*], Timnath; i.q. תִּמְנָה, with ה local.

תִּמְנַת חֶרֶס [*timnath' kheh'res*], Timnath-heres; *portion of the sun.* Compare תִּמְנָה above, and Appellative חֶרֶס.

תִּמְנַת סֶרַח [*timnath' seh'rakh*], Timnath-serah; by transposition for the preceding.

תָּמָר [*tāhmāhr'*], Tamar; *palm-tree.* Compare Appellatives.

תַּנְחֻמֶת [*tankhoo'meth*], Tanhumeth; *comfort, consolation.* From נָחַם, in the Piel, *to console, comfort.*

תֹּעוּ [*tōh-ngoo'*], Tou; *error.* From תָּעָה *to wander, err.* According to Simonis, *laughter, laughing.*

תֹּעִי [*tōh'ngee*], Toi; id. As an Appellative the form would properly have been תָּעִי, in pause תֶּעִי. Compare חֳלִי, in pause חֹלִי.

תַּעֲנָךְ [*tah-ngănāhkh'*], & תַּעְנָךְ [*tangnahkh'*], Taanach; *sandy soil.* From עָנַךְ (G.).

תַּפֵּחַ, תַּפּוּחַ [*tappoo'ăkh*], Tappuah; *apple,* i.e., *apple-region.* Compare Appellatives.

תָּקְחַת [*tok-hath'*], Tikovath; perhaps, *congregation.* From קהר, in the Samaritan, *to come together* (S.). It stands, 2 Chr. xxxiv. 22, for תִּקְוָה, 2 Ki. xxii. 14. Comp. the following.

תִּקְוָה [*tikvāh'*], Tikvah; *congregation.* Compare Niphal of קָוָה. Thus for the sake of agreement with the preceding, q.v.; else it may signify *hope.* Compare Appellatives.

תְּקוֹעַ [*t'kōh'ăng*], Tekoa; *a pitching of tents.* From תָּקַע *to pitch a tent.*

תְּקוֹעָה [*t'kōh-ngāh'*], Tekoah; id.

תְּקוֹעִי [*t'kōh-ngee'*], Tekoite; gentile noun of the preceding.

תְּקוֹעִית [*t'kōh-ngeeth'*], of Tekoah (2 Sa. xiv. 4, 9); fem. of the same.

תַּרְאֲלָה [*tar-ălāh'*], Taralah; perhaps, *a reeling,* i.q. Appel. תַּרְעֵלָה.

תִּרְהָקָה [tirhāh'kah], Tirhakah; *elevated, sublime;* properly, *elevation.* Collated with the Arabic (S.).

תֶּרַח [teh'rakh], Terah; *delay.* From תָּרַח, in the Chaldee, *to delay* (S.).

תִּרְחֲנָה [tirkhănāh'], Tirhanah; the signification is uncertain.

תָּרְמָה [tormāh'], Tormah; *thus,* according to the margin, Jud. ix. 31; but where it is best taken as an Appellative, *fraud, deceit,* from רָמָה; whence מִרְמָה, id.

תִּרְעָתִי [tir-ngāhthee'], Tirathite; gentile noun of a place, תִּרְעָה i. q. Chaldee תְּרַע *gate.*

תִּרְצָה [tirtsāh'], Tirzah; *pleasantness.* From רָצָה *to delight in* any thing or person, *to take pleasure in.*

תֶּרֶשׁ [teh'resh], Teresh; *severe, austere.* Collated with the Persic (S.).

תַּרְשִׁישׁ [tarsheesh'], Tarshish; *a breaking in pieces, destruction.* From רָשַׁשׁ *to break in pieces, to destroy.*

תִּרְשָׁתָא [tirshāh'thāh], Tirshatha; marg. (Ezr. ii. 63) *governor, severe, austere.* Compare תֶּרֶשׁ above, which may rightly be taken as an Appellative for *governor.*

תַּרְתָּן [tartāhn'], Tartan; the signification is uncertain.

תַּרְתָּק [tartāhk'], Tartak; *deep darkness,* or, *hero of darkness.* Collated with the Pehlvi (G.).

תִּשְׁבִּי [tishbee'], Tishbite; gentile noun from a city, תִּשְׁבָּה *captivity,* from שָׁבָה *to take,* or, *lead captivity.*

תַּתְּנַי [tat-t'nah'y], Tatnai; *gift.* Collated with the Persic (S.).

www.ingramcontent.com/pod-product-compliance
Lightning Source LLC
Chambersburg PA
CBHW070912160426
43193CB00011B/1436